The Microcomputer User's Guide to
INFORMATION ONLINE

The Microcomputer User's Guide to
INFORMATION ONLINE

Carol Hansen

HAYDEN BOOK COMPANY
a division of Hayden Publishing Company, Inc.
Hasbrouck Heights, New Jersey

Acquisitions Editor: DOUGLAS Mc CORMICK
Production Editor: ALBERTA BODDY
Text Design: JIM BERNARD
Compositor: PUBLISHERS PHOTOTYPE INC.
Printer: ARCATA BOOK GROUP/FAIRFIELD DIVISION
Cover Photo: RON SCALERA

Copyright © 1984 by HAYDEN BOOK COMPANY. All rights reserved. No part of this book may be reprinted, or reproduced, or utilized in any form or by any electronic, mechanical, or other means, now known or hereafter invented, including photocopying and recording, or in any information storage and retrieval system, without permission in writing from the Publisher.

Printed in the United States of America

	1	2	3	4	5	6	7	8	9 PRINTING
	84	85	86	87	88	89	90	91	92 YEAR

Preface

Knowledge is of two kinds. We know a subject ourselves, or we can find information upon it.

Samuel Johnson, April 18, 1775
(From James Boswell, *Life of Johnson*, 1791)

Johnson's words, written more than 200 years ago, take on new meaning in light of today's technology. In Johnson's time the amount of scientific and technical knowledge was less than one percent of what it is today and the kind of economic and business data we deal with, one of the byproducts of the industrial revolution, did not even exist. In our complex society, in which the quantity of relevant information in all but the narrowest fields is well beyond what an individual can be sure of finding out about, let alone absorb, Johnson's first type of knowledge—knowing a subject ourselves—is extremely difficult to come by. On the other hand, recent developments have made knowledge of the second type—knowing where to find information—easier to attain than at any time since the so-called "information explosion" began.

During the past 20 years a wealth of information has been put into computers and made available by "online" searching—that is, with immediate feedback—to virtually anyone willing to obtain the necessary equipment, pay the required fees, and learn the accessing procedures. While at first most computer searching was performed by intermediaries (librarians and other information professionals), the number of end users (people who want information) who perform their own computer searches is increasing. This book's aim is to tell end users what they need to know to use online systems to best advantage.

The trend toward end-user searching is being stimulated by a number of factors. Existing systems are being redesigned to be easier to use—to be more "user-friendly," in the parlance of the online industry. Organizations are developing new systems to be used right from the start by persons with little or no training. A good example of this type is the Dow Jones News/Retrieval for which the basic protocols can be learned in a few minutes. In addition, intensive research and development work has led to the creation of "transparent" microcomputer aids that actually help a novice user to perform a search with a sophisticated retrieval system. But by far the greatest stimulus is undoubtedly the fact that inexpensive microcomputers, which are becoming commonplace in homes and offices, can easily be adapted to act like the terminals needed to search online, remote databases.

People new to this area will be pleasantly surprised at how easily microcomputers can be used for searching; they will be truly amazed, however, by the vast information resources that are now available. From the home or office you can, within a few minutes, locate the latest prices of your stocks, purchase a refrigerator, check up-to-date airline schedules from New York to San Francisco, look for a job, examine race records of a particular thoroughbred, read an article from the *Harvard Business Review*, determine the percentages of men, women, and singles living in New York City, investigate the side effects of a drug, identify last year's Super Bowl winner, or obtain a bibliography of James Michener's books. The possibilities are increasing every day.

This book is meant to be a practical guide, not a technical manual. The questions it is designed to answer are: What information is out there? Does it serve my needs? How do I gain access to it? How much time and what kind of financial commitment are involved? What equipment and software are needed, and where can I obtain them? Although you will gain a general understanding of search techniques and the basic principles of online information retrieval, our intent is not to teach the specific details of how to use a particular system. The best sources of this information are the manuals produced by the organizations, called online vendors, that make remote databases available for online searching.

By the same token, this book does not contain an exhaustive listing of current database resources. It does, however, give enough detailed information to point you in the right direction without doing more extensive research. Liberal references and the names and addresses in the appendices are provided for those who want to learn more. Specific details change so rapidly that current information can only be obtained from vendors. You might consult the directories listed in the bibliography for consolidated information on large numbers of databases.

The first chapters provide a general explanation of the operation of online information systems and the broad range of information that can be accessed. Chapters 4 through 7 are descriptions of major systems and the most important or sample databases in the various service areas: 1. information utilities; 2. large vendors with databases on many subjects; 3. scientific, technical, and medical vendors and databases; 4. business, economics, news, and law vendors and databases. In addition to subject, some important differences exist among these groups. Some of the systems, like The Source, CompuServe, Dow Jones, and legal systems that make use of special user-friendly equipment, can be learned quickly. To search others effectively, it is necessary to spend time training or to purchase computer-search aids. Fortunately, the more complex systems are usually supported by excellent documentation, training programs, and consultants who are available through toll-free hotlines. The learning curve is quickly shortening as the highly technical systems are being simplified for use by persons who are not information professionals. Anyone who has been able to master a word processing or spreadsheet package should have little trouble using online systems and will have a lot of fun in the process.

Chapter 8 deals with equipment and communications software needed for online access. While it is assumed that most readers of this book are using microcomputer equipment, the availability and characteristics of simple terminals are also discussed. Chapter 9 follows with equipment and software-related topics of file transfer and computer-search aids. Chapter 9 also discusses what can be done with information after it is transferred to a local computer.

Owners of microcomputers fitted with communications equipment and software are not limited to information retrieval applications. They can also send mail, "talk" to others, form or become part of a special-interest group, receive free software, compute, program, use word processing packages, and so on. Since these activities are not central to the book's scope, they are not described in depth. However, you will be made aware of their possibilities in Chapter 10.

In the final chapter we look at what to expect next in this rapidly advancing area. Then, a classified bibliography of evaluated references provides sources for additional information on almost every online subject touched upon in this book. The last section, which contains the appendices, is one of the most important. It gives the names of vendor, database, and equipment organizations that are by far the best sources of up-to-date, specific information. These are the places to contact to get started.

Happy searching!

Acknowledgments

I would like to express my appreciation to my friends and co-workers who, without complaint, received much less from me than they should have reasonably expected while this book was being written. Specifically, I received much invaluable help from Joyce Plaza and Anne Tanner, who assisted with research and editing, respectively. Both adhered to my impossible deadlines. Chris Swisher took the photographs that appear in Chapter 8.

Contents

CHAPTER 1

Introduction   1
   Some Definitions   1
   Historical Background   2
   How it works   3
   Training Requirements   6
   Types of Searches   7
   Advantages of Online Searching   8

CHAPTER 2

Information Available Online   9
   Vendors   9
   Database producers   13
   Discussion   18

CHAPTER 3

The Search Process   19
   Introduction   19
   Menu-Driven Systems   19
   Command-Driven Reference Systems   22

CHAPTER 4

Information Utilities   34
   Overview   34
   The Source   35
   Compuserve   42
   Delphi   50

CHAPTER 5

Reference Vendors with Databases on Many Subjects   56
   Outside the United States   70

CHAPTER 6

Scientific, Technical, and Medical Vendors and Databases   73

  Databases   73
  Specialized Vendors   78
  Other Systems   100

CHAPTER 7

Business and Economic Vendors and Databases   103

  Databases   103
  Other Systems   124
  Specialized Services   125

CHAPTER 8

Equipment and Communications Software   126

  Terminals   126
  Microcomputer Communications   128

CHAPTER 9

Transferring Files, Search Aids, and Offline Software   140

  Introduction   140
  Transferring Files   141
  Integrated Communications and Offline Software   142
  Offline Packages   152
  Online Search Aids   153

CHAPTER 10

Computer-Mediated Communication and Other Online Applications   156

  Computer-Mediated Communication   156
  Computer-Assisted Instruction (CAI)   159
  Computer Bulletin Board Systems (CBBS)   160
  Other Timesharing Services   169

CHAPTER 11

The Future   172

  Vendors   172

Databases   173
Simplified Search Protocols   173
Extended Use   174
Integration of Technologies   174
Fee Structures   175
Societal Factors   175

GLOSSARY 177

BIBLIOGRAPHY 185

Bibliographies   185
Dictionaries   185
Directories   185
Monographs   187
Journals and Newsletters   188
Online Newsletters   190
For Further Reading   190

APPENDIX I
Networks and Major Vendors   **197**

APPENDIX II
Selected Databases   **202**

APPENDIX III
Selected Hardware and Software Manufacturers   **209**

Terminal Manufacturers   209
Communicating Word Processor Manufacturers   209
Modem Suppliers   210
Other Equipment Manufacturers   210
Communications Software Manufacturers   211

APPENDIX IV
Selected Bulletin Board Numbers   **216**

INDEX 217

The Microcomputer User's Guide to
INFORMATION ONLINE

CHAPTER 1

Introduction

The purpose of this book is to serve as a guide for the novice who wants to find information in *databases* by searching them *online* using *remote computers*. It also provides information on other types of online services and offers practical advice on using *telecommunications* to access computers.

SOME DEFINITIONS

Every effort has been made to keep this book as free of jargon as possible. An indication of how difficult this goal is to achieve is that four terms with which you may be unfamiliar have been introduced already: *databases*, *online*, *remote computer*, and *telecommunications*. Obviously, it is necessary to speak the basic language of a field in order to discuss it, and so before going further we shall define these words and a few other terms fundamental to online searching. We assume that everyone interested in this topic already has a general understanding of what computers can do.

A *remote computer* is simply a computer at a physical location removed from that of the person using it. A *database,* in the sense that it is used here, is a collection of *records* in computer-readable form. A *record* is a unit of related information; for example, in a bibliographic database, all information about one document (author, title, date, et cetera) is in one record, and the entire database consists of many such records representing many documents.

Databases may be searched *offline*—that is, at the computer center by a computer operator. Use of this method is becoming less common than that of *online* searching, which is searching in an interactive, conversational mode. With online access, feedback from the computer is immediate (unless there is an unusual problem). Databases for commercial use are made available by organizations called *vendors*; searching is done on large *timesharing* computers, machines that can be accessed by many persons at one time. Usually, vendors have more than one database on their computers, and some have more than one hundred.

As a potential user, you may be thousands of miles away from a vendor's computer. You will then need to use some type of *telecommunications network* to communicate with the remote computer. This can be the ordinary telephone system, but it is usually less expensive to use one of the national or international networks designed specifically for data transmission.

The minimal equipment you will need is a *terminal* and a *modem*. A *terminal* is a communication device with a keyboard similar to that of a typewriter and has either a printer, a video display, or both. You connect to the telecommunications network through a *modem*, which translates computer data into the types of signals that can be sent over telephone lines and vice versa. The modem may or may not be built into the terminal. Most popular microcomputers can be adapted to behave as terminals by using software designed for this purpose. The microcomputer is then said to *emulate* a terminal. A number of advantages micros have over terminals for online searching will be discussed in later chapters.

This is the basic vocabulary of online. You will learn additional definitions as other terms are introduced.

HISTORICAL BACKGROUND

The online information service industry is less than 25 years old. The impetus for the industry's growth has come from the need of persons in all professions for quick, easy access to information, a need that intensified as the amount and diversity of information increased. But these services would not have been possible without the convergence of several technological developments:

- Powerful timesharing computers
- Large, fast *random-access storage devices*
- Low-cost, fast terminals
- Low-cost telecommunications networks

Random-access storage devices are a type of equipment that allows data stored in computer-readable form to be read directly, no matter where they are located physically on the storage medium. At present the most common storage medium for large databases that are searched online is the disk. Magnetic tape, the previous medium for storing large databases, required *serial* searching—the process of examining each item sequentially until the right one is found. Serial searching is very slow compared to random-access.

Another technology in the bibliographic area, computer-driven *photocomposition* (creation of master-type plates for printing), contributed to the development of online services. During the early 1960s, publishers of large abstract and index services turned to photocomposition to reduce costs, to speed production, and to facilitate the publication of cumulations. This worked very well, and as a bonus, important by-products—databases—were produced.

At that point, virtually no additional expense was incurred by turning the databases over to vendors who made them available for online searching. The benefit to publishers—*database producers*—was additional income in the form of royalties based on online use of the databases. In the long term, online searching has had a profound effect on the economics of publication of abstracts and indexes, but in the beginning online access was seen simply as a way of deriving a small amount of additional revenue.

Although *publicly accessible* online systems (systems which can be used by persons not associated with the proprietary organization) have been used since the mid-1960s, widespread access did not begin until the early 1970s. Much credit for the developmental work can be given to two government agencies, The National Library of Medicine (NLM) and the National Aeronautics and Space Administration (NASA). These organizations had systems operating in 1970.

In 1972, System Development Corporation (SDC), which had developed the NLM system under contract, and Lockheed Information Services (a division of the aerospace company), which had played a similar role in the development of the NASA system, began commercial operation. One of the first databases on the commercial systems, ERIC (Educational Resources Information Center), gained immediate popularity in the educational community and continues to be used heavily.

The first online databases, with the exception of ERIC and a few others, were in science and technology. Business databases came next, followed by those covering social sciences, humanities, and popular materials. A third major vendor, Bibliographic Retrieval Services (BRS) entered the market in 1976. An outgrowth of the SUNY (State University of New York) Biomedical Communications Network, BRS at first was aimed primarily at academic libraries. In late 1982, BRS and Dialog (formerly Lockheed) developed an online service for direct access by *end users*. *End users* are persons who have information needs as opposed to *intermediaries* (librarians and other information professionals) who perform searches on behalf of end users.

The Source, an *information utility* introduced in 1979, was the first online information service designed expressly for the individual user. An *information utility* provides a broad range of online services such as messaging, information retrieval, and computing. CompuServe, the other major online utility, also began home-market service in 1979. There are now more than 200 vendors offering databases in news, law, business, economics, and just about every other subject area.

At present, online databases number 1500 and contain an estimated 150 million records. Together, the number of individual subscribers and those from business, libraries, schools, and laboratories is estimated to be in the tens of thousands, while the number of searches performed annually is over 10 million. All indications are that the online industry will continue to expand dramatically in the coming years.

HOW IT WORKS

There are four classes of participants in the online industry: 1. database producers who create computer-readable information; 2. vendors who make databases available for online searching; 3. intermediaries who perform searches on behalf of end users; and 4. end users. (See Fig. 1–1.) Within this general scheme are hybrids.

Some database producers, like the National Library of Medicine and Dow Jones, act as vendors for their own databases. Other organizations began as vendors and are now also producing databases. An example of a vendor-produced database is Pre-Med, a BRS database that contains very current biomedical information. More and more end users are choosing to do their own searches rather than delegate the work to intermediaries; indeed, this book is written for such persons.

Telecommunications

The very first step in executing a search is to dial the telephone number (or instruct your computer to dial the number) of your local telecommunications network node. Network *nodes*, access points to the network, are now available in over 1000 cities in the United States and in more than 30 foreign countries. Interna-

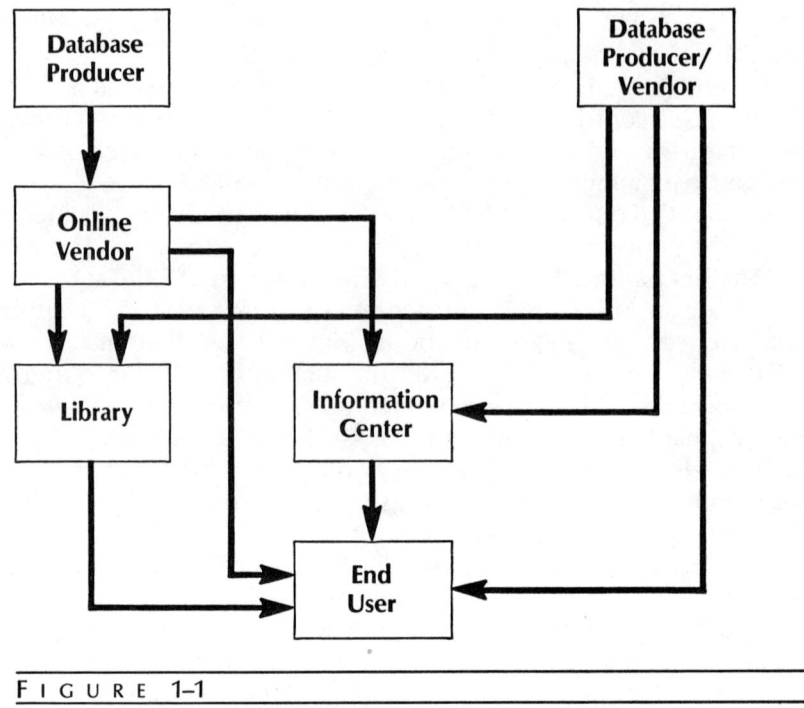

FIGURE 1-1

Flow of information from database producers to users

tional communication is achieved through satellite linkages. See Fig. 1-2 for a schematic of a worldwide telecommunications network.

If you are fortunate enough to live in the same geographic area as a vendor service, you may dial directly. In some sparsely populated areas it is sometimes more economical to use "800" numbers (if available) to dial directly rather than to go through a network.

The three major networks presently used by the online searching vendors are TYMNET (San Jose, California), TELENET (TELENET Communications Corporation of Vienna, Virginia), and UNINET (Roseland, New Jersey). You can access some online vendors through all three networks, others through only one or two networks, and still others through their own networks. The networks charge according to the length of time you are connected and then generally bill you through the vendors. Network charges are about $5 to $10 per hour during business hours, less in the evening. Lists of telephone numbers of authorized network nodes are supplied by vendors.

The flow of information on an individual basis during an online session is illustrated in Fig. 1-3. The signal that a connection has been made with the network varies according to the network, the modem, and the terminal equipment being used. Usually there is a light on the terminal or modem and a network prompt such as the words "PLEASE LOG IN " (given by TYMNET). This is among the friendliest prompts and means that you should now enter the commands necessary to become connected to the vendor computer. This process is called *logging on*. All vendor manuals provide instructions for logging on through the various networks. Networks function as the telephone system does—by routing messages over the fastest path available.

INTRODUCTION

FIGURE 1-2

Schematic of worldwide telecommunications network (courtesy of the Institution of Electrical Engineers)

After logging on, you key in statements and send them to the computer by pressing the RETURN key. The modem codes the data for transmission over telephone lines and the communications network to the computer. The computer decodes the message, responds, recodes for telecommunications, and directs the information back to you. After being translated back into machine-readable form by the modem, the computer's response is either printed on your terminal or displayed on a screen. The entire process happens so quickly that the response seems instantaneous.

Since you will probably want a hard-copy printout of your search results, you will want to use a print terminal rather than a video terminal. If you are using a microcomputer instead of a terminal, you can capture the search results on disk for later printing. This technique, called *downloading*, is discussed in Chapter 9.

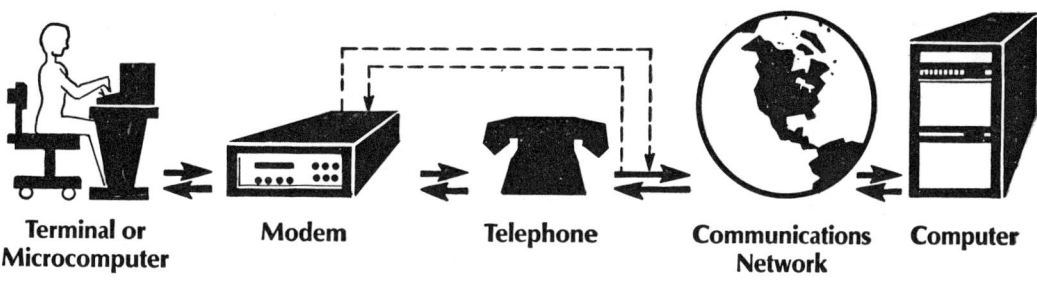

FIGURE 1-3

Flow of information to and from the remote computer

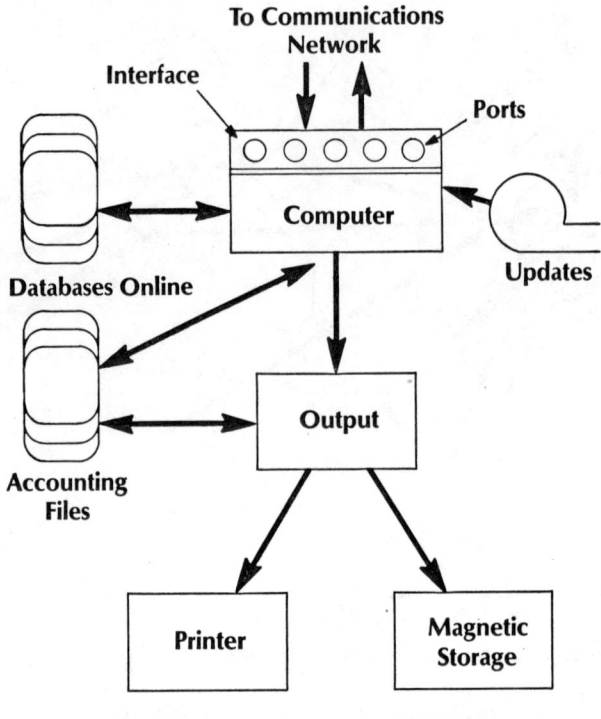

FIGURE 1-4
Schematic of computer system installation

The remote-computer installation is a complex operation (see Fig. 1–4). At its heart is the timesharing computer, or set of computers, that controls all calculations, performs logical operations, and moves information to and from peripheral devices. Databases are stored on large disks for instantaneous access, as are accounting files, which are used for automatic billing functions. Updates to each database must be entered regularly; computer installations produce printed or machine-readable output. Search results are often printed offline at the computer site when they are so large that online printing would be very costly.

The interface is a computer within a computer. It controls the *ports*—electronic passageways through which users gain access to the computer system. Some interfaces validate identification codes and passwords and send messages. The number of ports is limited. When the maximum number of persons is using a system, all ports will be full. If you try to log on at this time, you will receive a message such as "ALL PORTS BUSY".

TRAINING REQUIREMENTS

This book covers many different types of systems. Training requirements for users range from a few minutes to several weeks and depend partly on how thoroughly trained the user wishes to be. On-the-job, learn-by-doing training works very well for some online systems. You can retrieve basic stock quotes on Dow Jones after spending a brief time with the manual and then by keeping a crib sheet handy, but you probably need an hour or two to learn to use all the databases on Dow Jones. Similarly, with little preparation, you can access CompuServe and The Source with their menu-driven command languages, but time is needed to become familiar with the different databases and services.

At the other extreme, schools of library and information science give entire courses in online searching. The National Library of Medicine offers searchers of its system two full weeks of training. It is probably a safe bet that most intermediaries searching on Dialog, SDC, and BRS learned in one- to one-and-a-half-day workshops given by these vendors, but there are many searchers with informal training. And you should remember that, generally, since intermediaries are search professionals, they need to know more. Also, they must of necessity search subjects they do not understand well, and they need to search a wide variety of systems and databases.

Formal experiments with end users have shown that many are able to learn to search the bibliographic systems on their own through trial and error, although searches may not go as quickly or achieve as good results as they might if the user had received formal training. Chapter 3 provides general guidance on search strategy for those who want to perform their own bibliographic searches. But remember that the inexperienced searcher can always find someone at a local library who is willing to answer questions, give a demonstration, or even perform the actual search. There is no better method than watching a demonstration for learning what online searching is all about. Some observers of the field have suggested that end users may want to learn to do quick, simple searches themselves and use the information intermediaries for complex information problems. This makes a great deal of sense for the more sophisticated systems.

TYPES OF SEARCHES

Searches are, of course, customized. They are performed for hundreds of reasons, some of which may already be obvious to you. As with microcomputers, after you become more familiar with online systems, more uses become apparent.

Common types of searches (or, more strictly, information accesses) are:

Comprehensive bibliography: a search for *all* relevant references, covering all document types, going back in time as far as possible, and using several databases.

Selective bibliography: a fast search for a *few* relevant documents.

Author: a search for documents written by a particular author.

Cited author: a search for documents citing a particular author.

Citation: a search for documents citing a specific document.

Corporate: a search for publications by persons working for a specific organization.

Verification: a search to verify the accuracy or completeness of a bibliographic reference.

Identification: a search to complete a reference (e.g., "I'd like the Smythe article that appeared in *The Journal of the American Chemical Society* last May).

Patent: a search for relevant patent information.

SDI: a search for updates to databases. The purpose is to keep up to date on a subject.

Full text: a search for the full text of a document such as a law, a court decision, or a journal or encyclopedia article.

Statistical: a search for and possible manipulation of statistical data.

Dictionary: a search for handbook- or dictionary-type information such as definitions, chemical nomenclature, and physical properties.

Chemical substructure: a search for information on chemical compounds that satisfy certain structural criteria.

Document ordering: a search to order books or copies of articles online through a supplier.

Directory: a search for biographical information, airline schedules, or a list of good restaurants in a particular city.

Factual: a search for a piece of data such as the density of paraldehyde or the closing price of IBM stock on a particular day.

Messaging: sending or receiving messages, for example, through electronic mail, through direct, online communication or through reading or posting messages on bulletin boards.

Shopping: identifying and ordering items for purchase.

ADVANTAGES OF ONLINE SEARCHING

Online searching works very well. Most problems experienced in early years, such as slow response and frequent downtime, are now rare. A large number of databases is available, and the languages of the complex systems, which are very powerful, are being gradually redesigned to be simpler to use for persons with little training or experience.

Primarily, online searching has gained such rapid widespread acceptance because it is so fast. You can often perform in a few minutes a search that would take hours or even days to complete manually. Beyond that, online has made searches possible that were not even feasible manually. This is because there are so many more access points (*fields*) to the record that can be searched online than are available to a manual searcher. For example, manual searching for chemical compounds depends on nomenclature, whereas sophisticated online systems make it possible to search for a chemical substance on the basis of the structure. In some medical databases you can separate in a few seconds all human studies from animal studies, something that could not be accomplished in a manual search except by looking at all the original documents. You will see many more examples of the "online advantage" as you read descriptions of databases, vendors, and search languages in the following chapters.

CHAPTER 2

Information Available Online

This chapter provides an overview of the online industry and describes the types of information products and services that are available as well as the kinds of organizations that provide them. Chapters 4 through 7 and Chapter 10 contain details of the products and services in specific subject areas.

VENDORS

The essential characteristic of a vendor organization is that it provides a large timesharing computer containing databases that can be searched by many users simultaneously. A few major international vendors have well over a hundred databases, the users of which number in the tens of thousands; others have only a few databases and smaller numbers of users.

Table 2–1 shows the major categories of vendors that presently provide information services: utility, reference, and subject-specific. In the United States there are five organizations that clearly stand out in the first two categories, while there are more than a hundred subject-specific vendors. The major organizations in the information utility area are The Source in McLean, Virginia and CompuServe in Columbus, Ohio.

TABLE 2–1
TYPES OF VENDORS

TYPE	EXAMPLE
Information Utility	The Source CompuServe
Reference	Bibliographic Retrieval Services, Inc. Dialog Information Services, Inc. SDC Information Services
Subject-specific	Dow Jones News Retrieval Institute for Scientific Information National Library of Medicine Data Resources, Inc.

As mentioned already, an information utility is an online vendor that provides a broad range of services such as information, news, conferencing, and computing capability. The three primary *reference* vendors—organizations primarily in the business of providing information to the academic and business communities—are: Bibliographic Retrieval Services, Inc. (BRS) in Latham, New York; Dialog Information Services, Inc. in Palo Alto, California; and SDC Information Services in Santa Monica, California. The number of databases on these systems ranges from over 70 (BRS) to about 200 (Dialog). There are also a number of European vendors—called *hosts*—organized into a network called Euronet Diane, headquartered in Luxembourg. Several European systems are available in the United States through international communications networks such as TYMNET, while major U.S. systems are searched worldwide using these same networks.

Although subject-specific vendors cover nearly every field imaginable, they tend to concentrate on business, news, law, and the sciences. The Dow Jones News Retrieval Service, which provides up-to-the-minute stock quotes as well as other financial and news information, is marketed widely to home users. One of the first online databases, and probably the most heavily used bibliographic database, is the National Library of Medicine's MEDLINE.

In addition to the information services mentioned above, there are many other types of online services such as messaging, programming, word processing, file-building capability, and, simply, raw computer power. In fact, nearly anything that can be done with computers can be done online via an appropriate communications device.

Appendix I contains names and addresses of all vendors mentioned in this text and of other major vendors and networking organizations. In addition, the online directories provided in the first section of the bibliography give complete lists of vendors, and communications networks such as TYMNET provide descriptions of vendors using their systems. In Europe the best overall information source is Euronet Diane.

Types of Vendor Services

In addition to making databases available for searching, large vendors and some smaller ones as well provide most of the following support services.

User Aids—Any computer user knows that good documentation is critical. An online vendor provides it in the form of a user manual that generally consists of three parts: 1. directions on the means to access the system; 2. instructions covering the system command language (also called protocol—how to search the system); and 3. descriptions of the various databases.

How easy user manuals are to follow varies a great deal and tends to improve in later versions, as vendor companies mature. Dialog, SDC, and BRS all have excellent manuals. They are usually issued in loose-leaf, a format that facilitates frequent updates.

Manuals are essential for searching the more complex vendor systems. But some systems, like The Source, have fairly simple "menu-driven" protocols that you can learn in part while online. Even more technical systems have online HELP commands.

There are other types of user aids available. Some of the most important are *thesauri*, organized word lists that are vocabularies used to index, and therefore search, some databases. Although you can usually search a database without knowing the indexing vocabulary, use of a thesaurus can greatly improve results in many cases. Thus, you should acquire the database thesaurus if you're apt to search a particular database frequently. Thesauri are also often available online as part of a database.

Other kinds of user aids that vendors sometimes provide are classification schemes, word frequency lists, command charts (crib sheets), workbooks, codes, and lists of source documents for particular databases. An example of a situation in which codes are important is searching for information about specific companies in business databases (Disclosure, for example), which index by using the Security and Exchange Commission (SIC) codes.

Some producers of databases also supply manuals specific to their databases and to some other user aids mentioned here.

Newsletters—Most major vendors and several database producers regularly issue newsletters to keep users informed about system changes, schedules, available training workshops, and new databases. Some also contain articles about the online information world in general or news concerning the parent organization. Subscribers to the online service receive newsletters at no charge. To supplement newsletters, log-on messages often contain brief news items.

Training—Home-market vendors have designed their systems to be self-taught, and it is quite possible to learn most systems on your own. On the other hand, many people find vendors' training sessions worthwhile. Major vendors regularly schedule sessions (usually one to two days) in large cities throughout the United States, Europe, and certain other countries. They generally charge a nominal training fee.

Major database producers also provide training specific to their databases, sometimes in conjunction with vendor sessions. Advanced training in particular subject areas or in sophisticated search techniques is also available, and vendors will give on-site group instruction to members of one organization.

Hotlines—BRS, Dialog, SDC, The Source, CompuServe, the National Library of Medicine, Dow Jones, Mead Data Central, and many other vendors as well as database producers have toll-free hotlines that you can call for information such as training schedules, billing questions, requests for publications, and help with searching or with a system problem. For the most part, persons staffing these "help" desks are pleasant, knowledgeable, and willing to go out of their way to find answers. You will find hotline numbers as part of the descriptions of specific vendors in the following chapters and in Appendices I and II.

Document Delivery—With the widespread use of online searching for information retrieval, locating references to information about a topic has become much easier than locating the actual documents themselves. In order to fill this gap in the information chain, vendors have contracted with document suppliers (including some database producers) to supply documents, particularly photocopies of journal articles and hard-to-locate reports. You can order documents directly online using the vendor system, which will then bill you. There is also an encouraging trend, which has been accelerating recently, toward providing full text of documents online.

Final relief for the document delivery problem will probably not come until *all* full text is available online.

Selective Dissemination of Information (SDI)—Most vendors offer a current awareness service, called selective dissemination of information, that is a useful supplement to traditional methods of "keeping up"—scanning journals, attending professional meetings, et cetera. "Selective" refers to the individualized nature of SDI. A search strategy that reflects a user's research interests (called a *profile*) is stored in a vendor's computer and is matched automatically to each database update (usually monthly). The resulting printout of references reflects scanning of a wider range of journals than is possible for an individual to accomplish. SDI charges are approximately $3 and up per update.

Software and Private Files—An organization can maintain a private file, such as a database of internal company research reports, on a vendor computer. The owner controls access and pays fees based on input costs. Alternatively, an organization with large internal databases may find leasing vendor software more economical.

Selecting Vendors

In selecting a vendor, you must start in the obvious place: determining your information needs. Usually, *subject* matter of the available databases is the most important factor. To find which vendors have which databases, simply telephone the toll-free numbers in Appendix I and request basic information. Vendors will provide, free of charge, a listing of databases; some will send fairly extensive catalogs containing database descriptions. Or, you may take the opposite approach and call the producer of a database of interest to learn which systems have the database online. (See Appendix II for toll-free numbers of producers.) Another alternative, if a terminal is available, is to connect to the local TYMNET node to use TYMNET's subject index to list vendors using its network. See Chapter 3 for specific instructions. There is no charge for searching TYMNET.

Most large science and business databases are available through more than one vendor. Some are "up" on all three major U.S. reference vendors. Some smaller databases, however, are available exclusively with one vendor. Even organizations such as the National Library of Medicine and the Institute for Scientific Information, which vend their own databases, have made arrangements for access to some of their databases through other vendors.

Cost is another important consideration. Online services charge fees primarily according to *connect time*, the amount of time you are connected to the timesharing computer. Sometimes there is also a charge for online *hits* (the number of items retrieved). There is always a cost associated with offline retrieval (bibliographies or other information printed at the vendor site and mailed to the user). For the many vendors that do not require start-up fees or minimum use levels, there is no penalty for signing on and simply paying for what you use. You can sometimes obtain lower rates, however, in exchange for guaranteeing a minimum.

Vendor charges are usually the sum of three charges—database royalties, vendor service fees, and network fees. Network fees are relatively low. The royalty component tends to keep charges for particular databases fairly similar across vendors so that, with the exception of government systems to which access is somewhat restricted, cost differences among vendors are not usually large unless you have guaranteed a minimum on a system. Because certain searches may be facilitated (or made more difficult) by the command language of a particular vendor, direct comparison of costs is complicated.

By and large, however, *command languages* are all so similar that the inexperienced user should not select a vendor on this basis. Some very experienced searchers have developed a preference for one language over another, but this is often simply a preference for the language learned first.

DATABASE PRODUCERS

Database producers are the organizations that create the files mounted online by vendors. As mentioned earlier, some database producers, such as the National Library of Medicine, are vendors as well as producers.

The first databases were simply computer-readable forms of existing print products. File Number 1 on Dialog, for example, is ERIC, which consists of the information in *Resources in Education* and *Current Index to Journals in Education*. Similarly, COMPENDEX is nearly equivalent to *Engineering Index*, and SCISEARCH is the online counterpart of *Science Citation Index*. While you can still associate most databases with a print product, some have been created solely online—ABI/INFORM, for example.

The following section focuses on databases that were built by organizations primarily to provide information for public use; privately created databases, services such as electronic bulletin boards, and systems designed for computation or data manipulation are excluded. Chapter 10, however, includes a brief discussion of these other uses for remote-computer access. This distinction between database types is not clear-cut; some databases that are primarily informational can also be manipulated.

Types of Databases

There is a remarkable and somewhat confusing variety of online information. As an aid to understanding, databases can be categorized according to type, and the most logical place to start is to make a distinction between *bibliographic* (or literature-oriented) *databases* and *source databases*. Bibliographic databases contain references to documents. They do not provide answers to questions but rather tell you where to look for answers. For example, you might search for information on the use of Vitamin C in preventing colds and retrieve a reference to a book by Linus Pauling. To obtain the actual information, you would then have to locate the book and look through it.

Examples of source databases are directories (Electronic Yellow Pages), numeric databases (Dow Jones Quotes), dictionary databases (Chemline, which contains chemical nomenclature), and full-text databases (*Harvard Business Review* articles). These databases are one-stop information sources. You may not have to look further for the information you seek.

Table 2–2 contains some examples of popular databases in major subject areas, along with either the print counterpart or an indication of subject content. Almost any scientist, scholar, researcher, or businessperson should be able to find a familiar name in this list. You can also see that there are many sources of databases. Their

TABLE 2-2
SUBJECTS OF DATABASES

SUBJECT AREA	EXAMPLE	DESCRIPTION
Multidisciplinary	CDI	Comprehensive Dissertation Index
	LC/LINE	Books in the Library of Congress
Science	CA Search	Chemical Abstracts
	BIOSIS	Biological Abstracts and BioResearch Index
	BRS/DISC	Articles on microcomputing
Medicine	MEDLINE	Index Medicus
	EMBASE	Excerpta Medica abstract journals
Applied Science & Technology	COMPENDEX	Engineering Index
	NTIS	National Technical Information Service
Social Science	Social SCISEARCH	Social Science Citation Index
	PSYCINFO	Psychological Abstracts
Humanities	MLA Bibliography	MLA Bibliography
	Historical Abstracts	publication of ABC-Clio, Inc.
Business & Economics	Management Contents	articles from management journals
Popular Literature & News	Magazine Index	articles from popular journals
	Newsearch	newspaper articles
Law	Legal Resource Index	articles from law journals

producers include the private sector; the old, prestigious, scientific associations such as the American Chemical Society; and the government. Both government organizations and for-profit firms also serve as online vendors and carry databases from other economic sectors. Whether this is a healthy mix—especially in regard to the role of government, which charges lower rates for online and database services than the private sector does—is a matter of considerable debate within the online industry.

Table 2-3 illustrates another aspect of database variety: types of source documents covered. These databases contain, primarily, one type of document. Databases that cover journal articles commonly include chapters of multi-authored monographs, and some databases index many types of source documents; PSYCINFO comprises books, periodicals, technical reports, dissertations, and other monographs.

In 1978, McCarn (see bibliography) postulated that the most frequently searched bibliographic databases in the United States were those shown in Table 2-4. While use of other databases, particularly LEXIS, has undoubtedly grown considerably since then, it is likely that those on this list remain very important. The list reflects a continued emphasis on science and technology in online bibliographic databases.

INFORMATION AVAILABLE ONLINE

TABLE 2–3
SOURCE DOCUMENT COVERAGE

Source Document Type	Example	Description
Books	CATLINE	National Library of Medicine
Conference papers	Conference Papers Index	in the sciences
Congressional publications	CIS	Congressional Information Service
Dissertations	CDI	Comprehensive Dissertation Index
Government publications	GPO Monthly Catalog	GPO Monthly Catalog
Government reports	NTIS	National Technical Information Service
Journals (primarily)	SCISEARCH	Science Citation Index
Newspapers	Information Bank	The New York Times (and more)
Patents	Claims	publication from IFI/Plenum
Encyclopedia	Academic American Encyclopedia	full text

Table 2–5 offers some examples of source databases. While directory databases can be found in all subjects, numeric databases are concentrated in the sciences, economics, and business areas. Dictionary databases are found mainly in science, and full-text databases, although not common at present, are one of the most rapidly growing segments of the online industry. The ability to retrieve chemical substances according to their substructures—full-structure searching is also possible—is one of the most exciting recent developments in online information retrieval. Two full-text

TABLE 2–4
MOST POPULAR DATABASES

MEDLINE	National Library of Medicine
ERIC	Educational Resources Information Center
CA Search	Chemical Abstracts Service
PSYCINFO	American Psychological Association
BIOSIS	BioSciences Information Service of Biological Abstracts
NTIS	National Technical Information Service
The Information Bank	Mead Data Central

TABLE 2-5
SOURCE DATABASES

SOURCE DOCUMENT TYPE	EXAMPLE	DESCRIPTION
Directory	Electronic Yellow Pages	from telephone books in major cities
	Foundation Directory	describes foundations
Numeric	RTECS	Registry of Toxic Effects of Chemical Substances
	Dow Jones	stock quotes and other financial news
	PTS U.S. Time Series	time series, forecasts, and other business data
	Energy	Data Resources, Inc., on major energy resources
Dictionary	CHEMNAME	synonyms and data on chemical substances
	SUPERINDEX	index to many science handbooks
Full Text	Psychology Today	journal articles
	LEXIS	legal information
	Newsnet	newsletters
	Academic American Encyclopedia	encyclopedia
Substructure	CAS Online	substructures of chemical substances
Other	FIRSTWORLD	travel service
	Connexions	employment notices

newsletters *about* online are *The Online Chronicle*, which is on Dialog, and *The Online Hotline*, which is with an independent vendor. In the "Other" category in Table 2–5, home-market vendors provide whimsical items such as horoscopes and practical home-use services (e.g., the ability to shop by mail).

Evaluating Databases

In evaluating databases for a particular information need, subject is obviously the most important consideration. Even so, choices are often not obvious. For example, if you are looking for information about a particular drug, there are almost too many possibilities: International Pharmaceutical Abstracts, TOXLINE, Pharmaceutical News Index, SCISEARCH, BIOSIS, CA Search, or one of the general medical databases such as MEDLINE or Excerpta Medica. If the drug is psychoactive, you could try PSYCINFO; if it is an abused drug, ERIC could be appropriate; if it is used for cancer therapy, CANCERLIT would be a good choice. At the other extreme, you might want educational statistics for Ghana and be at a loss to find even one appropriate database.

All three major U.S. reference vendors have "databases of databases" to help you with this problem of database selection. These indexes to databases are called

Data Base Index (SDC), CROS (BRS), and DIALINDEX (Dialog). While all three work somewhat differently, the basic procedure is to request a search in the database index on a specific term or group of terms. The system responds with a list of databases and information on the frequency of occurrence of search term(s) in databases covered by the system. Rates for searching these database indexes are comparatively low.

TABLE 2–6

DATABASE EVALUATION CRITERIA

Subject Coverage
Type of Database
Availability of Source Documents
Cost
Size
Coverage Dates
Currency
Access Points

Table 2–6 lists other database evaluation criteria. "Type of Database" refers to bibliography, directory, dictionary, full text, numeric, et cetera. This is a crucial distinction. If the needed information is a chemical substance registry number, it would not make sense to search, for example, a bibliographic database, even one in chemistry, when registry numbers can be found so easily using one of the chemical dictionary databases. Similarly, you would not normally search a database of books for research information in a fast-moving field like biotechnology. Or, a high school student preparing a report on the effects of nuclear energy accidents on the environment would probably prefer a database like Magazine Index or the New York Times Information Bank rather than a highly technical database such as BIOSIS or ENVIROLINE.

You can check the content of databases in the database directories referenced in the first section of the bibliography; as mentioned above, the database documentation provided by vendors is quite helpful for this purpose.

Availability of Source Documents—Receiving terrific references to documents that you cannot obtain by the time you need them is useless. The online ordering systems of Dialog and SDC can help, but they are relatively expensive and take time. Sometimes you may want to limit your search to databases covering documents available in your local library.

Cost—Database costs vary from $5 per hour for CompuServe in non-prime time to well over $100 per hour for some very technical databases in other systems. There is no relationship between cost and quality. Some of the excellent large government databases are the least expensive.

Size—Size of databases usually ranges from a few thousand to hundreds of thousands of records.

Coverage Dates—Records in most databases go back to no earlier than the mid-1960s, when the necessary computer technology matured. A notable exception is CDI, which covers all *Dissertation Abstracts* back to the nineteenth century.

Another coverage consideration is whether the database is *segmented*—divided into parts that must be searched separately. Very large databases like CA Search and MEDLINE are segmented by date on all vendor systems. Sometimes it is only possible to search back files offline and have the results mailed to you; in BRS, you can retrieve offline results online the next day.

Currency—Update frequencies vary from every 15 minutes (Dow Jones Quotes/Current) to once a year or less often. Sometimes databases become "frozen" and are not updated for long periods of time because of problems with the database producer or vendor.

Access Points—There are many possible access points for searching; they differ by database. Some have classification schemes, and others control terms with a thesaurus. Various category codes, such as the previously mentioned SIC codes in Disclosure (a business database) or taxonomic codes in BIOSIS (a biological database), can be very important. Fortunately, you can search most bibliographic databases by title or abstract words even if they are indexed according to controlled vocabulary. Another very useful feature in many databases is the ability to limit searches by language in which the original document was written.

DISCUSSION

While reading the following chapters, you should keep in mind the fast-moving pace of the online field. Although we have made every effort to provide enough specific information to help you make informed choices now, information on available databases, vendors' pricing policies, training formats, equipment, and command languages—virtually everything—change continually. Therefore, if you are seriously interested in becoming an online user, you should contact vendors directly for the most up-to-date information.

CHAPTER 3
The Search Process

INTRODUCTION

Procedures for using online systems are different for each system, a fact that makes it difficult to generalize on the search process. Such discussions are only feasible if we divide the systems into three basic types:

- Menu-driven
- Comand-driven (reference)
- Command-driven (data)

This division presents problems, however, because few systems are strictly one type or another. Yet most fall into one category primarily or switch between modes, thus making this categorization helpful. Menu-driven systems are relatively simple to learn, at least at the start, but they have such diverse characteristics that few generalities can be taught. Command-driven data systems, some of which allow for manipulation of data, have such specific functions relative to particular data that little can be said about general strategies for searching them. There are, however, principles and techniques that can be applied to searching command-driven reference systems, and since you may never get formal training in these systems, but will probably use them, the major portion of this chapter will cover the process of searching bibliographic databases in online reference systems. First, though, to show the differences, we will give a brief description of menu-driven systems.

MENU-DRIVEN SYSTEMS

Exemplified by The Source, CompuServe, and Dow Jones, menu-driven systems ask the user questions, provide a "menu" of allowable responses, and explain how to select one. Extensive HELP commands (an occasional menu choice) provide you with a way of finding out what to do if it is not obvious. Menus are laid out in a series of levels as shown in Fig. 3–1.

You are shown the Entry Level menu immediately after logging on. After you select an item from an upper (more general) level, the computer shows you a lower (more specific) level. The actual information or program is at the lowest level. As a novice user, you may find it difficult to learn to move around the levels comfortably—that is, to exit from a lower level and return to a point where it is possible to start down the next desired path. Some commands are specific to certain hierarchies and

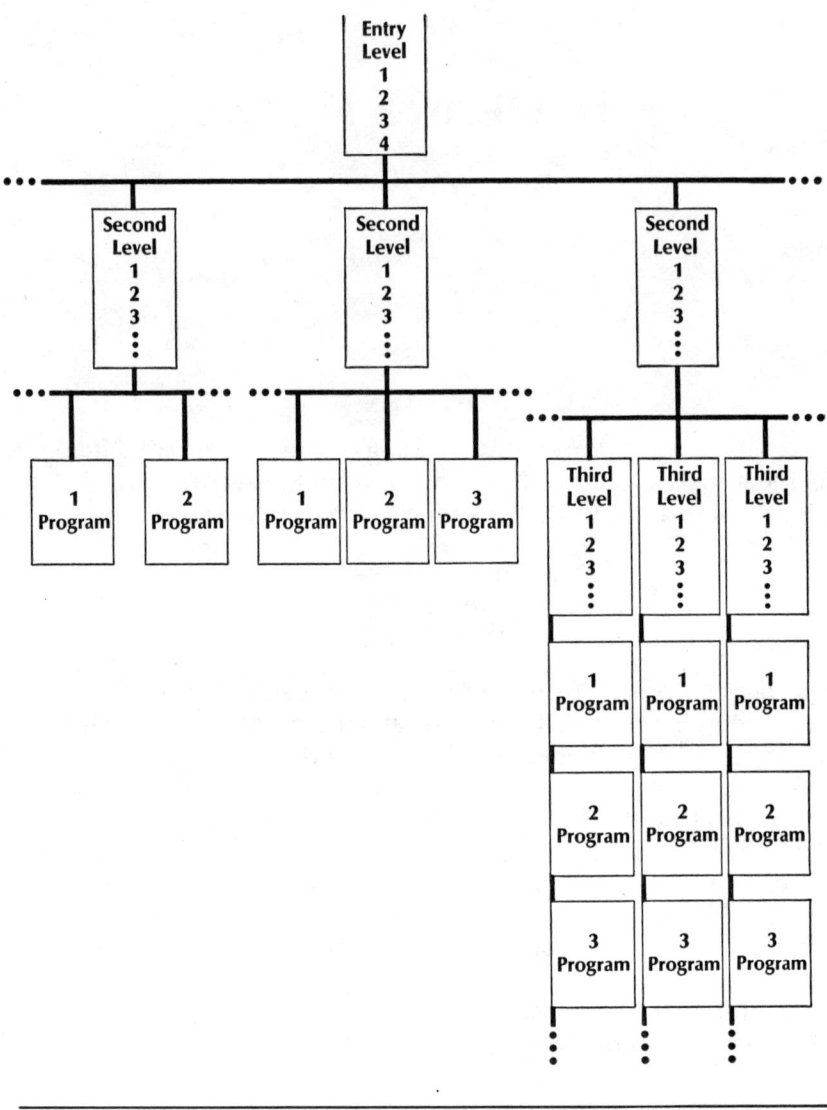

FIGURE 3-1

Section of level structure of a menu-driven system

do not work in others. Thus, it will not always be clear to you why an error message such as "INVALID COMMAND" is issued. Being aware of the menu structure helps.

In systems that are basically menu-driven, it is often possible to use commands to bypass menus and go directly to services, information, and programs. Also, frequently there are commands that you must learn in order to use certain services, information, and programs. You can nearly always find these commands through the HELP command.

The following example illustrates a simple search in a menu-driven system. The search is for a stock price.

THE SEARCH PROCESS 21

Fact Search (menu-driven system)

SYSTEM: This is the STOCKS Database

Enter Item Number or HELP

    1 Overview
    2 Instructions
    3 Bulletins
    4 Prices

USER: 2

SYSTEM: **Step 1:** To find a stock price select item 4 from the menu

         Step 2: Type the symbol for the stock you are interested in

         Step 3: Type SYMB and the name of the company if you do not know the symbol

         Step 4: Press RETURN key

Enter Item Number or HELP

    1 Overview
    2 Instructions
    3 Bulletins
    4 Prices

USER: 4

SYSTEM: Type in stock symbol

USER: IBM

SYSTEM: Close 126 5/8   09/23/83

Enter another stock symbol or press RETURN key to go back to menu or QUIT to discontinue STOCKS Database

USER: QUIT

SYSTEM: Type a new database name or HELP or OFF to exit the system

USER: OFF

SYSTEM: Off at (time, date)

    The advantage of the menu-driven system is that you are, in theory, told what to do every step of the way and so you do not have to learn and remember a system language. Although it is still possible to become confused, usually you can figure out what to do—eventually. This is not the case with command-driven systems, which require that the user learn at least a few basic commands to start. But once you master the commands, you can search these systems quickly and efficiently without waiting for menus and instructions to be displayed.

COMMAND-DRIVEN REFERENCE SYSTEMS

The following discussion applies to the situation in which a clinician, researcher, or scholar wants to find references to publications on a subject. This is one of the most widely performed types of searches and is facilitated by the large number of bibliographic databases that now cover most fields of knowledge.

Preparing for the Search

Whether it is necessary to spend time preparing for a search depends very much on the nature of your information need and the system you are using. Cost consciousness is also a factor, as a well-prepared search usually takes less online time (the primary online searching cost) to execute than a sketchily prepared one does. Naturally, you will take more time to prepare for a complex subject search than for a relatively simple search or for a search for articles by a particular author.

The first crucial step is to define your information need as precisely as possible. This is not as simple a matter as it seems. Online systems have many powerful options that can affect the outcome and cost of your search. For example, you may not be interested in reading articles written in languages other than English, and you will want to take steps to exclude them. Or, it may not be necessary to search back beyond a certain date—e.g., before 1976 for information about Legionnaire's Disease. Some other subject-related factors a prospective searcher might consider are: Does this question apply only to a certain age group? Does this drug-related question I am studying require information from animal experiments or only from human studies?

After defining the question as precisely as possible, the next step is to select a vendor service and a database; it is possible that you will search more than one database, and even use more than one service, to answer a single question. Chapter 2 and the following four chapters provide information to help make these decisions. See particularly the sections titled "Selecting Vendors" and "Evaluating Databases" in Chapter 2 and the discussion of SDC's Data Base Index in Chapter 6.

Another selection method that is both fun and *free* is to dial the local TYMNET node and type "INFORMATION" followed by a carriage return after the PLEASE LOG IN prompt. Respond to "PASSWORD:" with "SUN2SHINE" and just hit the RETURN key after "PROJ CODE:". Entering a question mark after the TYMNET prompt brings up instructions and the menu shown in Listing 3-1. Selecting "11" from the menu results in the index to TYMNET vendors. Terms are fairly broad, but you can use them to locate vendors that may have databases on your selected subjects.

Note: The convention used here and throughout this book on printout examples is that information typed by the computer is in regular font, and user responses are in underlined boldface.

Essentially, the search process is one of matching in both the macro and micro senses. In the macro sense you must match your information need to the information, wherever it is. In the micro sense you must enter search terms that match representations of required information stored in the computer. In online bibliographic searching, these representations are index terms. See Fig. 3-2.

Online computers respond as desired only when index terms match search terms on a character-by-character basis (although some allow for "wild cards," variable characters or alternate endings to words). Index terms in online systems typically consist of title words, words from abstracts, authors' names, corporate affiliations,

THE SEARCH PROCESS

LISTING 3-1

TYMNET INFORMATION SYSTEM

```
                    PLEASE TYPE YOUR TERMINAL IDENTIFIER d1
                    -2417-006-
    Does Not        PLEASE LOG IN: INFORMATION
     Display        PASSWORD: SUN2SHINE
     Return         PROJ CODE:

                    TYMSHARE H8  9/24/83   9:14
                                        TYMNET INFORMATION SYSTEM

User Response to → ENTER ITEM NUMBER OR A ? :2
  Receive Menu
                    Choose the information you would like from the following
                    menu.  Enter 'STOP' to abort an unwanted listing or 'QUIT' to
                    get out of the system.  All input must be in CAPITAL letters.

                    ITEM  FILE NAME              DESCRIPTION
                    ====  =====================  =====================================
                      1   @STATE                 TYMNET domestic access numbers by state
                      2   @TYMSAT                TYMNET public Tymsats sorted by node #
                      3   @CITY                  TYMNET domestic access numbers by city
                      4   @NEWPHONES             Domestic access numbers for cities added
                                                     during the last 90 days
                      5   @CHANGEPHONES          Changed and new access numbers for
                                                     cities already on the TYMNET network
                      6   @INTLPRT1COM           Info on TYMNET International access
                      7   @CONFIG                Configuration of TYMNET internationally
                                                     Includes speeds supported and network
                                                     names
                      8   @DPACACCESS            DATAPAC access numbers
                      9   @HOWTOUSETYMNET        Basic How to use TYMNET manual
                     10   @BLUSEARCHCOM          Computer and Data Services Available
                                                     Through TYMNET ( The BLUEBOOK )
                     11   @BLUEINDEX             Key word index to the Computer and
                                                     Data Services Available manual
                     12   @THUGSNEWS             Quarterly TYMNET Newsletter
                     13   @DATAPACTYMNET         Logging in from DATAPAC to TYMNET
                     14   @TYMNETDATAPAC         Logging in from TYMNET to DATAPAC
                     15   @PCFILE                Personal computer software certified
                                                     operational on TYMNET

User Response to → ENTER ITEM NUMBER OR A ? :11
    View Index
                    TYMNET SERVICES         Page     1
                    KEY WORD INDEX          03/09  17:43


                                    ACCOUNTING

                    BLOODSTOCK RESEARCH INFORMATION SERVICE, INC.
                    CYBERSHARE LTD.
                    DIALCOM, INC.
                    DTSS INCORPORATED
                    OPTIMUM SYSTEMS, INC. (OSI)
                    PROPRIETARY COMPUTER SYSTEMS  (PCS)
                    ROCKIE SMITH ENTERPRISES, INC. (RSE)


                                    ACTUARIAL

                    M & R SERVICES, INC.
                    POLYSYSTEMS, INC.


                               ADVERTISING & MARKETING
```

LISTING 3-1 (continued)

```
THE NEW YORK TIMES

       AEROSPACE

EUROPEAN SPACE AGENCY/INFORMATION MANAGEMENT

       AGRICULTURE

BIBLIOGRAPHIC RETRIEVAL SERVICES (BRS)
COMPUSERVE INCORPORATED
DATA RESOURCES, INC. (DRI)
DIALOG INFORMATION SERVICES, INC.
EUROPEAN SPACE AGENCY/INFORMATION MANAGEMENT

       AIRLINES

COMPUSERVE INCORPORATED
DIALCOM, INC.
LOCKHEED DATAPLAN, INC.
PROPRIETARY COMPUTER SYSTEMS (PCS)
THE COMPUTER COMPANY
    •
    •
    •
```

classification codes, and other special items; some databases have index terms (assigned by indexers) in addition to title and abstract terms, and some do not. In databases with assigned indexes, terms are usually *controlled*—selected from a *thesaurus* or other specially constructed vocabulary. This means that you cannot perform the best search by using *Russia* or *Vitamin C* when the approved index terms are *USSR* and *Ascorbic Acid*. As computers are very particular, *U.S.S.R.* would not work either. The intellectual challenge in searching controlled vocabulary is to find the appropriate, approved term—the one in the database vocabulary.

When searching *uncontrolled* vocabulary—mainly title words, but also abstract words (in those databases that have abstracts)—the problem is to include all possible synonyms, variant forms, and alternate spellings as they might appear in the text. Thus, to perform a complete search, you would have to use *Russia, USSR, U.S.S.R.* and, possibly, specific cities such as *Moscow* and *Leningrad*; both *Vitamin C* and *Ascorbic Acid; sulphur* and *sulfur; paediatrics* and *pediatrics; UFO* and *Unidentified Flying Object*. Word endings can be a problem, as it is tedious to type *learn, learning,*

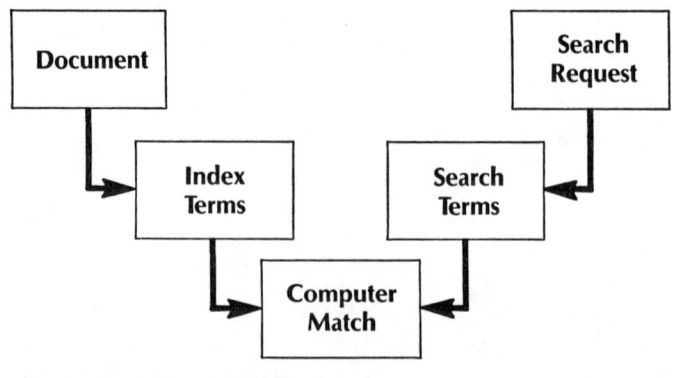

FIGURE 3-2

The online matching process

learned, learns, et cetera; many systems solve this problem by allowing for *truncation*. For example, in the SDC system, the single search term *LEARN:* will match the four terms mentioned above and any others beginning with the five letters, L-E-A-R-N. Conventions of this type are documented in the vendor manuals that you receive when you sign up with a vendor.

You should also consult these manuals to find which fields are available for searching in a database. As already mentioned, fields are access points such as language, title words, index terms, authors, codes, et cetera. A full record consists of many fields. See Listing 3-2 for an illustration of a *full record* from the Microcomputer Index on the Dialog system.

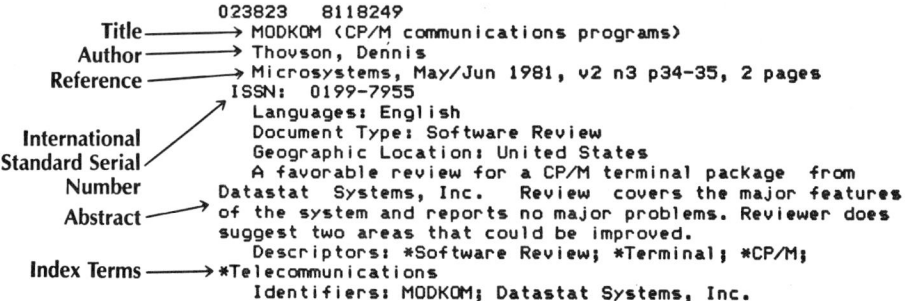

LISTING 3-2

PRINTOUT OF FULL RECORD
System: DIALOG   Database: MICROCOMPUTER INDEX

If you are familiar with the printed counterpart of a database, you have the advantage of understanding subject coverage and indexing language. You should also know that differences between printed and online indexes go beyond physical form. As clearly illustrated by Listing 3-2, an online database has far more access points: journal title, document type, language, geographic location, descriptors, identifiers, all title words, and all abstract words. In fact, you can search for almost every word in the record (though not months, volume, issue numbers, or pagination). *Identifiers* are index terms freely assigned to articles to supplement *descriptors*, which are chosen from the controlled vocabulary.

Manuals also give format conventions for fields. For example, an author's name might appear in various databases as *Smith, Jr; Smith Jr; Smith, Jane R.; Smith, Jane Roberta.* If the author is a Jr., Sr., II, or III, the situation becomes slightly more complex.

Case Study

The following example will help you to understand the online process and the search-strategy suggestions made above. Let us assume that you are a microcomputer user using online systems. You are interested in upgrading your modem and communications package and would like to do background reading. You decide to perform a search of Dialog's Microcomputer Index to find articles on this subject in microcomputer journals. Since your computer is CP/M based, it makes sense to limit the search to this type of operating system.

Step 1: Develop Strategy—In developing a strategy for searching, the first step is to identify search *concepts*, the separate ideas implied by a topic. In this case the concepts are:

Modems
Communications packages
CP/M-based systems

Since the database is devoted exclusively to microcomputers, all articles in it are related to microcomputers; thus, you need not include microcomputers as a concept.

The next step is to translate concepts into search terms that best match the index terms of the database. Subject index terms on Microcomputer Index on Dialog are title words, abstract words, descriptors assigned by indexers from the thesaurus, and identifiers, also assigned by indexers. These are merged into a term list called a *basic index*. A section of the Dialog basic index, which is available online through the EXPAND command, is shown in Listing 3–3. Almost all bibliographic systems have an index similar to this one. In simple subject searching, *it is this basic index that the user is trying to match.*

If a thesaurus is available, use it at this point to locate subject terms. If not, as we assume here, you are on your own to develop an appropriate set of terms. To do a comprehensive search, it is very important to think of all possible synonyms for each concept. In this case, the terms in Table 3–1 are adequate for starting.

Question marks are truncation symbols. They instruct Dialog to search for any terms beginning with this string of characters. *Modem?* retrieves both *modem* and *modems*. *Packages* was determined to be unnecessary, and some popular microcom-

---

LISTING 3–3

BASIC INDEX ON DIALOG-MICROCOMPUTER INDEX DATABASE

```
Expand Command ──▶  ?e modem
                    Ref  Items   Index-term
                    E1      39   MODELING
                    E2      24   MODELS
                   ┌E3     139   *MODEM
                   │E4       1   MODEM I
Term "Expanded"────┤E5       3   MODEM 80
         On"       │E6       1   MODEMCARE
                   │E7       1   MODEMLAND
                    E8      44   MODEMS
                    E9       1   MODEM80
                    E10      1   MODERATE
                    E11      1   MODERATED
                    E12      1   MODERATELY
                                    For more, enter PAGE

Expand Command ──▶  ?e communication
                    Ref  Items   Index-term
                    E1       3   COMMUNICATES
Term "Expanded"     E2      11   COMMUNICATING
         On"      ↘ E3      70   *COMMUNICATION
                    E4       1   COMMUNICATION WORKERS
                                   OF CANADA
                    E5     165   COMMUNICATIONS
                    E6       1   COMMUNICATIONS WORKERS
                                   OF AMERICA
                    E7       4   COMMUNICATOR
                    E8       4   COMMUNITREE
                    E9      36   COMMUNITY
```

THE SEARCH PROCESS

TABLE 3-1
CONCEPT-TO-TERM TRANSLATION

CONCEPTS	TERMS
Modems	*Modem?*
Communications packages	*Communicat?*
CP/M-based systems	*CP/M*
	IBM
	Zenith
	DEC
	Osborne

puter brand names were added to the CP/M concept because articles about communicating with these computers may not mention CP/M specifically. Note that you could have added *Coupler?* to the modem concept, *Telecommunications* to the communications concept, and more microcomputer names. Developing a search strategy is an art, not a science, and you cannot identify a perfect strategy beforehand. In selecting search terms, there is a cost/benefit tradeoff that you must consider within the context of your information need. With experience, you will learn to look at probabilities when deciding which concepts or terms to include.

Step 2: Log On—Listing 3-4 shows the Dialog log-on procedure through TELENET. After prompts appear, you provide a terminal identifier (D1 for most microcomputers), the Dialog TELENET address, and then the password, which is struck over for security reasons. The LOG-ON message contains the date and time. The "?" prompts you to respond. You then type "B 233" (begin Microcomputer Index) to go to that database.

Note: Information typed by the user is underlined.

LISTING 3-4
LOGGING ON TO MICROCOMPUTER INDEX IN DIALOG

```
                          TELENET
                          215 8A
Terminal Identifier → TERMINAL=d1
   Dialog TELENET → ac 41520
          Address
                          415 20 CONNECTED
             Date
   User Password     ENTER YOUR DIALOG PASSWORD
    (Struck Over) →            LOGON File6 Wed 23feb83 20:26:42 Port864
             Time
                       ? b233
Instruction to Go to              23feb83 20:27:18 User1762
     Microcomputer        $0.23  0.005 Hrs File6*
    Index (File 233)      $0.04  Telenet
                          $0.27  Estimated Total Cost

   Coverage Dates → File233:Microcomputer Index - 81-82/Jun
                    (Copr. Micro. Info. Serv. Inc. 1982)
                          Set Items Description
```

LISTING 3-5

SELECTING AND COMBINING TERMS
Search for Information on Communications Packages and Modems for CP/M-based Systems
System: DIALOG   Database: MICROCOMPUTER INDEX

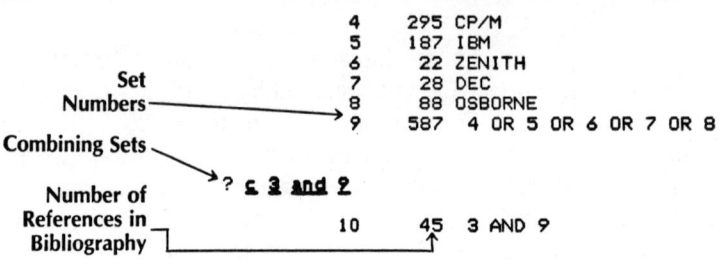

```
Selecting Terms ——→ ? ss modem? or communicat?
                         1    112  MODEM?
                         2    196  COMMUNICAT?
                         3    282  1 OR 2

Selecting Terms ——→ ? ss cp/m or ibm or zenith or dec or osborne
                         4    295  CP/M
                         5    187  IBM
                         6     22  ZENITH
      Set                7     28  DEC
   Numbers ————→         8     88  OSBORNE
                         9    587  4 OR 5 OR 6 OR 7 OR 8
Combining Sets
   Number of      ? c 3 and 9
 References in
  Bibliography        10     45  3 AND 9
```

Step 3: Selecting and Combining Terms—Listing 3-5 shows the searching portion of the session. After the "?" prompt, you key in *SS modem?* or *communicat?* to ask the computer to search for all references containing *either* term. It does not matter whether upper case, lower case, or a combination of the two is used. The computer responds with the number of references to each term in a record and with the number in which either or both appear (*set** number 3). Proceed in a similar manner for the CP/M concept; this results in set number 9. The final search statement combines ("C") sets 3 *and* 9 which specifies references that have *both* a term from set 3 and a term from set 9. Notice how drastically this final step reduces the number of references.

OR and AND are called *Boolean operators*, named for George Boole, a nineteenth-century mathematician. You will use them frequently in online information systems in the manner illustrated above. Indeed, the capability for making such combinations is a major advantage of online systems. Another operator, NOT, is generally available but rarely needed.

Figure 3-3 illustrates the logical processes by means of Venn diagrams (after the logician, John Venn). Look at the circles to see why OR logic expands the number of references retrieved and why AND logic reduces retrieval. NOT logic must be used with caution. For example, you might consider the following strategy for the example search:

Modem?		*MS-DOS*
OR	NOT	OR
Communicat?		*PC-DOS*

The problem is that this strategy eliminates articles that discuss, for example, *both* PC-DOS and CP/M communications.

*Group of records retrieved in response to a search statement

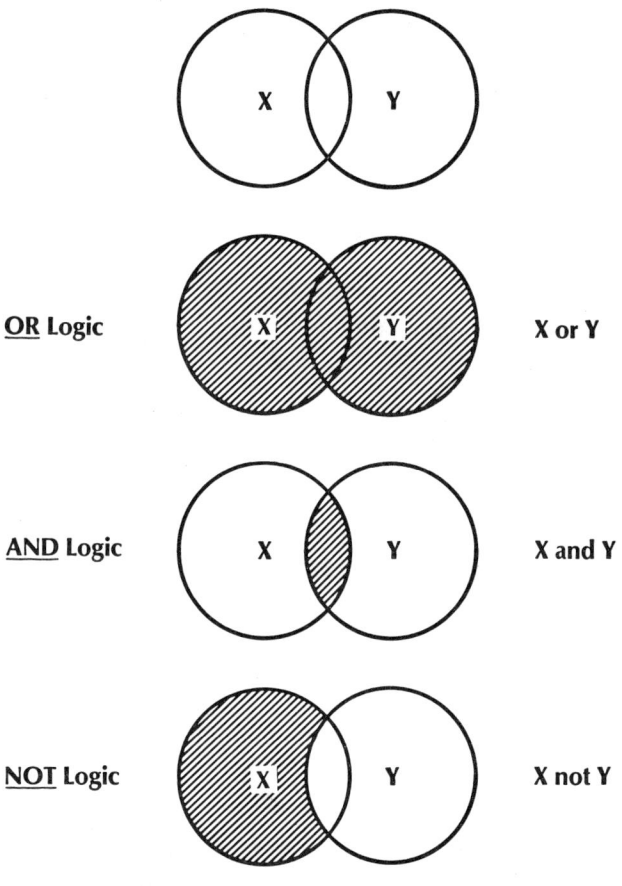

FIGURE 3-3

Logical operators with Venn diagrams

Step 4: Printing References—You can print references online or display them online and download them to a diskette or other storage medium to be printed later. Or, you may print them offline at the computer site and have them mailed to you, a process that takes several days. Online printing can be expensive, but it is always more convenient to have your references immediately. Usually, only large bibliographies, for which the cost differential can be great, are ordered to be printed offline.

In Dialog the print command is T (for type) followed by the set number, the format, and the range of references to be printed. Most Dialog files have eight print formats that vary according to the amount of printed information. In Listing 3-6, the command given is to print the first five references from set number 10 in format 3, which gives Dialog and Microcomputer Index accession numbers, the title, author, journal reference, and the International Standard Serial Number for the journal.

Step 5: Logging Off—Online sessions end with a log-off procedure like the one shown in Listing 3-7. The system gives the date, time, cost (broken

INFORMATION ONLINE

LISTING 3-6

PRINTING REFERENCES
Search for Information on Communications Packages and Modems for CP/M-based Systems
System: DIALOG   Database: MICROCOMPUTER INDEX

Set Number ──┐
Format Number ──┐

? t **10/3/1-5**

Number of
References to Be
Printed

```
10/3/1
035676    8212169
    Communicating with the heavyweights: IBM, Osborne flex
terminal muscles
    Derfler, Frank
    Kilobaud Microcomputing, May 1982, v6 n5 p18-27, 6 pages
    ISSN:0192-4575

10/3/2
033383    8204671
    Now micros can talk mainframe
    Vose, G. Michael
    Microcomputing, Mar 1982, n27 p382, 1 page ISSN: 0199-6789

10/3/3
```
Accession Numbers ──→ `029242    8137219`
Title ──→ `The General...a multi-purpose communications program`
Reference ──→ `    Hunt, Daniel`
`    Interface Age, Oct 1981, v6 n10 p104-107+, 10 pages`
Journal Serial
Number ──→ `ISSN:0147-2992`

```
10/3/4
026598    8128233
    Model IIs talking to IBMs thanks to new progams
```
Author ──→ `    Latamore, Bert`
```
    80 Microcomputing, Aug 1981, n20 p66-68, 2 pages
    ISSN: 0199-6789

10/3/5
023823    8118249
    MODKOM (CP/M communications programs)
    Thovson, Dennis
    Microsystems, May/Jun 1981, v2 n3 p34-35, 2 pages
    ISSN: 0199-7955
```

LISTING 3-7

LOGGING OFF DIALOG

Date ──┐
Time ──┐
User Identification ──┐
Number

? **logoff**

```
                23feb83 20:42:36 User1762
```
Dialog Connect ──→ `$12.06    0.268 Hrs File233*`
Time and Cost ──→ `$2.68    Telenet`
TELENET Cost ──→ `$14.74   Estimated total cost`
Log-off Time ──→ `LOGOFF 20.42.43`
Address Disconnect
Message ──→ `415 20 DISCONNECTED`
TELENET Prompt ──→ `a`

down according to Dialog and TELENET cost), and a message that the connection has been broken. At this point you are back in the TELENET network and may proceed directly to log on to another system without re-dialing.

Improving a Search

Frequently, searches do not proceed in the straightforward manner shown above. You can improve them, however, by adding more synonyms, by eliminating search terms that are too general or not on target, by adding or eliminating concepts, by limiting by language, date, or other special features, and so forth. Systems are designed to be *interactive*. The most common search problem is missing *relevant* references as opposed to retrieving references that are *irrelevant,* simply because it is much easier to eliminate irrelevant references that you can see than to know what is missing. As a new searcher, you may often feel that the one or two terms you first select will be adequate to cover a concept when actually more synonyms or variant forms are needed. Some troubleshooting approaches are given in Table 3-2. One "trick" used by experienced searchers is to look at index terms of retrieved references for ideas for either additional search terms or for terms to eliminate. Sometimes you may have no idea how to structure a search, but you know one or two relevant references. A good approach in this situation is to retrieve the known references online and look at how they are indexed.

After you have mastered the search techniques described above and have done a fair amount of searching, you may want to explore some of the more sophisticated

TABLE 3-2

TROUBLESHOOTING

Problem	Question

Fewer references than wanted or expected	Was logic correct?
	Term misspelled?
	Need more synonyms?
	Truncate when appropriate?
	Use variant spelling forms?
	   (e.g., fetal and foetal, WHO and W.H.O.)
	Were vague or unnecessary terms used?
	   (e.g., factor, product; or education or children in an educational database)
	Eliminate a concept?

Too many references	Was logic correct? Remove least specific synonyms? Add a concept? Limit by language, date, or document type or other factor?
Irrelevant references	Was logic correct? Were subject terms appropriate? Add a concept? Use NOT logic?

search capabilities of the major system languages to improve efficiency and results. Some of these are:

- Selecting terms from online vocabulary displays
- Searching terms that are adjacent to or a certain distance from each other
- Automatically searching hierarchically related terms
- Saving searches for later execution or execution in a different database
- Displaying a compact history of the search
- Erasing commands
- Sorting references online
- Merging references from different databases before printing
- Obtaining time and cost data while online
- Sending messages to and receiving messages from the system
- Ordering documents
- Entering and modifying a selective dissemination of information profile

Mistakes and Problems

It is not unusual for people just beginning to search to worry that they will harm the system. That just will not happen. Online timesharing systems are completely protected from users. The worst thing that can happen is that you can waste money. There are two basic ways to make mistakes: through strategic errors—selecting wrong or inadequate search terms or not combining them in the right way; through mechanical errors—selecting a wrong command or making typing errors. The first type of error is the most serious because you do not always know when it has happened. When you make a mechanical error, the system usually responds with some kind of clue such as "NO POSTINGS" (usually means that a search term has been misspelled) or "INVALID ENTRY" (to signal that a command has not been entered properly).

An extremely frustrating situation is to be "bumped" off the system, or even worse, to have the system "crash." Fortunately, "bumps" and "crashes" do not happen very often, and when they do, it is often possible to recover at the point where the search was interrupted. At other times you may receive a signal such as "ALL PORTS BUSY" when attempting to log on. In essence, this means that the vendor computer is full, that as many people as it can accommodate simultaneously are searching at that time. Usually, another call in a few minutes will produce results.

Systems also, on occasion, become very slow in responding, a condition that is frustrating not only because of the time wasted, but also because you are being charged for connect time during the computer pauses. Usually, experienced searchers will log off a system when it is responding poorly and will return later. It is advisable, too, to log off when you encounter line noise, another kind of problem. Line noise occurs most often when you search at high speeds or in geographic areas that do not have high-quality telephone wiring. It manifests itself in extra or incorrect characters or in meaningless strings of characters being printed or displayed even when you are not keying.

Online systems, though not infallible, very, very rarely make mistakes. Sometimes, however, you may receive results far different from what you expected. With enough diligence and imagination, you will almost always find the cause. If not, you can obtain a diagnosis from the vendor by sending a copy of the online transaction and the results along with a query letter.

CHAPTER 4
Information Utilities

OVERVIEW

The two best known and most widely used general services are The Source in McLean, Virginia and CompuServe in Columbus, Ohio. For want of a better term—certainly not because of their corporate structure or financial goals—these companies are called *information utilities*. They provide not only a wide range of business and home-use information services but also electronic messaging and other online computing capabilities similar to those of computer service bureaus.

The Source and CompuServe are both very young organizations that have grown quickly. Founded in June 1979, The Source Telecomputing Corporation was purchased by Reader's Digest in September 1980 and is now a subsidiary of the Reader's Digest Association, Inc. Control Data Corporation bought a minority interest in April 1983. Calling itself "America's Information Utility," The Source now has over 40 databases providing more than 750 specific services to over 30,000 subscribers.

CompuServe Information Service is part of CompuServe, Inc., a remote computer services organization that became in 1980 a wholly owned subsidiary of H. & R. Block, Inc. The information service was begun in August 1979 to provide information and computing services specifically for personal-computer and home-terminal users. Now CompuServe subscribers, numbering over 40,000, have access to information on over 170 main topics and more than 400 subtopics.

The capabilities and applications of The Source and CompuServe are so diverse and far-reaching that they are difficult to categorize. You can read a book, "converse" with a friend, check details of a company's financial situation, read hometown news, send and receive messages, play blackjack, buy furniture—the list is nearly endless. Still, most applications fall into the following areas:

- News databases such as the UPI wire service, or editions of newspapers
- Financial information such as stock market quotes or corporate financial information
- Communications services including conferencing, electronic mail, and bulletin boards
- General entertainment; for example, games, puzzles, horoscope readings, and poetry
- Consumer information services such as movie reviews, restaurant guides, and health tips

INFORMATION UTILITIES

- Reference databases
- Aids to shopping
- Computing services

A very recent entrant into the market served by The Source and CompuServe is the Delphi system of General Videotex Corporation in Cambridge, Massachusetts. While Delphi offers fewer services at present, the system provides direct computer-to-computer links to other services such as Dialog and Dialcom and can even be used to send mail to subscribers of The Source and CompuServe.

THE SOURCE

NAME: The Source Telecomputing Corporation
1616 Anderson Road
McLean, VA 22102

TELEPHONE:
(800) 336-3366 (Business)
(800) 336-3330 (Hotline)
(703) 734-7500 (Virginia and outside U.S.)

NUMBER OF DATABASES:
42 (more than 750 services)

HOURS:
Service: 24 every day
Hotline: Monday–Friday 8AM–1AM EST
Saturday, Sunday 9AM–1AM EST

COST: (October 1, 1983)

*Registration fee:** $100 (one-time, refundable after 30 days if not satisfied)

Hourly connect time charges: (local time)

	SPEED	WEEKDAYS 7AM–6PM	WEEKENDS HOLIDAYS 6PM–7AM
THE SOURCE	300 baud**	$20.75	$ 7.75
	1200 baud	$25.75	$10.75
SOURCE*PLUS	300 baud	$39.75	$34.75
	1200 baud	$44.75	$37.75

**Baud is a measure of speed. Three hundred baud is about 30 characters per second.

Monthly minimums: $1 for account maintenance
$9 usage
$.25 each time connect fee

Storage charge based upon number of additional blocks.

*May be waived. See Subscription Information below.

Connect time charges include communications except for WATS line at $15 per hour.

Billing may be to a company or credit card.

SUBSCRIPTION INFORMATION:
You can order the Subscriber Kit ($100) directly from The Source or purchase it at a computer store. Contents are a manual, a Source Command Guide (a directory of services), a copy of *Sourceworld* (the subscriber newsletter), a sign-on card, a new subscriber agreement, and a postage-paid envelope in which to return the agreement.

The Source has made a number of arrangements to "bundle" a subscription with microcomputer software and hardware. For example, the registration fee has been waived for purchasers of certain Zenith microcomputer models, and some Philips word processors. Such arrangements are subject to change.

USER AIDS:
The Source User's Manual   (included with registration; $19.95 separate)
An Introductory Guide to Programs and Services   gratis
Command Guide   gratis
Update   gratis
Sourceworld newsletter   gratis

COMMUNICATIONS:
TYMNET, TELENET, UNINET, SOURCENET, Direct Dial in the Washington, D.C. area, WATS line

300 and 1200 baud

TRAINING: The Source offers no formal training; you learn by reading the manual and takin advantage of the online HELP commands. Online commands are more specific than those in the manual.

DESCRIPTION: Since space does not permit discussion of all The Source databases and services here, we describe only major areas and key databases.

Communications Services:
The user account number (also called ID number) serves as the code to identify participants in all the communications services.

MAIL
All subscribers to The Source have at their disposal what is, in effect, an electronic mailbox which can be used to send and receive messages. With the simple MAILCK command, you can check quickly to see if messages are waiting. If so, there are many options, which include ignoring the message, reading it and replying, forwarding it to another user, saving it, or deleting it. Mail can be sent to as many as 200 Source users at one time. Some of the sending capabilities are delayed-delivery and creation of a mailing list file.

INFORMATION UTILITIES 37

CHAT
To "chat" (talk to another online user), you display online the ID numbers of people currently connected to The Source, then select one and type the command "CHAT ABC123" in which ABC123 is the ID number of the person selected. This user chooses or refuses to chat. Subscribers to The Source who did not know each other previously have become electronic pen pals and have been married after learning of mutual interests through a file that lists interests (DISEARCH) or through the electronic bulletin board (POST).

Readers of this book are invited to chat or send messages to me (ID:STJ511) through The Source.

POST
POST is The Source's classified ad and bulletin board section. There is no charge for posting. Notices are deleted automatically every 14 days. Arrangement is by subject categories (about 75), which are listed in the user manual. The following sampling of topics should provide a feel for the potential of Post: Antiques, Apple, Atari, Disability, Help Wanted, Music, Photography, Property/Houses Swap, Software Sale, Sports, Visicalc, Weekend Getaway.

PARTI
PARTI stands for PARTICIPATE, computer conferencing at a fairly high level. See Chapter 10 for a discussion of conferencing.

*Source*Plus:* A group of relatively sophisticated services for which a higher access rate is charged, Source*Plus includes several business databases such as Management Contents and Media General, which provide stock analyses.

Business: Business services in addition to those in Source*Plus give stock data and business news and make available spreadsheet and accounting software.

Catalog Shopping: The Source has specialized services for bartering and/or ordering records, tapes, books, and classic radio programs, and a discount shopping service for which a membership fee is charged.

Education and Careers: This section contains teaching programs such as drills in mathematics and grammar at several levels, information on college financial assistance, and EMPLOY, an employment opportunity and resume database broken down by more than 40 professions. Any subscriber may add a resume to the EMPLOY database. As you would expect, "Computers" is one of the professional employment categories.

Government and Politics: Here you will find congressional legislation tracking (Source*Plus), news commentary and interviews, and access to the United Press International wire service.

Home and
Leisure: In the consumer area, there are games such as blackjack, poker, adventure, and backgammon; biorythms; familiar quotations, a home medical guide; personal financial services such as income tax advice; energy-saving tips; toll-free telephone numbers of consumer organizations.

News and Sports: In addition to the UPI wire service, which is online minutes after release, you will find the U.S. News and Washington Letter.

Science and
Technology: Mainframe computing capability is available for performing statistical computations and other mathematical routines and for modeling in engineering and in the sciences.

Travel, Dining,
and
Entertainment: For travelers and persons seeking entertainment, there are airline schedules, a travel club, restaurant guides, wine guides, and movie reviews. You can use the travel club for making hotel and airline reservations; it also offers money-saving tour packages.

Creating and
Computing: It is possible to use The Source to create your own files. This feature can be used, for example, by a private special-interest network to file mail or to capture information from other Source files. One intriguing use is to market your own publication. A private file may be created, tested through advertising in POST, and submitted to PUBLIC, the database of user-built files. If accepted, the creator will receive royalties based upon use of the file. Some examples of PUBLIC files are "The IBM PC Gazette," "Be Your Own Lawyer," and "Find Your Ancestors." The Source's text writing and editing functions facilitate creation of files.

The Source supports Basic/VM, Fortran 66, Pascal, a modeling package, and calculations; it also has other computing capabilities.

SYSTEM PROTOCOLS:
There are two basic ways to reach information that is contained in The Source. From the *Command Level,* indicated by the prompt "->", you can go directly to a program or information service by typing the appropriate command. Or, at the Command Level, you can type MENU and be guided by the choices that appear at each step. Other than MENU, the critical commands a beginner needs to know are QUIT (to return to the Command Level) and OFF (to exit from the system). OFF must be entered at the Command Level.

CASE STUDIES: The two case studies that follow illustrate typical uses of The Source. Case 1 demonstrates the electronic bulletin board capability and uses menus. The second case shows access by commands.

INFORMATION UTILITIES

Case 1: A new Apple computer owner is shopping for an inexpensive printer and decides to look at The Source bulletin board, POST, to see if there are any printer "specials" listed or if anyone is offering a secondhand printer for sale. See Listing 4-1. In the example, all user responses are underlined, and information from The Source is not underlined.

The very first step is to log on to the system, a procedure that is similar in all online systems and is illustrated in Chapter 3. After logging on to The Source, the user is led from the WELCOME message (Level 1) to THE SOURCE MAIN MENU (Level 2) to MAIL AND COMMUNICATIONS (Level 3) and finally to POST. Once in POST,

---

LISTING 4-1

SEARCH ON THE SOURCE FOR INFORMATION ON APPLE PRINTERS

```
                    WELCOME TO THE SOURCE

                    1  USING THE SOURCE
                    2  TODAY
                    3  BUSINESS UPDATE
         Level 1    4  THE SOURCE MAIN MENU
                    5  WHAT'S NEW
                    6  COMMAND LEVEL

                    Enter item number or HELP 4


                    THE SOURCE MAIN MENU

                    1  NEWS AND REFERENCE RESOURCES
                    2  BUSINESS/FINANCIAL MARKETS
                    3  CATALOGUE SHOPPING
                    4  HOME AND LEISURE
         Level 2    5  EDUCATION AND CAREER
                    6  MAIL AND COMMUNICATIONS
                    7  CREATING AND COMPUTING
                    8  SOURCE*PLUS

                    Enter item number or HELP 6


                    MAIL AND COMMUNICATIONS

                    1  MAIL
                    2  CHAT
         Level 3    3  POST
                    4  PARTICIPATE
                    5  MAILGRAM MESSAGES

                    Enter item number or HELP 3


                    POST

                    1  OVERVIEW
                    2  INSTRUCTIONS
                    3  READ
         Level 4    4  POST
                    5  PURGE
                    6  SCAN

                    Enter item number or HELP 3
```

LISTING 4-1 (continued)

Selecting Category → `<C>ategory,<U>ser ID,<D>ate,<K>eyword:`**c**

Narrowing Search → `Categories, or <H>elp:`**apple**
`Searching...`
`244 notices valid.`

`<N>arrow, <E>xpand or Return for all :`**n**

`<C>ategory,<U>ser ID,<D>ate,<K>eyword:`**k**

`Keyword(s) or <H>elp:`**printer**
`Searching...`
`5 notices valid.`

Carriage Return (not printed) — `<N>arrow, <E>xpand or Return for all :` ↓
`Wait..`

Browsing Header → `Category:APPLE`
`Subject:SILENTYPE PRINTER`
`From:TCK807`
`Posted:20 FEB  9:57 pm`

Carriage Return — `<N>ext,<PO>st, or Return for text-` ↓

`I HAVE A SILETYPE PRINTER I'D LIKE TO`
`SELL--$250. ALSO HAVE A APPLE SERIAL`
`CARD I'LL SELL FOR $75 AND A MODEL 33`
`TELETYPE FOR $65.`
`CONTACT GENE AT TCK807.`
`THANKS.`

---

the user chooses to read and is asked what parameter (category, user ID, date, or keyword) is to be searched. Categories are general and are listed in the user manual. The remainder of the interaction and some of the other possibilities in POST are explained in the response to the HELP READ command, Listing 4-2.

Case 2: An executive is traveling to Houston in a few days and would like to entertain some colleagues in a fine French restaurant. In order to ensure that all goes smoothly, she wants to make the reservation ahead of time. The Source is consulted to identify the best restaurant. See Listing 4-3.

At the WELCOME message, the searcher selects the command level, then types the command "USREST" to go directly to the restaurant guide. The remainder of the interaction is almost self-explanatory. After finding that a total of 64 restaurants is listed for Houston, the searcher asks for a search for the French ones by giving the FIND command (which means "I want to search a subject") and then FRENCH after the prompt. The 30 French restaurants are "scanned" for name, address, and rating. Then the full description of the four-star restaurant, Courtlandts, is printed.

INFORMATION UTILITIES   41

LISTING 4–2

RESPONSE TO "HELP READ" COMMAND IN THE SOURCE

```
READING NOTICES
---------------

    STEP   1:  BEGIN YOUR SEARCH.........Enter  the   command READ at  the first
               prompt. You will  be asked to  specify how you  want to call up
               entries. You can select by <C>ategory, <U>ser ID, <D>ate, or
               <K>eyword.

               Select  CATEGORY to  see  notices in  any category you  select.
               Select USER ID  to see notices  posted by any user you specify.
               Select DATE to  see notices posted on the day or range of dates
               you specify. The  best form for entering dates is: 16 JAN 1982.
                    Enter date ranges like this: 16 JAN 1982,19 MAR 1982.
               Select KEYWORD to see all the notices that contain the keyword
               you select.

-More-
           NOTE: After selecting  any of the search attributes listed above, you
                 can  enter just  the first few  letters of your  search word to
                 keep your selection as large as possible.

              EX: After selecting  USER ID, entering  the first part of an ID
                  number, STC for  instance, will  narrow your selection to the
                  notices posted by users whose account numbers begin with
                  STC.

                  Similarly, after selecting CATEGORY, entering A will narrow
                  your  selection of  valid entries  to  notices  posted in
                  categories that begin with the letter A.
    STEP   2:  NARROWING  AND EXPANDING YOUR  SEARCH....Once you've made  your
               selection, the number  of  notices available  for  reading will
               appear, and you  will be able to further narrow or broaden your
               selection by <C>ategory, <U>ser ID, <D>ate, or <K>eyword.

               At  the  prompt   "<N>arrow or <E>xpand  your Selection or Press
               Return to See All Valid Entries" enter N or E depending on what
               you  want  to  do,  and the  <C>ategory,  <U>ser ID,  <D>ate, or
               <K>eyword:" prompt will appear again. There  is no need  to re-
-More-
               enter anything you've already entered. If  you are <E>xpanding,
               your new entry  will ADD all the notices that  match it to  the
               number of already valid entries. If  you are <N>arrowing,  your
               entry will call up only the  entries that contain all the char-
               acteristics you've specified.
```

LISTING 4–3

SEARCH ON THE SOURCE FOR A GOOD FRENCH RESTAURANT IN HOUSTON

```
WELCOME TO THE SOURCE

             1  USING THE SOURCE
             2  TODAY
             3  BUSINESS UPDATE
Level 1      4  THE SOURCE MAIN MENU
             5  WHAT'S NEW
             6  COMMAND LEVEL

             Enter item number or HELP 6
             -> usrest

Welcome to the Mobil Restaurant Guide, your window into fine dining.

Enter "help" for further instructions.
```

LISTING 4–3 *(continued)*

Choosing City → Enter City,State (for example, CHICAGO,IL):<u>houston,tx</u>
64 restaurant(s) found in Houston,TX.   64 total.
City,State or <cr> to search:

64 restaurant(s).

Choosing → Select scan, find, backup, print, restart,
Restaurant Type or help for more instructions:<u>find</u>
Search for:<u>french</u>

30 restaurant(s) with "FRENCH".

Select scan, find, backup, print, restart,
or help for more instructions:<u>scan</u>

The following   30 restaurant(s) have "FRENCH"
in their descriptions.

Restaurant(s) in Houston, TX

Scanning Directory →
```
        .
        .
     5  **    BUD BIGELOW'S CHARCOAL HOUSE.    7939 Westheimer Rd (77063), 1
                mi W. 782-0430.
     6  **    CADILLAC BAR.    1812 Sheperd Dr (77007), 3 mi W of I-10.
                862-2020.
     7  ***   CHARLEY'S 517.    517 Louisiana (77002). 224-4438.
     8  ****  COURTLANDTS.    3200 Louisiana St (77006), at Stuart, 1 mi SW,
                59 Louisiana St exit. 526-3247.
     9  ***   D'AMICO'S.    2407 Westheimer (77098), 4 mi W. 524-5551.
                Westheimer Rd. 782-3888.
        .
        .
```

Select scan, find, backup, print, restart,
or help for more instructions:<u>print 8</u>

The following   30 restaurant(s) have "FRENCH"
in their descriptions.

Restaurant(s) in Houston, TX

Printing
Full Description
**** COURTLANDTS.   3200 Louisiana St (77006), at Stuart, 1 mi SW, 59
Louisiana St exit. 526-3247. Hrs: 11:30 am–2 pm, 6–10 pm. Closed Sun;
major hols. A/C. Continental menu. Bar. Semi–a la carte. Lunch,
$6.95–$17.95; dinner, $13.95–$22.50. Specialties: rack of lamb, beef
Wellington, veal Oscar. Own pastries. Background music. Entertainment
(piano bar) exc Sun. Georgian decor. Jacket required. Cr cds: A, D, MC, V.
Spoken: Spanish,French.

COMPUSERVE

NAME: CompuServe Information Service
5000 Arlington Centre Boulevard
Columbus, OH 43220

TELEPHONE: (800) 848-8990   (Hotline)
(800) 848-8199   (Business)
(614) 457-8600   (Ohio)

NUMBER OF DATABASES:
170 main topics (400 subtopics)

INFORMATION UTILITIES 43

HOURS: *Service:* 24 hours (5AM—8AM as available)
Hotline: Weekdays 8AM—Midnight EST
Weekends 2PM—Midnight EST

COST: (January 1, 1983)

Registration fee: Included in packages described in Subscription Information.

Hourly connect time charges: (local time)

	SPEED	WEEKDAYS 8AM–6PM	EVENINGS WEEKENDS 6PM–5AM
CompuServe	300 baud	$22.50	$ 5.00
CompuServe	1200 baud	$35.00	$17.50

Higher rates for certain services.

Fees for online storage and for printing.

Connect time charges include communications when using the CompuServe network. TYMNET $2/hour from contiguous United States. WATS $20/hour weekdays and evenings and $10/hour on weekends.

Billing by credit card or direct with a surcharge.

SUBSCRIPTION INFORMATION:

There are numerous options. You may order a sign-up kit directly from CompuServe or purchase one in a computer store. It costs $39.95 and includes five hours of free time. The kit consists of the fairly brief *CompuServe Information Service User's Guide*, the *Dow Jones Information Service User's Guide*, a list of access numbers and log-on procedures for the CompuServe network, a CompuServe ID number and secret password, a description of the CompuServe service continuation terms and conditions, a CompuServe service continuation request and agreement, Dow Jones News/Retrieval user code, Dow Jones agreement, and one hour of free time on Dow Jones. At Radio Shack Computer Centers a similar packet, called the Universal Sign-Up Kit, is available for $19.95, but offers only one hour of online time; the price for a one-hour kit including communications software for the Radio Shack computers is $29.95. The idea is to log on using the limited-time password, try the system, and sign up as a permanent customer online using a credit card number. You must also send in the written agreement included in the kit.

CompuServe presently has agreements with some microcomputer manufacturers—Commodore and Atari, for example—to include a subscription with some of their products.

USER AIDS: CompuServe Information Service Guide (included with kit)
Programming Area Guide $3.95
Microquote User's Guide $6.95
User's Guide $4.95
SIG Instruction Manual $3.95
Supplement II: EMAIL $2.50
EMI Flight Planning Users Guide $5.95
Other manuals may be ordered online
Today magazine $30 per year
Update newsletter   gratis

COMMUNICATIONS:
CompuServe network in about 100 U.S. cities and Canada, TYMNET, WATS

300 or 1200 baud

TRAINING: Self-instruction user's manual and online HELP commands.

DESCRIPTION: CompuServe is like The Source in that it has communications capabilities, information services, and computing software.

Communications Services: CompuServe has four communications services, three of which parallel Source functions.

EMAIL
Like MAIL, EMAIL is a person-to-person system for delivering messages. You can read and send mail, check to see whether an addressee has received something you sent, and file mail. It is simple to edit messages before sending them on EMAIL.

If anyone would like to communicate with me on CompuServe about this book or any other matter, my ID number is 72115,620.

CB
As with CHAT in The Source, CB (standing for Citizen's Band) allows for an online conversation with another user. One of CompuServe's most popular services, CB also functions as a CB radio network or telephone party line on which many users can interact at once.

INFORMATION UTILITIES 45

BULLET
Analogous to POST, BULLET is an electronic information exchange bulletin board to which any user can add a message.

FEEDBK
FEEDBK is a method for communicating with CompuServe. You can use it at no charge to report problems, ask questions, and order documentation. FEEDBK and the customer service hotline complement each other.

User Information: This selection has information and services that should be of interest to all users. Included are the "What's New" feature; directions for specifying terminal defaults, for changing your password, for reviewing charges, and for changing credit card information; and answers to frequently asked customer questions.

Personal Computing Services: Here you have access to shop-at-home, special-interest groups, and the programming area that allows you to create a program or text file, to exchange software, and to use business and educational programs. Public domain software is available for downloading.

Home Services: Under Home Services you will find newspapers; weather information for most major U.S. cities; electronic banking; games and entertainment features; and a reference library of publications, movie reviews, and a travel guide.

Business and Financial: This area contains business and financial news, Standard and Poor's data, stock quotes, and the Value Line database. Most of the business and financial services have a surcharge.

SYSTEM PROTOCOLS:
The CompuServe system functions in a manner very similar to that of The Source. A top menu is like the Main Menu in The Source. The T command returns you to the top menu. Typing GO XXX-N, in which XXX is a service code and N is a page number, enables you to go directly to a service without cycling through the menus.

There is an online index of topics accessible through the top menu; you can search this index by keyword for any subject. Updated versions of the index are printed sometimes in the CompuServe magazine and newsletter that are sent to subscribers. New

INFORMATION ONLINE

users will find the menu structure diagram printed in the user's manual very helpful.

CASE STUDIES:

Case 1: A ski enthusiast is planning a weekend trip to New England. To find out if conditions are satisfactory and to select the particular area to visit, she accesses the ski reports on CompuServe. See Listing 4–4.

LISTING 4–4
FINDING NEW ENGLAND SKI REPORT THROUGH COMPUSERVE

```
                        COMPUSERVE INFORMATION SERVICE

                        19:36 EST   MONDAY     28-FEB-83

                        WHAT'S NEW
                        INFORMATION ON DEMAND
                        BHG ADDS FOOD BUYLINE
Log-on Message →        L-5 SOCIETY CHAPTER - SPACE SIG
                        SKI REPORTS AVAILABLE
                        AVIATION INSURANCE GUIDE
                        MEDICAL INFORMATION FROM AAMSI

                        FOR DETAILS, SEE WHAT'S NEW
                        ENTER: GO NEW AT THE ! PROMPT
                        ON ANY PAGE.

Carriage Return         KEY <ENTER> FOR NEXT PAGE: ↓
  (not shown)

                        COMPUSERVE              PAGE CIS-1

                        COMPUSERVE INFORMATION SERVICE

                        1 HOME SERVICES
                        2 BUSINESS & FINANCIAL
                        3 PERSONAL COMPUTING
Top Menu →              4 SERVICES FOR PROFESSIONALS
                        5 USER INFORMATION
                        6 INDEX

                        ENTER YOUR SELECTION NUMBER,
                        OR H FOR MORE INFORMATION.

                        !6

                        COMPUSERVE              PAGE IND-1

                        INFORMATION SERVICE INDEX
                        -------------------------

                        1 TO SEARCH INDEX
Index Menu
                        2 COMPLETE INDEX LIST

                        LAST MENU PAGE. KEY DIGIT
                        OR M FOR PREVIOUS MENU.

                        !1

                        COMPUSERVE              PAGE IND-99

                        THE CIS INDEX PROGRAM ALLOWS
                        YOU TO SEARCH FOR TOPIC AREAS
                        BASED ON KEY WORDS.

                        PLEASE ENTER KEYWORD
Index Search →          : SKI

                        SKI CONDITIONS                WEA
```

INFORMATION UTILITIES 47

LISTING 4-4 *(continued)*

Command to Go to → KEY: GO PAGE#
the Weather → OR <ENTER> TO CONTINUE: **GO WEA**
Section
COMPUSERVE   PAGE WEA-1

WEATHER   PAGE WX-3

   1 STATE FORECASTS
   2 EXTENDED FORECASTS
   3 FORECAST EXPLANATION
   4 PROBABILITY OF PRECIP.
   5 MARINE FORECASTS
   6 SPORTS FORECASTS
   8 WEATHER WARNINGS
  12 AVIATION WEATHER MENU

Selecting Sports → SELECTION: **6**
Weather

SPORTS

ENTER IDENTIFIERS
OR <H> FOR HELP

Asking for Help → ID: **H**

SPORTS WEATHER CONTAINS REPORTS
ON WEATHER CONDITIONS IN MAJOR
RECREATIONAL AREAS, SUCH AS
NATIONAL PARKS AND SKI AREAS.
SNOW REPORTS FOR MAJOR SKI
CENTERS (ALB, BOS, DEN, SLC)
ARE AVAILABLE IN THE WINTER.

KEY <ENTER> FOR NEXT PAGE:

AT THE ID: PROMPT YOU MAY ENTER:
 - A 3 LETTER LOCATION ID (RNO)
 - A LIST OF ID'S (SLC,RNO)
 - A QUOTE (") TO REUSE LAST IDS
 - A DIGIT ON MENU WX-2 OR WX-3
   (E.G. ID: 5   FOR NOTAMS)
 - A COMMAND:
     H OR ? - THIS HELP TEXT
     M - RETURN TO LAST MENU
     LIST - LIST ALL LOCATION IDS

LAST HELP PAGE
Request to List → KEY <ENTER> TO RESUME:**LIST**
Locations

ALB ARB BOI BOS CHI DEN FAT GRB
GRR GTF HTL LAS LAX MKE MQT PHX
RDU RNO SEA SFO SLC SSM
Selecting → ID: **BOS**
Boston Area

NEW ENGLAND SKI AREAS COUNCIL OFFICIAL SUMMARY OF SKIING CONDITIONS
AT NEW ENGLAND SKI AREAS AS OF NOON, FEBRUARY 28, 1983.

SKIING CONDITIONS ARE SUBJECT TO CHANGE DUE TO WEATHER, SKIER
TRAFFIC AND OTHER FACTORS. BE AWARE OF CHANGING CONDITIONS.

LEGEND: NEW-INCHES OF NEW SNOW IN LAST 24 HOURS. PDR-POWDER SNOW.
PP-PACKED POWDER. LSGR-LOOSE GRANULAR. FRGR-FROZEN GRANULAR. WET
GR-WET GRANULAR. WHERE TWO SUCH TERMS APPEAR, THE FORMER SHOWS
CONDITIONS ON 70 PERCENT OR MORE TERRAIN, AND THE LATTER THE NEXT
MOST PREVALENT CONDITION. VC-VARIABLE CONDITIONS. TC-THIN COVER.
MM-SNOW MADE IN LAST 24 HOURS. WBLN-WINDBLOWN SNOW. NO-NOT
OPERATING. OPR-OPERATING. NS-NIGHT SKIING AVAILABLE.

   .
   .
   .

Listing 4-4 (continued)

```
NEW HAMPSHIRE.
WILDERNESS PP LSGR 11 TRAILS 2 LIFTS.
WILDCAT PP ICY SPOTS 25 TRAILS ALL LIFTS.
BRETTON WOODS PP LSGR 12 TRAILS 3 LIFTS OPEN TOP TO BOTTOM.
CANNON MOUNTAIN PP LSGR 20 TRAILS 5 LIFTS & TRAM.
WATERVILLE VALLEY LSGR 18 TRAILS 7 LIFTS OPEN TOP TO BOTTOM.
KING RIDGE LSGR 13 TRAILS 4 LIFTS.
CROTCHED MTN. LSGR PP 15 TRAILS 5 LIFTS NS.
  .
  .

VERMONT.
JAY PEAK PP FRGR 28 TRAILS ALL LIFTS.
SMUGGLERS' NOTCH PP LSGR 25 TRAILS ALL LIFTS.
STOWE PP LSGR 38 TRAILS MM ALL LIFTS.
BOLTON VALLEY PP LSGR 23 TRAILS ALL LIFTS NS.
  .
  .
```

The user does not know where ski reports are within the menu structure and so decides to use the online index, which is entered from the top menu. Through the index she learns that the reports are part of the "Weather" section. She types GO WEATHER, as directed. In the Weather menu, number 6 (SPORTS FORECASTS) appears to be most appropriate for ski information. Then, not knowing how to respond to ENTER IDENTIFIERS, she keys in H for HELP, a frequent option in CompuServe. A description of SPORTS WEATHER and directions for using it then appear. Not knowing the location identifiers for New England, she asks for a list of possibilities and guesses that BOS (for Boston) will give the New England conditions. Information is up-to-date and is preceded by a legend that clearly explains the codes.

This is a good example of both how CompuServe guides and assists the user *most of the time* and how it sometimes can be very confusing. Here everything is obvious—except what the location codes stand for. Unless someone is either very lucky or very astute, he or she can undergo considerable trial and error to figure them out.

Case 2: A consultant who works from his home in Houston wants to travel to Philadelphia on June 1 and decides to look at the *Official Airline Guide* on CompuServe to locate appropriate flights and fares. See Listing 4-5. Rather than step through the menus, he types the GO OAG command to go directly to the *Guide*. After he selects the menu choice to access the *Guide*, a printed message states that there is a surcharge for this service and asks the user to agree to the charge by pressing RETURN ENTER. A "+" at the next choice gives *OAG* instructions on how to format a request. The consultant then

INFORMATION UTILITIES 49

LISTING 4–5

LOCATING AIRLINE SCHEDULES AND FARES ON COMPUSERVE

Go to *Official* → !**GO OAG**
Airline Guide

```
OAGEE                    PAGE OAG-1

    OFFICIAL AIRLINE GUIDE EE

    1. HOW TO USE OAG EE
    2. OAG EE FEEDBACK
  $ 3. ACCESSING OAG EE

    OAG HELP DESK: 800-323-4000

    LAST MENU PAGE. KEY DIGIT
    OR M FOR PREVIOUS MENU.
```

Select Choice to → !**3**
Access the *OAG*
```
OAGEE                    PAGE OAG-30
```

Surcharge Notice →
```
          * PLEASE NOTE *
    IF YOU PROCEED, THE FOLLOWING
    SURCHARGES WILL BE INCURRED
    OVER AND ABOVE COMPUSERVE RATES:
    $21/HR STANDARD SERVICE
    $32/HR DURING PRIME TIME HOURS
    TO RETURN TO COMPUSERVE FROM OAG
    ENTER /Q.

    OAG EE MAY BE UNAVAILABLE FROM
    12 MIDNIGHT-4 A.M. CENTRAL TIME.

    KEY <ENTER> TO ACCESS OAG EE.
```

User Types a → !
RETURN
```
OAGEE                    PAGE OAG-200


    REQUEST RECORDED,
    ONE MOMENT, PLEASE

    CONNECTED TO 080AG

    WELCOME TO THE OFFICIAL AIRLINE GUIDE
    (OAG), COPYRIGHT 1983, OFFICIAL AIRLINE
    GUIDES, INC., OAK BROOK, ILLINOIS 60521


    ENTER /I OR + FOR OAG MENU
```
Select *OAG* Menu → **+**

```
          ** OAG COMMAND MENU **
```
OAG Instructions → ENTER:/I FOR INFORMATION AND ASSISTANCE
```
         /S FOR SCHEDULE DISPLAYS
         /F FOR FARES DISPLAY
    NOTE: YOU MAY USE CITY NAMES OR CODES.
         IF YOU OMIT ANY PART OF THE ENTRY,
         THE SYSTEM WILL PROMPT YOU FOR IT.
```
OAG Examples → EXAMPLE:
```
         /S MIA;DALLAS 1SEP 3P
         /F MIAMI;DALLAS 1SEP
    OTHER COMMANDS FOR USE LATER:
         /M TO RETURN TO THIS MENU SCREEN.
         /S SCHEDULES FOR A NEW CITY PAIR.
         /F FARES FOR A NEW CITY PAIR.
         /Q TO EXIT FROM THE OAG.
```

LISTING 4–5 (continued)

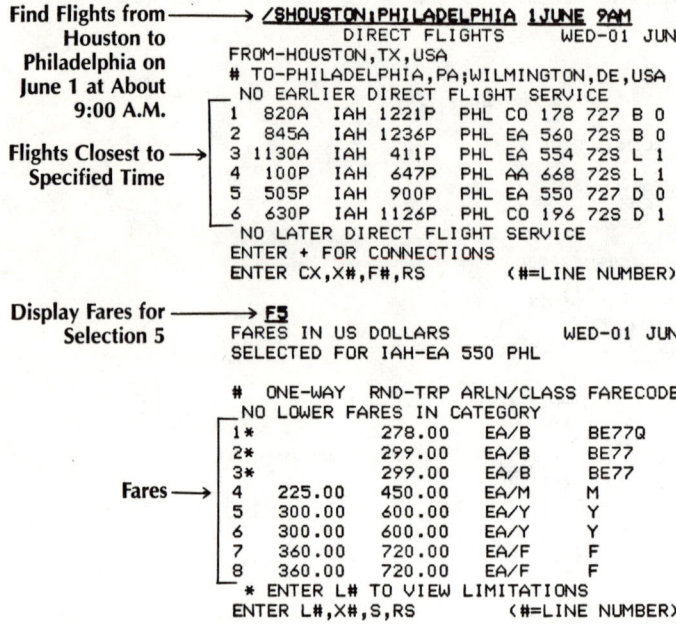

Find Flights from Houston to Philadelphia on June 1 at About 9:00 A.M. → `/SHOUSTON;PHILADELPHIA 1JUNE 9AM`

Flights Closest to Specified Time

Display Fares for Selection 5 → `F5`

Fares

```
 /SHOUSTON;PHILADELPHIA 1JUNE 9AM
         DIRECT FLIGHTS     WED-01 JUN
FROM-HOUSTON,TX,USA
# TO-PHILADELPHIA,PA;WILMINGTON,DE,USA
  NO EARLIER DIRECT FLIGHT SERVICE
1   820A  IAH 1221P  PHL CO 178 727 B 0
2   845A  IAH 1236P  PHL EA 560 72S B 0
3  1130A  IAH  411P  PHL EA 554 72S L 1
4   100P  IAH  647P  PHL AA 668 72S L 1
5   505P  IAH  900P  PHL EA 550 727 D 0
6   630P  IAH 1126P  PHL CO 196 72S D 1
  NO LATER DIRECT FLIGHT SERVICE
ENTER + FOR CONNECTIONS
ENTER CX,X#,F#,RS         (#=LINE NUMBER)

F5
 FARES IN US DOLLARS        WED-01 JUN
 SELECTED FOR IAH-EA 550 PHL

#  ONE-WAY  RND-TRP  ARLN/CLASS FARECODE
  NO LOWER FARES IN CATEGORY
1*           278.00   EA/B      BE77Q
2*           299.00   EA/B      BE77
3*           299.00   EA/B      BE77
4  225.00   450.00   EA/M      M
5  300.00   600.00   EA/Y      Y
6  300.00   600.00   EA/Y      Y
7  360.00   720.00   EA/F      F
8  360.00   720.00   EA/F      F
 * ENTER L# TO VIEW LIMITATIONS
ENTER L#,X#,S,RS          (#=LINE NUMBER)
```

asks for flights from Houston to Philadelphia; by keying F5, he requests the fares. He could have also looked at restrictions on special fares by entering L1, L2, or L3.

DELPHI

NAME: DELPHI
General Videotex Corporation
3 Blackstone Street
Cambridge, MA 02139

TELEPHONE: (800) 544-4005 (Hotline)
(617) 491-3393 (Massachusetts)

NUMBER OF DATABASES:
36 plus Dialcom and Dialog services

HOURS: *Service:* 24 every day
Hotline: Monday–Friday 8AM–Midnight EST
Weekends 8AM–10PM EST

INFORMATION UTILITIES

COST: (January 1, 1983)

Membership fee: $49.95

Hourly connect charges: (local time)

SPEED	WEEKDAYS 8AM–6PM	EVENINGS WEEKENDS HOLIDAYS
300 baud	$13–18.00*	$ 5.00
1200 baud	no differential	

Additional charges for certain features.

Storage charges based on number of characters.

No minimums.

Connect time charges included.

Billing is to a credit card.

SUBSCRIPTION INFORMATION:
Membership applications are obtained by writing or calling General Videotex.

USER AIDS: Delphi Handbook (included with subscription; $19.95 for additional copies)

COMMUNICATIONS:
TYMNET or Delphinet (in selected cities)

300 or 1200 baud

TRAINING: Self-instruction user's manual and online HELP commands.

DESCRIPTION: Delphi is the new kid on the block, having initiated service late in 1982. The range of services at start-up was similar to those of The Source and CompuServe, although services were fewer in number.

Communications Services: Delphi offers bulletin boards, conferencing, and mail with the usual provisions for entering, sending, and deleting messages. A unique and useful feature of the Delphi MAIL service is the ability to send mail to users of other systems—The Source, CompuServe, Dialcom, and ONTYME—using the addressee's identification numbers on

*Lower rates due to volume discounts.

those systems. You can also use a telegram service that converts your electronic mail to U.S. mail, telegram, telex, or wire.

Readers of this book are invited to communicate with me through my Delphi member name, CAROLJANE.

Information Services: An intriguing information service is ORACLE, a group of people with expertise in a great variety of areas, particularly personal computing. You can ask the ORACLE absolutely anything and receive a reply in your Delphi mailbox within a few days.

For an hourly fee, you can request a literature search by a librarian and receive the results via MAIL. Or, you can sign on to Dialog Information Services through the Delphi computer and be billed by Delphi—the fees are the same as those charged by Dialog. Access is also available through Delphi to a restricted set of Dialcom Computer Services, which include wire service news and about a hundred programs, mostly in the accounting, mathematical, scientific, and statistical areas. Provision of Dialog and Dialcom is a *gateway* service, meaning that the remote host computer being searched is distant from the computer initially accessed (Delphi).

A database belonging to Delphi is the Kussmaul Encyclopedia, a general reference work at the adult level with more than 20,000 entries. Since the encyclopedia is revised and updated continually, the editor invites feedback through Delphi.

Home Services: Delphi provides a banking service that will pay your bills and will even help reconcile your checkbook. You can auction or bid on goods and services on BAZAAR, shop at home, and make travel arrangements including airline, hotel, and car reservations. SCHEDULER helps keep track of appointments.

Entertainment: About a dozen of the popular games are available, and the member publishing service INFOMANIA features newsletters, collaborative novels, polls on significant and trivial issues, writing by members, and in PUNCHLINE any kind of comment. Writing services such as programs to upload, format, and download text help members to create files to be "published" in INFOMANIA.

Computing: In addition to providing computing services through Dialcom, Delphi plans to support several popular programming languages and offer typesetting by which you can produce camera-ready copy.

SYSTEM PROTOCOLS:

The Delphi menu-driven language is similar to those of The Source and CompuServe. New subscribers can make extensive use of the

INFORMATION UTILITIES 53

HELP command and online instruction to learn the system. There is a well-organized manual that contains a description of every service; the descriptions, however, are not as detailed as the online text. Delphi has some very helpful control commands for stopping and starting printing and for bypassing unwanted text, but there is no GO-type command for moving directly from one place to any other part of the service. Plans are underway to implement such a command in the near future.

CASE STUDIES:

Case 1: After being a user of Delphi for about one month, I decided to look at my mail. See Listing 4–6. The experience begins with an unusual

---

LISTING 4–6

READING AND REPLYING TO MAIL ON DELPHI

Log-on Message ⟶
```
Welcome to DELPHI
Version 1.2
Copyright (c) 1983
General Videotex Corporation

You love peace.

Latest updates to Delphi BB's:
   MEMBER-SERV 3/1/83
   OPERATIONS 2/23/83
   SYSTEM 3/15/83

MAIN Menu:

   APPOINTMENT-CALENDAR
   BULLETIN-BOARDS
   CONFERENCE
   DELPHI-ORACLE
   EXIT
   FINANCIAL SERVICES
   GAMES
   GUIDED TOUR
   HELP
   INFOMANIA
   LIBRARY
   MAIL
   NEWS
   ONLINE-MARKETS
   PROFILE
   TRAVEL
   WRITERS-CORNER
```

Selecting Mail from ⟶ `MAIN>What do you want to do?` **mail**
the Main Menu
```
MAIL Menu:

   CATALOG
   EXIT
   HELP
   MAIL
```

Selecting Mail from ⟶ `DMAIL>What do you want to do?` **mail**
the Mail Menu
`You have 2 new messages.`

LISTING 4-6 *(continued)*

```
Requesting Mail  →  MAIL> Directory
   Directory         #  From              Date          Subject

                     1  GYRO              15-MAR-1983   Greetings!
                     2  JIMJONES          18-MAR-1983   Reply to your message in BB.MEMBERSERV

Reading First    →  MAIL> read
   Message
                     From:  GYRO              15-MAR-1983 21:10
                     To:    CAROLJANE
                     Subj:  Greetings!

                     Welcome -- and sorry for the trouble you had in getting logged in.
                     We hope you enjoy the system, and that its use profits you in some
                     way or other.

                     Gyro

Reading Second   →  MAIL> read
   Message
                     From:  JIMJONES          18-MAR-1983 22:23                    MAIL #2
                     To:    CAROLJANE
                     Subj:  Reply to your message in BB.MEMBERSERV

                     Subject:  Introduction

                     Hello. Who are you? What do you do? How did you learn about Delphi?
                     I publish VIDEO-DIAL, a monthly newsletter on micro telecommunications.
                     JIM JONES.

Replying to Second → MAIL> reply
   Message
                     Subj:  Micro telecommunications Newsletter
                     Enter your message below. Press CTRL/Z when complete, CTRL/C to quit:
                     I am a librarian who is writing a book on using online systems.
                     Would like to hear more about VIDEO-DIAL. How can I subscribe?
                     CarolJane
```

log-on message known as the "fortune cookie" ("You love peace") and the Main Menu. Selecting MAIL from the Main Menu brings up the Mail Menu from which I again select MAIL and learn that I have two messages. Next, I isssue the DIRECTORY command, which is found in the manual, and look at the sender's user names and at the dates and subjects of the messages. The final steps, which are obvious from the printout, are to read and to reply.

Case 2:   A high school student is preparing a report on the Battle of Gettysburg and decides to start by looking in the Kussmaul Encyclopedia on Delphi. See Listing 4–7. The student selects LIBRARY from the Main Menu and receives the Library Menu. She next issues the LOOKUP command, which she found in the Delphi Manual, and responds with GETTYSBURG after the prompt. Not finding an exact match on GETTYSBURG, the computer suggests GETTYSBURG, BATTLE OF. That is just what the student wanted, and so she asks that the text be printed.

INFORMATION UTILITIES

LISTING 4-7

SEARCH ON DELPHI'S KUSSMAUL ENCYCLOPEDIA FOR INFORMATION ON THE BATTLE OF GETTYSBURG

```
MAIN Menu:

  APPOINTMENT-CALENDAR
  BANKING
  .
  .
  LIBRARY
  .
  .
  WRITERS-CORNER

MAIN>What do you want to do?  library

LIBRARY Menu:

  DIALCOM
  EXIT
  HELP
  LOOKUP
  RESEARCH-LIBRARY
  XREF

LIBRARY>What would you like to do?  lookup
Search for:  gettysburg
Unrecognized entry \GETTYSBURG\ - scanning...
GETTYSBURG
Do you want GETTYSBURG, BATTLE OF?  y

GETTYSBURG, BATTLE OF (July 1--3, 1863), greatest
battle of the CIVIL WAR, occurring in S Pa.  This
battle was a severe defeat for the Confederate
forces under Gen. Robert E.  LEE, and with the
simultaneous surrender of the S army at Vicksburg,
Miss., it determined the outcome of the Civil War.
Confederate defeat destroyed any possibility of
diplomatic recognition by foreign countries and
thus cut off the prospect of important military
aid, especially from Great Britain.  Lee decided,
following his victory on May 5 at
CHANCELLORSVILLE, Va., to invade the North in
order to save S territory from further
depredations of battle and to attack and isolate
Harrisburg, Pa., an important N railroad hub and
  .
  .
  .
```

CHAPTER

5
Reference Vendors with Databases on Many Subjects

Three major vendors in the United States provide files in a broad range of subject disciplines. This chapter covers these vendors—Dialog Information Services, Bibliographic Retrieval Services (BRS), and SDC Information Services—and then adds a brief discussion of their Canadian and European counterparts. Dialog, SDC, and BRS are full-support vendors in that they offer the key support services mentioned in Chapter 2—well-developed documentation, frequent training at sites throughout the country, monthly newsletters, and toll-free hotlines for technical help.

The main differences among the three vendors are the databases, the command languages, and the peripheral services they provide. While there are major databases such as BIOSIS Previews and ERIC (Educational Resources Information Center) on all three systems, many databases are "up" on only two of these vendors or are unique to one. Vendors add databases regularly and sometimes remove them, so the availability of databases changes constantly. As mentioned previously, vendors' catalogs are the best source of information on database availability.

Regarding command languages, with the partial exception of BRS services designed for end users, all are command- rather than menu-driven. All have a few basic commands for logging on, searching and combining subject terms, displaying and printing references, and logging off. These must be learned before using the system. Differences among protocols for accomplishing these tasks are for the most part a matter of format.

The three command languages, however, provide more powerful techniques such as the ability to retrieve terms depending on their proximity to each other, the ability to sort references, and the ability to use terms retrieved in one database as search terms in another without re-keying. These techniques, which vary significantly among the vendors, can improve retrieval and efficiency. However, they are not necessary for performing successful searches in most cases and need not concern the new or infrequent searcher.

One of the most important peripheral services is online document ordering, a capability of both Dialog and SDC. Another is low-cost, off-hour access at reduced rates, introduced late in 1982 by both Dialog and BRS. Called the "Knowledge Index" (Dialog), and "BRS After Dark," these services are designed specifically for the home microcomputer user.

In the discussion and examples below, there is a disproportionate emphasis on social science, humanities, and general-interest databases. This is done simply to provide information not available anywhere else in this book and to minimize overlap with Chapters 6 and 7, which are devoted entirely to scientific, technical, and business applications. The reader should not lose perspective because of the examples but should keep in mind that, by far, the majority of databases and searches are in science, technology, and business.

DIALOG

NAME: Dialog Information Services, Inc.
3460 Hillview Avenue
Palo Alto, CA 94304

TELEPHONE:
(800) 227-1927 (Marketing)
(800) 227-8282 (Training)
(800) 982-5838 (California)
(415) 858-3785 (Outside U.S.)

INTERNATIONAL OFFICES:
Haymarket, New South Wales, Australia   Tel: 02-264-6344
Oxford, England   Tel: (0865) 730 969
Toronto, Ontario, Canada   Tel: (416) 593-5211
Tokyo, Japan   Tel: (03) 463-4391 or (03) 272-7211

NUMBER OF DATABASES:
190

HOURS:
Service: Monday–Thursday   Midnight–10PM EST
Friday   Midnight–8PM EST
Saturday   8AM–8PM EST
Hotline: Monday–Friday   9 AM–8:15PM EST

COST: (January 1, 1983)

No registration fee.

From $15 to $300 per connect hour depending on the database, plus offline print charges and some online display fees. Most common range is $40 to $60 per connect hour.

No minimums. Substantial discounts are available for organizations willing to guarantee various levels of minimum usage.

Communications charges are not included. They are:

TYMNET: $10/hour
TELENET: $10/hour
UNINET: $6/hour
WATS: $18/hour
Direct Dial: No charge

Billing is monthly.

58 INFORMATION ONLINE

SUBSCRIPTION INFORMATION:
To subscribe, an individual or responsible person within an organization need only sign a service contract.

USER AIDS: Making the Dialog Connection with a Personal Computer   gratis
Dialog in Brief   gratis
Basic System Guide $40
Lab Workbook $10
Database Documentation Chapters $5 each
Chronolog newsletter   gratis
Dialog through LEXIS/NEXIS User's Manual $10
Various brochures one copy   gratis

COMMUNICATIONS:
TYMNET, TELENET, UNINET, WATS, and Direct Dial

300 and 1200 baud

TRAINING: System Seminar for new users: 1 1/2 days $135.
Advanced Seminars: 1/2 day $45.
Expanded Subject Seminars: One day $115.

Dialog holds training seminars regularly throughout the United States and abroad. On-site training is also available. Each person who attends a system seminar receives $100 of free online time in one of the ONTAP practice files.

In addition, the first Monday of every month is "Dialog Day," a kind of open house that includes an introduction for potential customers in the morning and a clinic for current customers in the afternoon. Dialog Day is conducted in Chicago, Houston, Boston, New York, Philadelphia, Palo Alto, Los Angeles, and Washington, D.C. It is free, but reservations are required.

DESCRIPTION: Largest of the three broad-spectrum vendors, Dialog has databases in all areas of science and technology, business, economics, law, government, current affairs, social science, humanities, and education. It also provides extensive coverage of patents.

Among the major social science databases, a Dialog strength, are PSYCINFO (Psychological Abstracts), which is also on Knowledge Index; Sociological Abstracts; and Social SCISEARCH (counterpart of *Social Sciences Citation Index* from the Institute for Scientific Information). ERIC, the first Dialog database, continues to be used heavily by educators.

For the humanists, there is, foremost, the MLA Bibliography produced by the Modern Language Association. Other important databases in the humanities are Historical Abstracts, Philosopher's Index, and Artbibliographies Modern.

Comprehensive Dissertation Index (CDI), based on *Dissertation Abstracts*, is one of Dialog's most important multidisciplinary databases. A small amount of information in CDI is duplicated in other places. While most databases go back to the mid-1960s, CDI is an index to virtually all American, and some foreign, doctoral dissertations dating back to 1861!

Dialog covers a number of important national directories: *American Men and Women of Science*, the *Encyclopedia of Associations*, *Marquis Who's Who*, *Ulrich's International Periodical Directory*, and *The Foundation Directory*. A unique set of Dialog databases is the Electronic Yellow Pages (with sections on: Construction, Financial Services, Manufacturers, Professionals, Retailers, Services, Wholesalers), which is put together from the Yellow Pages of over 4000 telephone books.

A useful Dialog feature is the set of ONTAP files, each of which contains a small segment of a regular file. These files may be used at the low rate of $15 per hour by searchers who feel that they need online practice. As mentioned, each person who attends the system seminar receives $100 of free search time on these files. Currently there are 10 ONTAP files, and this number will grow.

To help searchers select the correct database to use for a specific subject, Dialog has produced an index to its databases: DIALINDEX. Using DIALINDEX, you can perform a pre-search on many databases at one time to come up with the number of matching items in each. Databases with the highest retrieval results are the obvious choices for searching.

SYSTEM PROTOCOLS:
Dialog has a powerful command language with nearly all the sophisticated features available on any system. These include saving searches for future use across files, sorting references, searching for terms according to their proximity to one another, and reviewing word lists online. You may also obtain SDI service and order documents online through Dialog.

CASE STUDY: See Chapter 3 for an example of a Dialog search.

NOTE: The information above describes the regular Dialog service. Below is comparable information for "Knowledge Index," the Dialog service that is primarily for end users. The main differences are that available databases are fewer, some databases cover shorter time periods, costs are lower, hours are restricted to evenings and weekends, and search commands have been simplified.

KNOWLEDGE INDEX

NAME: Knowledge Index
Dialog Information Services, Inc.
3460 Hillview Avenue
Palo Alto, CA 94304

TELEPHONE: (800) 227-1927 (Marketing)
(800) 227-5510 (Hotline)
(415) 858-3796 (Hotline, California)

NUMBER OF DATABASES:
23

HOURS: *Service:* Monday–Thursday 6PM–5AM (local time)
Friday 6PM–Midnight (local time)
Saturday 8AM–Midnight (local time)
Sunday 3PM–5AM (local time)
Hotline: Monday–Friday 7PM–11PM EST

COST: (January 1, 1983)

Registration fee: $35. Entitles user to two free hours of connect time.

$24 per connect hour.

No minimum.

Communications charges are included.

Billing is to a credit card only.

SUBSCRIPTION INFORMATION:
To subscribe, an individual must sign a customer agreement and give a valid credit card number.

USER AIDS: Knowledge Index User's Workbook (included with registration)

COMMUNICATIONS:
TYMNET, TELENET, UNINET, and Direct Dial

300 and 1200 baud

TRAINING: A self-instruction manual is at your disposal, and, in addition, you may access a set of online HELP commands.

DESCRIPTION: Although it is limited at present to 23 databases, Knowledge Index, like Dialog, has broad subject coverage. Knowledge Index databases are: AGRI1 (AGRICOLA database of the U.S. National Agricultural Library); BOOK1 (Books in Print); BUSI1 (ABI/INFORM database of Data Courier, Inc.); COMP1 (INSPEC database of the Institution of Electrical Engineers); CORP1 (business news from Standard & Poor's); EDUC1 (ERIC database of the National Institute of Education); ENGI1 (ENGINEERING LITERATURE INDEX from Engineering Information, Inc.); GOVE1 (publications of the Government Printing Office); GOVE2 (NTIS); MAGA1 (popular magazines from the MAGAZINE INDEX of Information Access Corporation); MEDI1, MEDI2, MEDI3 (the National Library of Medicine's MEDLINE database dating back to 1966); MEDI5, MEDI6, MEDI7 (BIOSIS Previews); NEWS1 (daily news from *The New York Times, The Wall Street Journal,* and *The Christian Science Monitor*); NEWS2 (same as NEWS1, but from 1979 on); PSYC1 (the PSYCINFO database of the

American Psychological Association); MEDI4 (International Pharmaceutical Abstracts); LEGA1 (Legal Resource Index); and BUSI2 (Trade and Industry Index). For microcomputer users there is the INTERNATIONAL SOFTWARE DATABASE (10,000 listings of software for micros and minis) and MICROCOMPUTER INDEX (covering over 40 journals such as *Byte, Personal Computing,* and *Infoworld*). Other databases will be added.

SYSTEM PROTOCOLS:

In addition to hours, cost, and number and size of databases, there are system differences between Dialog and Knowledge Index. Knowledge Index is a simplified version of Dialog. Some sophisticated features such as proximity searching by a range of options, offline printing, saving searches, and selective dissemination of information have been removed, and protocols for entering search terms and displaying references online are slightly different. Otherwise, to an experienced Dialog user, Knowledge Index looks very familiar.

As with Dialog, Knowledge Index allows the user to order documents online. Through Dialog you have more control over ordering, as you are able to choose a vendor from a vendor directory with price lists that are part of Dialog documentation. In Knowledge Index, the document supplier is selected by the vendor, and the charge is $4.50 plus $.20 per page copied for articles and $4.50 plus the actual cost for other documents. When cost of connect time is added, online document ordering can become an expensive procedure. But the cost is balanced by the fact that online ordering is fast and convenient.

CASE STUDY:

Citizens opposed to construction of a nuclear power plant near their homes are considering staging a large demonstration to attract attention to their cause. They are interested in the legal implications and potential effectiveness of their plans and want to read about nuclear protest demonstrations conducted elsewhere. A member of the group decides to perform a search on Knowledge Index using MAGAZINE INDEX, a database of popular journals. See Listing 5–1 for the results.

Similarities between Dialog search commands and Knowledge Index commands should be apparent. Knowledge Index uses the FIND command to substitute for both S and C in Dialog; the Knowledge Index command to show references is D for DISPLAY, with choice of formats limited to Short (S), Medium (M), and Long (L). Otherwise, for a relatively simple search such as this one, basic format and logical operations are the same. Note that "Atomic powerplants-" appears as the initial part of a descriptor in both printed references. A logical way to extend this search is to add this term to the strategy.

LISTING 5-1

SEARCH OF MAGAZINE INDEX DATABASE ON KNOWLEDGE INDEX FOR INFORMATION ON NUCLEAR POWER PLANT DEMONSTRATIONS

```
begin maga

 3/ 1/83  20:20:33 EST
Now in MAGAZINES (MAGA) Section
  Magazine Index (MAGA1) Database
  (Copyright 1982 Information Access Corp.)

?find nuclear and power and plant?

           5745 NUCLEAR
          13304 POWER
           9237 PLANT?
     S1    935 NUCLEAR AND POWER AND PLANT?

?find demonstrat?

     S2   2268 DEMONSTRAT?

?find s1 and s2

     S3    21  S1 AND S2

?d s3 /1
              Display 3/L/1
1398627
  Raiders of Diablo Canyon.
  Rogers, Michael
  Rolling Stone   p11(5)   Nov 12   1981
  CODEN: RLGSA
  illustration; photograph
  GEOGRAPHIC CODE: NNUSWCA    SIC CODE: 1629
   DESCRIPTORS: atomic power-plants-California; earthquakes and
 atomic power-plants-safety devices and measures; Diablo Canyon
 Nuclear     Power     Plant-demonstration,    1981;    Abalone
 Alliance-demonstration, 1981; Greenpeace International-demonstr-
 ation, 1981

?d
              Display 4/L/2
1308357
   Legal  showdown  at  Shoreham.   (Shoreham Nuclear Power Plant
 protests)
   Jaffe, Susan
   Nation    v232    p334(3)    March 21    1981
   CODEN: NATNB
   illustration
   SIC CODE: 1629
   DESCRIPTORS: Long Island Lighting Co.-cases; Shoreham Nuclear
 Power    Plant-cases;    atomic    power-plants-cases;    SHAD
 [Alliance-cases; demonstrations-cases
```

BRS

NAME: Bibliographic Retrieval Services, Inc.
1200 Route 7
Latham, NY 12110

TELEPHONE: (800) 833-4707 (Hotline)
(518) 783-1161 (New York state)

NUMBER OF DATABASES:
70

REFERENCE VENDORS WITH DATABASES ON MANY SUBJECTS 63

HOURS: *Service:* Monday–Saturday 6AM–4AM EST
Sunday 6AM–2PM, 7PM–4AM EST
Hotline: Monday–Friday 8AM–1AM EST

COST: (May 1, 1983)

No registration fee.

From $16 to $110 per connect hour.

Online print charge of $.03 per record for records containing the journal reference or abstract.

Offline print charges and other fees.

No minimum required.

Discounts available for organizations willing to guarantee a minimum.

Communications charges not included. They are:

TYMNET: $11/hour
TELENET: $7/hour
UNINET: $6/hour
WATS: $26/hour
Direct Dial: $3/hour

Billing is monthly.

SUBSCRIPTION INFORMATION:
Subscribing only requires filling out and signing a service contract.

USER AIDS: BRS System Reference Manual $18
BRS Training Workbook $15
Searching the Medlars Database $9
Database Guides $2.50 each

COMMUNICATIONS:
TYMNET, TELENET, UNINET, WATS, Direct Dial

300 or 1200 baud

TRAINING: Introduction: One day $35 (user) $50 (non-user)
Subject Seminars: One-half day $25 (user) $50 (non-user)
One day $50

Conducted regularly in the United States and abroad.

DESCRIPTION: Although fewer than those on Dialog, the 70 BRS databases touch on all fields of knowledge and include all but one (The Information Bank) of the most popular databases named in Chapter 2: BIOSIS, Chemical Abstracts, ERIC, MEDLINE, NTIS, and PSYCINFO.

BRS is unlike Dialog and SDC in that it does not provide document delivery, but it is the first of the major bibliographic systems to offer the full text of journals online. At present, the total *Harvard Business Review* can be searched and printed by BRS online. Other full-text BRS databases are the Academic American Encyclopedia, a group of Elsevier medical journals, and 18 American Chemical Society journals.

Two unique BRS databases are Pre-Med and Pre-Psych. These are small BRS-produced databases that contain medical and psychological information more current than that found in the MEDLINE or PSYCINFO databases. As with Dialog, BRS provides an index to its databases.

SYSTEM PROTOCOLS: As illustrated in the case study below, BRS's search language has the same basic capabilities as Dialog's. Only the conventions are different. In the BRS system, you enter search terms directly instead of using SS (or SELECT), as in Dialog or FIND, as required by the Knowledge Index protocol. The same Boolean operators, (AND, OR, and NOT), are used, but the commands to display and print items are different. For the experienced searcher, BRS has a set of very useful commands for sorting and then merging references that are retrieved from different databases.

CASE STUDY: The Nobel Prize-winning scientist, James Watson, will give an honorary lecture at Universal University tomorrow, and the Chairman of the Department of Biology will introduce him. The chairman has requested a Curriculum Vitae from Dr. Watson's office, but it has not arrived yet. Although he is generally familiar with Watson's work, the Chairman urgently needs a few specifics concerning the scientist—his exact current title, the name of the institution from which he received his doctorate, and the year he won the prize. The solution: an online search of the biographical reference source, *American Men and Women of Science*, on BRS. See Listing 5–2. Keeping in mind the principles explained in the Dialog and Knowledge Index examples, the reader should be able to follow this search easily. The only search term is Watson's name, entered in the prescribed BRS format, which includes hyphens between words and the "$" truncation symbol.

NOTE: We have described regular BRS service above. Specifics for BRS After Dark, the home-computer service, follow. Major differences are cost, number of online databases, hours, and the availability of non-information services such as electronic mail and at-home shopping services on After Dark. Also, After Dark's protocol is simpler than BRS's and is partly menu-driven.

REFERENCE VENDORS WITH DATABASES ON MANY SUBJECTS

LISTING 5-2

SEARCH OF AMERICAN MEN AND WOMEN OF SCIENCE DATABASE ON BRS FOR BIOGRAPHICAL INFORMATION ABOUT JAMES WATSON

Database Code for American Men and Women of Science → ENTER DATA BASE NAME_: **mwsc**

```
*SIGN-ON   19.56.23              03/01/83:

BRS - SEARCH MODE  - ENTER QUERY
```

Search Term → `1_: watson-james-d@`

```
          RESULT        1

     2_:   ..print 1 all/doc=1
```

Print Statement ↑

```
AN 124505. 0000.
AU Watson-James-Dewey.
PS BORN: Chicago, Ill, Apr 6, 28.
DC MOLECULAR BIOLOGY.
SU 200700.
ED Univ Chicago, BS, 47; Ind Univ, PhD, 50.
HD DSc, Univ Chicago, 61, Ind Univ, 63, Long Island Univ, 70, Adelphi
   Univ, 72, Brandeis Univ, 73, Albert Einstein Col Med, 74, Hofstra
   Univ, 76 & Harvard Univ, 78; LLD, Univ Notre Dame, 65; Rockefeller
   Univ, 80.
EX Nat Res Coun fel, Copenhagen Univ, 50-51 & Cambridge Univ, 51-52.
   Nat Found Infantile Paralysis fel, 52-53.
   sr res fel biol, Calif Inst Technol, 53-55.
   from asst prof to assoc prof, 56-61, PROF BIOL, HARVARD UNIV, 61-.
   DIR, COLD SPRING HARBOR LAB, 68-.
CP Mem, Nat Cancer Bd, 72-74.
HA Co-recipient, Nobel Prize in Med, 62.
   John Collins Warren Prize, Mass Gen Hosp, 59.
   Eli Lilly Biochem Award, 60.
   Lasker Prize, Am Pub Health Asn, 60.
   co-recipient, Res Corp Prize, 62.
   John J Carty Medal, Nat Acad Sci, 71.
   Presidential Medal of Freedom, 77.
ME Nat-Acad-Sci.
   Am-Acad-Arts-Sci.
   Royal-Danish-Acad.
   Am-Soc-Biol-Chemists.
   Am-Asn-Cancer-Res.
RE Induction of cancer by viruses.
AD Cold Spring Harbor Lab.
   Cold Spring Harbor, NY. 11724.
SX M.
YR 28..
DG 50..
CC A.
```

Field Names (arrows pointing to EX, CP, HA, ME)

BRS AFTER DARK

NAME: BRS After Dark
1200 Route 7
Latham, NY 12110

TELEPHONE: (800) 833-4707 (Hotline)
(518) 783-7251 (New York state)

NUMBER OF DATABASES:
28

HOURS: Service: Daily 6PM–4AM (local time)
Hotline: Monday–Friday 8PM–3AM EST
Saturday 8AM–5PM EST
Sunday 8AM–2PM EST

COST: (January 1, 1983)

Registration fee: $50

$6 to $15 per connect hour.

Minimum is $12 per month.

Communications charges are included.

Billing is to credit cards.

Monthly, detailed use statements sent by BRS.

SUBSCRIPTION INFORMATION:
To subscribe, send a small form giving pertinent credit card numbers and other information.

USER AIDS: BRS After Dark User's Manual (included in registration fee)

COMMUNICATIONS:
UNINET, TELENET

300 or 1200 baud

TRAINING: A self-instruction manual is included.

DESCRIPTION: After Dark has 28 databases in the sciences, medicine, business, finance, reference, education, social sciences, humanities, energy, and the environment. Among major ones are AGRICOLA (National Agricultural Library), BIOSIS Previews (BioSciences Information Service), Chemical Abstracts, Mathematical Reviews, MEDLINE (National Library of Medicine), NTIS (National Technical Information Service), ABI/INFORM (Data Courier, Inc.), Management Contents, Patdata (U.S. patents), ERIC (Educational Resources Information Center), Books in Print, PSYCINFO (American Psychological Association), and, in full text, both the Harvard Business Review and the Academic American Encyclopedia.

In addition to offering traditional bibliographic functions, BRS After Dark plans to include services similar to those of The Source and CompuServe: electronic mail, a data processing newsletter, shop-at-home, and instant software delivery programs.

CASE STUDY: To continue the BRS search question, the Biology Department chairman decides that he also wants to see a list of Watson's publications to supplement the biographical information found in *American Men and Women of Science*. He decides to first search the Books in Print database in BRS After Dark to identify Watson's books. See Listing 5–3.

The searcher is led to the database through a series of menus. Once in the Books in Print database (BBIP), he receives on request a brief description of the database. It is noteworthy that the online description does not contain instructions in *use* of BBIP. The printed manual is required to perform a search and to print answers.

BRS is currently developing a third system, COLLEAGUE, for health professionals. See Chapter 6 for a description.

REFERENCE VENDORS WITH DATABASES ON MANY SUBJECTS

LISTING 5-3

SEARCH OF BOOKS IN PRINT DATABASE ON BRS AFTER DARK FOR BOOKS BY JAMES WATSON

```
                    WELCOME TO BRS AFTER DARK

Desired Screen      PLEASE TYPE IN SCREEN LINE LENGTH (20, 40, OR 80)
     Width    ────→  40

                    TONIGHT'S MENU IS.....................
                                                          .
                    NUMBER       ITEM                     .
                                                          .
                       1         LOOKING FOR INFORMATION?....
                                 SEARCH SERVICE           .
                                                          .
                       2         WANT TO HEAR THE LATEST?....
                                 NEWSLETTER SERVICE       .
                                                          .
                       3         NEED A PROGRAM?.....SOFTWARE
                                 SERVICE                  .
                                                          .
                       4         KEEP IN TOUCH!....ELECTRONIC
                                 MAIL SERVICE             .
                                                          .
                       5         LET'S MAKE A DEAL!......SWAP
                                 SHOP                     .
                                                          .
                       6         WANT A SNEAK PREVIEW?.COMING
                                 ATTRACTIONS              .
                                                          .
                       7         WANT TO CHANGE YOUR SECURITY
                                 PASSWORD?  ...SECURITY   .

                    TYPE IN MENU ITEM NUMBER THEN HIT ENTER
                    KEY FOR DESIRED SELECTION:            .
Select Menu Item 1 ──→ 1

                    YOU ARE NOW CONNECTED TO THE BRS AFTER.
                    DARK SEARCH SERVICE . THE FOLLOWING   .
                    CATAGORIES OF DATABASES ARE AVAILABLE .
                    FOR SEARCHING:                        .
                    CATEGORY     DESCRIPTION              .
                                                          .
                         1       SCIENCE AND MEDICINE     .
                         2       BUSINESS AND FINANCE     .
                         3       REFERENCE                .
                         4       EDUCATION                .
                         5       SOCIAL SCIENCE/HUMANITIES.
                         6       ENERGY AND ENVIRONMENTAL .

                    TYPE IN CATEGORY NUMBER THEN HIT  ENTER
                    KEY FOR DATABASES DESIRED             .
Select Menu Item 3 ──→ 3

                    REFERENCE DATABASES                   .
                    *******************
                    DATABASE name                    LABEL
                                                          .
                    BOOKS IN PRINT                    BBIP
                    DISC                              DISC
                                                          .
                    TYPE IN LABEL FOR DATABASE DESIRED:
Database Label for ──→ bbip
   Books in Print
                    ARE YOU A NEW AFTER DARK USER?   PLEASE
                    TYPE IN YES OR NO:     no
                    WOULD YOU LIKE A DESCRIPTION OF THE
                    DATABASE? (Y OR N) y
        Database   ⎧ The BRS/Books In Print database is a
     Description   ⎨ premium source of information on
                   ⎩ virtually all books currently in print
                     and any titles scheduled to be
                     published within the next six months.
```

LISTING 5-3 (continued)

```
         The database includes popular,
         scientific and technical, medical,
         business and economics, religious,
         large type, children's and paper back
         books. R.R. Bowker COMPANY PRODUCES
         THIS DATABASE AND UPDATES IT MONTHLY.
             Total Price = $16.00 (Includes $10
         royalty to producer)
         TYPE IN SEARCH TERMS
```

Search Term → `S1 --> watson-james-d.`

```
         A1    4 ITEMS FOUND
         ENTER COMMAND    p
         ME WATSON-JAMES-D.
```
Reference to One → `TI THE DNA STORY. A DOCUMENTARY HISTORY`
of Watson's Books
```
            OF GENE CLONING.
         AE TOOZE-JOHN.
         PD SEP, 1981.
         NT ILLUSTRATED.
         PR TEXT ED    $24.95. 0-7167-1292-X.
         PB W-H-FREEMAN.
         SC ACTIVE ENTRY (AE).
         SU GENETICS (0019072X).
            DEOXYRIBONUCLEIC ACID (00127012).
         PG 605.
           .
           .
           .
```

SDC INFORMATION SERVICES

NAME: SDC Information Services
         2500 Colorado Avenue
         Santa Monica, CA 90406

TELEPHONE: (800) 421-7229   (Outside California)
              (800) 352-6689   (California)
              (800) 336-3313   (Outside Virginia)
              (703) 790-9850   (Virginia)

INTERNATIONAL OFFICES:
         Sydney, Australia   Tel: (02) 922-9308
         Berkshire, England   Tel: (44) 734-866811
         Toronto, Ontario, Canada   Tel: (416) 489-6640
         Tokyo, Japan   Tel: (03) 349-8520

NUMBER OF DATABASES:
         77

HOURS: Service: Monday–Thursday   All day except 9:45–10:15PM EST
                    Friday 3AM–8PM EST
                    Saturday 8AM–7PM EST
                    Sunday 7PM–3AM EST

         Hotline: Monday–Friday 8AM–5PM PST (Santa Monica, CA)
                    Monday–Friday 8AM–5PM EST (McLean, VA)

REFERENCE VENDORS WITH DATABASES ON MANY SUBJECTS 69

COST: (January 1, 1984)

No registration fee, but one of three start-up packages is required. See Subscription Information.

From $35 to $160 per connect hour plus offline print charges and online display charges for some databases.

$100 monthly minimum.

Discounts are available for organizations willing to guarantee larger minimums. Automatic discounts given for over five hours of use per month on selected databases.

Communications charges are not included. They are:

TYMNET: $ 8/hour
TELENET: $ 8/hour
WATS: $24/hour
Direct Dial: No charge

Billing is monthly.

SUBSCRIPTION INFORMATION:

Gaining access to SDC requires signing a service contract and taking advantage of one of three start-up training packages: (a) Workbook package, which contains a self-instruction workbook, and $300 of online searching time over a three-month period. Cost: $125. (b) Workshop package entitling user to two spots in a New User Training Workshop, a training workbook, and $150 of online searching time over a six-month time period. Cost: $200. (c) Custom Package, which is a training session for up to 12 people at the user site, and $400 of online time over a six-month time period. Cost: $400 plus travel expenses for the instructor. All packages include the ORBIT System User Manual, the Quick Reference Guide, and five individual database manuals of your choice.

USER AIDS: ORBIT System User Manual $40
Quick Reference Guide $15
Database Manuals $7.50
Self-Instructional Workbook $15

COMMUNICATIONS:

TYMNET, TELENET, WATS, Direct Dial

300 or 1200 baud

TRAINING: ORBIT Basic Skills Seminar: One day $150 including $150 connect time credit on special files
ORBIT Advanced Skills Seminars: One day $100
Special Subject Seminars: One day $100

ORBIT Basic Skills Primer (contact SDC)
Custom Training (contact SDC)

DESCRIPTION: SDC databases also tap into all fields of knowledge and include most major databases; SDC is known, however, for its in-depth coverage of science and technology. SDC has some important databases that are not found on any other systems: APILIT (American Petroleum Institute), and the Derwent publications—PESTDOC (pesticides, herbicides, plant protection), RINGDOC (pharmaceutical literature), VETDOC (veterinary literature), STANDARD DRUG FILE (SDF) (drug compendia), and WPI (World Patents Index). PESTDOC, VETDOC, SDF, and RINGDOC are available only to subscribers of the comparable printed services, while WPI is an example of a database for which subscribers are charged substantially less than non-subscribers.

SDC has both document ordering and a database index to help searchers choose proper databases. As of this writing, a simplified, less expensive service (similar to those offered by Dialog and BRS) for home microcomputer users is not planned. However, SDC recently announced development of ORBIT Search Master, a microcomputer software package that simplifies access. See Chapter 9.

SYSTEM PROTOCOLS:
The case study illustrates ORBIT's system commands for searching terms, combining references, and printing and displaying. Although forms are different from those of Dialog and BRS, basic functions are again the same, including use of Boolean operators (AND, OR, and NOT).

CASE STUDY: Mr. and Mrs. Jones have a three-year-old daughter who they feel is particularly quick and bright compared to her playmates. They wonder if she should be in a special educational program to develop her full potential. But they realize that, as parents, they maybe biased and would like information on how to identify gifted preschoolers. They decide to perform a search of the Educational Resources Information Center (ERIC) database on SDC. See Listing 5–4.

Search terms are entered directly, without specific commands; set numbers can also be combined directly. In the example, two terms, *high* and *achiever*, have been combined into a synonym equivalent to *talent* and *gifted* before being "ORed" with these two terms. See Search Statement 1. This technique is called *nesting*. The SDC truncation symbol is ":".

OUTSIDE THE UNITED STATES

Outside the United States, notably in Canada and Europe, there are online vendors that provide services similar to Dialog, BRS, and SDC. Some of their databases are the same as those searchable on U.S. systems; others are unique to the countries of origin.

LISTING 5-4

SEARCH OF ERIC DATABASE ON SDC FOR INFORMATION ON IDENTIFICATION OF GIFTED CHILDREN

```
SS 1 /C?
USER:
(high and achievers) or talents or gifted

PROG:
SS 1 PSTG (5733)

SS 2 /C?
USER:
identifs and preschool

PROG:
SS 2 PSTG (1354)

SS 3 /C?
USER:
1 and 2

PROG:
SS 3 PSTG (45)

SS 4 /C?
USER:
print 2

PROG:

-1-
AN  - EJ190536
TI  - Identifying and Educating Gifted/Talented Nonhandicapped and
      Handicapped Preschoolers
AU  - Karnes, Merle B.; Bertschi, Jane D.
SO  - Teaching Exceptional Children; v10 n4 p114-19 Sum 1978 (1978)
IS  - CIJMAR79

-2-
AN  - EJ004804
TI  - The Use of the Wechsler Preschool and Primary Scale (WPPSI) in
      the Early Identification of Gifted Students
AU  - Rellas, Archie J.
SO  - Calif J Educ Res; 20; 3; 117-119 (1969 May)
IS  - CIJE69
```

In Canada, the two primary vendors of bibliographic databases are Q/L Systems and CAN/OLE (both Ottawa, Ontario). Q/L's databases are primarily science and business databases with a Canadian orientation, while CAN/OLE covers about 20 databases, with a concentration in science and technology.

In Europe, over 50 national systems, referred to as *hosts*, are connected by an umbrella organization, EURONET Diane, which is based in Luxembourg and which became operational in 1980. One of the most desirable features of the EURONET systems is the creation of the Common Command Language, a single command language for basic searching of most European hosts.

A recent survey (see Collier, 1982, in the bibliography for Chapter 5) reveals that, in spite of these national systems, Dialog is by far the most heavily used online service in Europe, followed by ESA-IRS (Rome, Italy). The third and fourth most popular systems were SDC and Blaise (the British Library System, London). Other European systems are Citere (France), Data-Star (England), Datacentralen (Denmark), DIMDI (West Germany), Echo (Luxembourg), FIZ Technik (West Germany), Inka (West Germany),

Telesystemes Questel (France), Pergamon Infoline (England), and Spidel (France). Complete names, addresses, and telephone numbers for these organizations are given in Appendix I.

There are strong indications that the number of searches of U.S. databases by Europeans is far greater than the reverse. Most databases that are important in the U.S. are available there; cost is lower in the U.S. because communications charges to Europe are higher than communications charges within the U.S. Also, communications tend to be more reliable within the U.S. Nevertheless, European vendors have become interested in the U.S. market, and two, Pergamon Infoline and Telesystemes Questel, have opened offices in the Washington, D.C. area. See Appendix I. Europeans and Canadians have some unique databases and services to offer, especially European economic and business data, and some U.S. searchers have begun to take advantage of them.

CHAPTER

6

Scientific, Technical, and Medical Vendors and Databases

Through technical libraries and information centers, scientists have been among the heaviest users of online information services since inception. Primarily, this is because all the major scientific disciplines' abstracting and indexing publications, such as *Chemical Abstracts* and *Biological Abstracts*, and several important technical government databases came online in the early years.

Managers of corporate libraries serving research and development departments were quick to recognize the value of online services—particularly their advantage of cost-effectiveness over manual literature searching—and were willing to commit substantial funds to online information.

Rapid acceptance of online in the medical community in the early 1970s was due to the development of the Medical Literature and Analysis System (MEDLARS) by the National Library of Medicine (NLM). A then state-of-the-art system, with an excellent large database called MEDLINE based on *Index Medicus*, MEDLARS was at first free of charge to the academic medical library community. While fees were eventually initiated and have been raised gradually, NLM charges are still below commercial rates for comparable service.

DATABASES

Today, one can gain access to all major scientific, technical, and medical databases, including MEDLINE, through Dialog, BRS, and SDC. You can search several databases through all three systems. See Table 6–1.

That a database is on a particular system, as indicated by the table, does not imply strict equivalence. Access points—i.e., the searchable fields—may vary among the systems, and more important, the number of years that can be searched online differs for some databases. In particular, coverage dates are likely to be shorter on Knowledge Index and BRS After Dark. You should also be aware that names of databases are not necessarily the same across systems. For example, the National Library of Medicine database is called MEDLINE on Dialog, MEDI on Knowledge Index, and MEDLARS or MESH by BRS and BRS After Dark.

The three major vendors provide many other databases in science, technology, and medicine. Some are mentioned below in groups arranged by subject area. Also, see Appendix II for a list of major databases. In addition, it is important to remember that many multidisciplinary databases, such as Comprehensive Dissertation Index, contain substantial scientific and technical information.

TABLE 6-1
AVAILABILITY OF MAJOR SCIENTIFIC, TECHNICAL, AND MEDICAL DATABASES THROUGH DIALOG, BRS, AND SDC SERVICES

DATABASE	DIALOG	KI*	BRS	DARK**	SDC
AGRICOLA***	X	X	X	X	
Biological Abstracts	X		X	X	X
Chemical Abstracts	X		X	X	X
Engineering Index	X	X	X		X
Excerpta Medica	X				
Mathematical Reviews	X		X	X	
MEDLINE	X	X	X	X	
NTIS****	X		X	X	X
Science Citation Index	X				
SPIN *****	X				

```
*       Knowledge Index
**      BRS After Dark
***     from the National Agricultural Library
****    National Technical Information Service
*****   Searchable Physics Information Notices
```

Chemistry

Chemical Abstracts, with close to six million records, dominates the chemistry area. Some useful, specialized-subject supplements to Chemical Abstracts are Paperchem (pulp and paper industry), Chemical Industry Notes, Chemlaw, and the TSCA (Toxic Substances Control Act) list. Several patent files are also important sources of chemical information, and chemists have online access through BRS to the complete articles of 18 American Chemical Society Journals.

Very helpful aids to chemical searchers are chemical dictionary databases on Dialog (Chemname, Chemsearch, Chemsis, and Chemzero) and on SDC (Chemdex, Chemdex 2, and Chemdex 3). Each of these databases contains information on nearly six million substances. A dictionary record has a registry number (a unique identification number assigned by Chemical Abstracts Service to every chemical substance it indexes), a molecular formula, ring data, nomenclature such as synonyms and the eighth and ninth collective index names, and other useful information about the substance. Unless the registry number is already known, most searches of Chemical Abstracts begin with a search of one of these dictionary files.

Listing 6–1 is a printout of a search for *dioxin* in the SDC Chemdex file. The full-record terms and their codes are registry number (RN), molecular formula (MF), collective index name (N), ring structure (RSD), and synonyms (SYNM). Any term, or part of a term separated by hyphens, such as *dibenzo*, could have been used as a search term to locate this record. Of course, a common chemical name fragment such as *dibenzo* would retrieve thousands of records and would need to be combined with other terms to perform a useful search.

You may use the Chemdex registry number for *dioxin*, 1746-01-6, to search the Chemical Abstracts database and other chemical databases without needing to determine its proper nomenclature.

SCIENTIFIC, TECHNICAL, AND MEDICAL VENDORS AND DATABASES

LISTING 6-1

SEARCH FOR DIOXIN ON THE SDC CHEMDEX 3 FILE

```
                      USER:
Enter the ──────→ file chemdex3
CHEMDEX3 File
                      PROG:
                      ELAPSED TIME ON ORBIT: 0.01 HRS.
                      YOU ARE NOW CONNECTED TO THE CHEMDEX3 DATABASE.
                       FILE CONTAINS 858,487 COMPOUNDS, THRU 4RD QUARTER 1981
                      SUPPLEMENT(8104), WHICH ARE NEW COMPOUNDS AND UPDATES TO COMPOUNDS IN
                      CHEMDEX AND CHEMDEX2.  THIS FILE SHOULD ALWAYS BE USED IN CONJUNCTION
                      WITH CHEMDEX (1,638,531 COMPOUNDS FROM 36-88-4 THRU 56700-44-8) AND
                      CHEMDEX2 (1,358,125 COMPOUNDS FROM 56700-46-0 THRU 72028-13-8).
                      ****
                      USE CROSSFILE SEARCHING OF REGISTRY NUMBERS TO RETRIEVE ADDITIONAL
                      INFORMATION FOR AND FROM COMPOUNDS IN CHEMDEX AND CHEMDEX2.

                      SS 1 /C?
                      USER:
Search for Dioxin ──→ dioxin
        Record
                      PROG:
                      SS 1 PSTG (1)

                      SS 2 /C?
                      USER:
Print the Record ──→ print full
                      PROG:

                      -1-
                      RN  - 1746-01-6 (SEE ALSO 56795-67-6)
                      MF  - C12H4Cl4O2
                      N   - Dibenzo(b,e)(1,4)dioxin, 2,3,7,8-tetrachloro-
                      RSD - 3 RING(S), C4O2,C6,C6 (OC2OC2)
                      SYNM- Dibenzo-p-dioxin, 2,3,7,8-tetrachloro-  (Also 8CI);
                            2,3,7,8-Tetrachlorodibenzo-p-dioxin;   TCDBD;
                            2,3,7,8-Tetrachlorodibenzo-1,4-dioxin; Dioxin (herbicide
                            contaminant);  TCDD;  2,3,7,8-Tetracholorodibenzo-p-dioxin;
                            Dioxin
```

A unique and powerful type of chemical information retrieval, searching on the basis of structure alone, is possible through the search systems of Chemical Abstracts Service and Questel, which are described under SPECIALIZED VENDORS later in this chapter.

Energy and the Environment

In the energy and environment areas, APILIT (publications) and API-PAT (patents) from the American Petroleum Institute, Energyline, Enviroline, GeoRef (geology), Oceanic Abstracts, Derwent's PESTDOC, Pollution Abstracts, and many more databases supplement the coverage of major databases such as Chemical Abstracts, Biological Abstracts, and Engineering Index.

Sometimes the number of databases with information on a subject is astounding. Listing 6–2, for example, shows a search for databases containing the word *dioxin* in SDC's Data Base Index (DBI). Thirty-five of the SDC databases have at least one refer-

LISTING 6-2

SEARCH OF SDC'S DATA BASE INDEX FOR DATABASES CONTAINING INFORMATION ON DIOXIN

```
                            USER:
                           ┌►file dbi
                           │ PROG:
        Enter Database ────┤ ELAPSED TIME ON ORBIT: 0.01 HRS.
           Index File      │ YOU ARE NOW CONNECTED TO THE DATA BASE INDEX DATABASE.
                           │ THIS IS THE MASTER INDEX TO ALL SEARCH SERVICE DATABASES.
                           └ UPDATED WITH NEWEST FILES AS OF 6/3/83

                           ┌ SS 1 /C?
      Search Statement ────┤ USER:
                           └►dioxin

                             PROG:
                             SS 1: (35) DATABASES

 Print Seven Records ─────┐ SS 2 /C?
       (in Decreasing     │ USER:
       Order by Number    └►print 7
       of Dioxin
       References)          PROG:
                              ┌►-1-
  Chemical Abstracts ────────┤ DN   - CAS6771
        (1967-71)             └ PSTG- AT LEAST 551.

                              ┌►-2-
  Chemical Abstracts ────────┤ DN   - CAS77
        (1977-81)             └ PSTG- AT LEAST 391.

                              ┌►-3-
  Biological Abstracts ──────┤ DN   - BIOSIS
      (1980-Present)          └ PSTG- AT LEAST 311.

                              ┌►-4-
  Biological Abstracts ──────┤ DN   - BIO7479
        (1974-79)             └ PSTG- AT LEAST 301.

                              ┌►-5-
     Newspaper Indexes ──────┤ DN    - NDEX
                              └ PSTG- AT LEAST 231.

                              ┌►-6-
   Chemical Abstracts ───────┤ DN    - CAS7276
         (1972-76)            └ PSTG- AT LEAST 171.

                              ┌►-7-
     Pestdoc (Derwent) ──────┤ DN    - PESTDOC
                              └ PSTG- AT LEAST 151.
```

ence to dioxin! Data Base Index lists them in decreasing order by number of references—as shown by the postings (PSTG).

Life Sciences

Most major databases—MEDLINE, Chemical Abstracts, Biological Abstracts, Excerpta Medica, and Science Citation Index—are important in the life sciences. Depending on your particular search topic, you might also want to look at PSYCINFO (Psychological Abstracts), VETDOC (veterinary medicine), Health Planning and Administration, the Life Sciences Collection of Cambridge Scientific Abstracts, or the

Zoological Record. Two new databases in the expanding biotechnology field are TELE-GEN and Biotechnology Index from Derwent. Major subject databases for pharmaceuticals are RINGDOC, International Pharmaceutical Abstracts, and Pharmaceutical News Index. The key drug compendia, "Martindales The Extra Pharmacopoeia" and "Facts and Comparisons," are scheduled to join Derwent's Standard Drug File online soon. Since producers update online publications continually, bringing up these compendia databases will vastly improve retrieval of very current factual drug information.

BRS and the American Medical Association (in conjunction with GTE TELENET) have designed online clinical services for direct use by the physician. The BRS system, called COLLEAGUE, initially will cover bibliographic databases in biomedicine and the full text of key textbooks of major medical publishers and about 10 primary medical journals such as *The New England Journal of Medicine*. COLLEAGUE uses a simplified command language.

AMA/NET, a cooperative service of the American Medical Association and GTE, is designed to provide socio-economic as well as clinical information directly to physicians and other health professionals. It consists of the full text of *AMA Drug Evaluations*, other AMA publications, and an electronic mail service. See the full description below.

Physical Sciences and Technology

In addition to Engineering Index, NTIS, SPIN, Mathematical Reviews, and other databases already mentioned, important technology databases are INSPEC (Institution of Electrical Engineers) (London), TRIS (Transportation Research Information Services), METADEX, and World Textiles. You may be particularly interested in Microcomputer Index and International Software Database.

Patents

You can find patent information in databases devoted exclusively to patent coverage or as part of other indexes such as Chemical Abstracts. Covering patents exclusively are World Patents Index on SDC, the IFI/Plenum CLAIMS databases on Dialog, PATDATA on BRS and BRS After Dark, and PATSEARCH on Pergamon Infoline (below).

Superindex

An information breakthrough occurred in 1983 with the online availability of Superindex on BRS. An immense database, Superindex is the product of more than 15 years of development by a company owned by CRC Press. It contains the "back-of-the-book" indexes of over 600 reference works from approximately 25 of the leading publishers in science, engineering, and medicine. These publishers include the American Chemical Society, CRC Press, Elsevier, McGraw-Hill, Prentice-Hall, John Wiley, Van Nostrand, and Williams and Wilkins. The most comprehensive service of its type in the world, with two million index entries, Superindex comprises hundreds of merged indexes from key works such as *CRC Handbook of Chemistry and Physics*, *Merck Index*, *Physician's Desk Reference*, and *McGraw-Hill Encyclopedia of Science and Technology*.

A companion database to Superindex is Datafield, which consists of tabular data from reference books. With Datafield, you can retrieve actual data such as values, properties, or standard constants of materials, substances, and compounds.

SPECIALIZED VENDORS

Some of the above-mentioned database producers (on Dialog, SDC, and BRS systems), as well as other database producers in the sciences, are also vendors. The first producer/vendor and still largest is the National Library of Medicine, but in the past few years Chemical Abstracts Service and the Institute for Scientific Information, which publishes *Science Citation Index,* have also become vendors. Below, we discuss these organizations and other major specialized science vendors individually and then briefly describe science vendors with less widespread use in the United States at present.

NATIONAL LIBRARY OF MEDICINE

NAME: MEDLARS
National Library of Medicine
8600 Rockville Pike
Bethesda, MD 20209

TELEPHONE: (301) 496-6193

NUMBER OF DATABASES:
18

HOURS: Service: Monday–Friday 3AM–9PM EST
Saturday 8:30AM–5PM EST
Hotline: Monday–Friday 8:30AM–5PM EST

COST: (January 1, 1983)

No registration fee.

From $15 to $75 per hour depending on particular databases and whether the searching is done in prime (10:00AM to 5:00PM EST Monday through Friday) or non-prime (other) time.

Additional fees are assessed for offline printouts and Selective Dissemination of Information searches.

Minimum charge is $15 per month. Communications charges are included.

Plans are to institute a new pricing algorithm based on connect time, "computer work," and characters printed or displayed.

Billing is monthly.

SUBSCRIPTION INFORMATION:
To use NLM, an individual or organization must sign a memorandum of understanding *and* send an individual for at least three days of a one-week training workshop at the National Library of Medicine or at one of a few other selected U.S. sites.

SCIENTIFIC, TECHNICAL, AND MEDICAL VENDORS AND DATABASES   79

USER AIDS: Online Services Reference Manual $15
Medical Subject Headings-Annotated Alphabetic List $17
Medical Subject Headings-Tree Structures $12
Medical Subject Headings-Supplementary Chemical Records $22
The NLM Technical Bulletin   gratis (provided to users only)

COMMUNICATIONS:
TYMNET, TELENET, WATS, and Direct Dial

300 and 1200 baud

TRAINING: Beginning user: Three to five days   No charge
Advanced: Five days   No charge
Abbreviated advanced: Three days   No charge

Training is conducted regularly at the National Library of Medicine and at regional centers (currently two) and occasionally at a few other selected major cities. To date, the requirement that any organization wanting access to the NLM system must send someone to the formal training has meant that most NLM online users are information professionals, but NLM is currently designing a training program more suited to end users.

NLM holds updates annually in various regions of the country at no charge.

DESCRIPTION: NLM's MEDLINE database may well be the most heavily used of all online databases. At $22 per hour (prime-time) and $15 per hour (non-prime), MEDLINE is less expensive through NLM than through any other service except BRS After Dark. Of course, After Dark has fewer search capabilities and you cannot search it during regular business hours.

MEDLINE, a high-quality database with excellent indexing, extensively covers journal articles (1966–present) and chapters of selected multi-authored works (1975–1981) in all areas of clinical medicine, biomedical research and health sciences education, administration, and practice. Another key NLM database is TOXLINE, which is a merged compilation of drug and toxicology databases, primarily part of MEDLINE, International Pharmaceutical Abstracts, Chemical-Biological Activities, and Health Effects of Environmental Pollutants. The last three databases originate at other producers, the American Society of Hospital Pharmacists, Chemical Abstract Service, and BioSciences Information Service, respectively.

NLM also has a "small" chemical dictionary database, CHEMLINE, containing just over 500,000 records, a database of biomedical audiovisuals (AVLINE), and a database devoted to books and serials catalogued by the National Library of Medicine (CATLINE). Some

NLM databases in subfields of medicine are BIOETHICS, CANCERLIT, HEALTH (health economics, administration, and planning), and HISTLINE (history of medicine).

NLM provides two data files that you can use to retrieve specific facts rather than citations. One file is the Registry of Toxic Effects of Chemical Substances (RTECS), which contains toxicity data compiled by the National Institute of Occupational Safety and Health for over 50,000 substances. RTECS records have chemical identification information as well as references to data sources and standard values such as the aquatic toxicity rating. The Toxicology Data Bank (TDB) records consist of 60 different fields in several categories: 1. descriptive (e.g., chemical names and CAS registry numbers); 2. excerpts (e.g., laboratory methods); 3. index strings (e.g., interactants); 4. values (e.g., minimum fatal dose); 5. pharmacology/toxicology (e.g., antidote and treatment); 6. manufacturing data (e.g., manufacturers); and 7. chemical and physical properties (e.g., solubility).

SYSTEM PROTOCOLS:

System Development Corporation developed the MEDLARS command language, ELHILL, under contract to NLM. Basic features resemble those on SDC. In recent years the languages have evolved differently; NLM has not implemented some features introduced by SDC, such as true-adjacency searching. However, NLM does have a method of adjacency searching and has added some fairly sophisticated features on its own.

CASE STUDIES:

Case 1: A MEDLINE user just discovered that he has cancer and wants to investigate all therapeutic possibilities. He has read in the lay press and in some publications obtained through health food stores about the benefits of using laetrile as a therapeutic agent in cancer treatment and wants to find if there is any validity to the claims. Knowing that there has been some serious research on this topic, the user performs a search of MEDLINE for articles limited to clinical trials, because they are most likely to give hard, comparative data. See Listing 6–3. MEDLINE might also have articles on socio-economics, legal, and psychological aspects of laetrile use.

The user enters the term *laetrile*, which automatically searches *amygdalin*, the scientific name. The 77 retrieved references are then combined with *clinical trials* to give 12 references, five of which have been printed. Note that MEDLINE covers editorials and news in addition to substantive articles. Three articles come from two prestigious medical journals: *The New England Journal of Medicine* and *Journal of the American Medical Association (JAMA)*.

Case 2: An industrial chemist considers using the solvent, methanol, in a new product and wants data on the health effects of this product.

LISTING 6-3

SEARCH FOR INFORMATION ON LAETRILE CLINICAL TRIALS ON THE MEDLINE DATABASE FROM NLM

```
                    HELLO FROM ELHILL AT NLM.
                    YOU ARE NOW CONNECTED TO THE MEDLINE FILE.

                    SS 1 /C?
                    USER:
Search Statement →  laetrile
                    PROG:
                    SS (1) PSTG (77)

                    SS 2 /C?
                    USER:
Limit Set 1 to   →  1 and clinical trials
Clinical Trials     PROG:
                    SS (2) PSTG (12)

                    SS 3 /C?
                    USER:
                 →  print 5
Print Five Records  PROG:

                    1
                    TI  - A verdict against laetrile [editorial]
                    SO  - NZ Med J 1982 Mar 24;95(704):184-5

                    2
                    AU  - Young CW
                    TI  - Lessons of the laetrile study.
                    SO  - Clin Bull 1981;11(3):99-101

                    3
                    TI  - National Cancer Institute begins laetril clinical trial [news]
                    SO  - JAMA 1980 Aug 8;244(6):538

                    4
                    AU  - Moertel CG
                    AU  - Fleming TR
                    AU  - Rubin J
                    AU  - Kvols LK
                    AU  - Sarna G
                    AU  - Koch R
                    AU  - Currie VE
                    AU  - Young CW
                    TI  - A clinical trial of amygdalin (Laetrile) in the treatment of
                          human cancer.
                    SO  - N Engl J Med 1982 Jan 28;306(4):201-6

                    5
                    AU  - Moertel CG
                    AU  - Ames MM
                    AU  - Kovach JS
                    AU  - Moyer TP
                    AU  - Tinker JH
                    TI  - A pharmacologic and toxicological study of amygdalin.
                    SO  - JAMA 1981 Feb 13;245(6):591-4
```

She decides to search the Registry of Toxic Effects of Chemical Substances, a database of the National Institute of Occupational Safety and Health, on NLM. See Listing 6–4 for the straightforward interaction. The printed record shown gives both specific data and references. People not familiar with the coding conventions can use the NLM manual to ascertain their meanings.

Listing 6–4

SEARCH OF RTECS DATABASE ON NLM FOR METHANOL DATA

Enter RTECS Database → **file rtecs**
```
PROG:
YOU ARE NOW CONNECTED TO THE RTECS FILE.
TOXICITY DATA IN NIOSH'S RTECS HAVE NOT BEEN CRITICALLY EVALUATED.

SS 1 /C?
USER:
```
Search Term → **methanol (n1)**
```
PROG:

SS (1) PSTG (1)

SS 2 /C?
USER:
prt full
PROG:
```

	SI	– NIOSH/PC1400000
Systematic Name →	N1	– METHANOL
	RN	– 67-56-1
Concentration That Will Kill 50% of Exposed Organisms Within 96 Hours →	AQ	– AQUATIC TOXICITY RATING: TLm96:over 1000 ppm WQCHM* "Water Quality Characteristics of Hazardous Materials," W. Hann, and P.A. Jensen, Environmental Engineering Division, Civil Engineering Department, Texas A & M University, Volumes 1-4, 1974 3,-,74
	TR	– TLV-TWA 200 ppm; STEL 250 ppm (skin) DTLVS* "Documentation of Threshold Limit Values for Substances in Workroom Air," Cincinnati, Ohio, American Conference of Governmental Industrial Hygienists, 1980 4,263,80
Toxicology and Cancer Review →	TR	– TOXICOLOGY REVIEW MEDIAV Medicine. 32,431,53//CLCHAU Clinical Chemistry. 19,361,73//FNSCA6 Forensic Science. 2,67,73//JTEHD6 Journal of Toxicology and Environmental Health. 1,153,75//MJAUAJ Medical Journal of Australia. 2,483,78
Standards and Regulations →	SR	– OSHA STANDARD-air:TWA 200 ppm (SCP-E) FEREAC Federal Register. 39,23540,74
	SR	– DOT-FLAMMABLE LIQUID, LABEL:FLAMMABLE LIQUID FEREAC Federal Register. 41,57018,76
NIOSH Criteria Documents →	NC	– CRIT DOC. OCCUPATIONAL EXPOSURE TO METHYL ALCOHOL recm std-air:TWA 200 ppm;CL 800 ppm/15M NTIS** National Technical Information Service.
	ST	– "NIOSH MANUAL OF ANALYTICAL METHODS" VOL 1 247, VOL 2 S59 NIMAM*
Status →	ST	– REPORTED IN EPA TSCA INVENTORY, 1980
	ST	– EPA TSCA 8E NO:03780108-FOLLOWUP SENT AS OF APRIL, 1979
	ST	– MEETS CRITERIA FOR PROPOSED OSHA MEDICAL RECORDS RULE FEREAC 47,30420,82

INSTITUTE FOR SCIENTIFIC INFORMATION

NAME: ISI Search Network
Institute for Scientific Information
3501 Market Street
Philadelphia, PA 19104

TELEPHONE: (800) 523-1850
(215) 386-0100 (Pennsylvania)

SCIENTIFIC, TECHNICAL, AND MEDICAL VENDORS AND DATABASES

INTERNATIONAL OFFICES:
Uxbridge, Middlesex, England   Tel: 44-895-30085
Toronto, Ontario, Canada   Tel: (416) 922-0608
Offenbach Am Main, West Germany   Tel: 0611-889077
Randwijk, The Netherlands   Tel: 08889-207
Mexico City, Mexico   Tel: 651-3181
Singapore   Tel: 2526762
Also, agents in Japan, India, and Taiwan

NUMBER OF DATABASES:
4

HOURS:
Service: 24 hours a day except Friday 11PM–4AM EST
Hotline: Monday–Friday 8AM–5PM EST

COST:
(January 1, 1983)

No registration fee.

Connect charges are $50 per hour for subscribers to the comparable print product and $150 for all others.

Additional fees for offline prints and for saved-search strategies.

No minimums.

Communications charges are not included. They are:

TYMNET: $7/hour
TELENET: $7/hour
Direct Dial: No charge

Billing is monthly.

SUBSCRIPTION INFORMATION:
To subscribe, it is only necessary to sign a contract.

USER AIDS:
ISI Online Data Bases Guide $25
Index to Research Fronts in ISI/BIOMED $25*
Index to Research Fronts to ISI/CompuMath $25*
Index to Research Fronts in ISI/GeoSciTech $25*

*$25 to users, $50 to non-users

COMMUNICATIONS:
TYMNET, TELENET, and Direct Dial

300 and 1200 baud

TRAINING:
Introductory, one-day workshop: $25

ISI holds workshops regularly throughout the United States and abroad.

DESCRIPTION: There are four databases on the ISI Search Network; these are listed below with their corresponding print products to which users must subscribe in order to obtain lower online connect rates.

DATABASE	PRINT PUBLICATION
ISI/BIOMED	Science Citation Index (in part)
ISI/ISTP&B	Index to Scientific and Technical Proceedings and Books
ISI/CompuMath	CompuMath Citation Index
ISI/GeoSciTech	GeoSciTech Citation Index

None of these databases covers all the information that is on the entire Science Citation Index database on Dialog. However, BIOMED contains about two-thirds of this material, the part relating to the biomedical sciences for the three most recent years and for the current year. Dialog's SCISEARCH, by comparison, dates from 1970.

CompuMath includes 360 journals in their entirety and draws selectively from over 6000 more to cover mathematics, computer science, statistics and related disciplines. GeoSciTech indexes 350 key journals in their entirety and more than 6000 selectively for information on geology and related fields such as petroleum science, atmospheric science, oceanography, and metallurgy. ISTP&B provides access to single-author papers published in proceedings and multi-authored books in virtually every scientific and technical discipline.

SYSTEM PROTOCOLS:

The ISI Search Network commands have the same basic functions as those on the other large systems. They resemble Dialog commands more closely than those of any other system.

Two search capabilities are unique to the ISI databases. You can search by cited reference or by cited author—that is, you can retrieve articles on the basis of an author's having cited another article or author. This is a very powerful capability that sidesteps the difficulties involved in finding just the right subject terms to include in a search; it can be used alone or as a useful supplement to the more traditional type of subject searching.

You can perform straightforward citation searching on the ISI Search Network and on ISI databases mounted on systems such as Dialog and BRS. But the ISI Search Network is the only vendor system designed for searching by *research front specialties*. A research front specialty is defined as an intense research activity area that is actually identified through analysis of citation patterns. A search of this type retrieves a bibliography of current papers that cite the core literature of the specialty.

Research front specialty searches are easy to perform. The search term is simply the specialty number, which you can obtain either from the Index to Research Front Specialties in the printed version (see USER AIDS above) or online. Nearly 8000 research fronts have been identified for BIOMED, while CompuMath and GeoSciTech have more than 3000 each. As it is a different type of database, ISTP&B does not have research fronts.

ISI has developed a search aid for microcomputer users. Called Sci-Mate, it in essence translates the ISI system language (and other system languages as well) from a command to a menu-driven format that you can use with little instruction. See Chapter 9 for examples of ISI database searches using Sci-Mate.

NIH/EPA CHEMICAL INFORMATION SYSTEM (CIS)

NAME: NIH/EPA Chemical Information System
Computer Sciences Corporation
6565 Arlington Boulevard
Falls Church, VA 22046

TELEPHONE: (800) 368-3432 (Hotline)
(703) 237-2000 x7121 or x7129 (Virginia)

NUMBER OF DATABASES:
19

HOURS: *Service:* 24 hours every day except for maintenance times, which are scheduled in advance
Hotline: Monday–Friday 9AM–5PM EST

COST: (February 1, 1983)

Subscription fee of $300 per year except for non-profit degree-granting institutions and tax-supported public libraries (called "exempt" customers). Exempt customers are also entitled to $100 per month of free use of CIS (excluding communications). An exempt organization may have up to three separate accounts.

No minimums or discounts.

Connect charges range from $30 per hour for electronic mail to $150 per hour. Most databases are in the $55 to $85 range.

Communications charges are not included. They are:

TYMNET: $7/hour
TELENET: $7/hour
Direct Dial: No charge

Billing is monthly.

SUBSCRIPTION INFORMATION:

To subscribe, an individual or responsible person within an organization need only sign a contract. CIS is unusual in that two organizations, the National Institutes of Health (NIH) and the Environmental Protection Agency (EPA), provide the databases, while the National Technical Information Service (NTIS) handles contracts and billing, and Computer Sciences Corporation is responsible for user support services such as training, exhibits, manuals, the CIS newsletter, and answering all questions that do not deal with contracts.

USER AIDS: Manuals for each database $11.50
CIS Newsletter   gratis

COMMUNICATIONS:

TYMNET, TELENET, and Direct Dial

300 and 1200 baud

TRAINING: New User Training: One- or two-day $100 per day

CIS holds training regularly in Falls Church and occasionally at selected sites throughout the United States and abroad.

DESCRIPTION: CIS comprises a mix of files, primarily numeric, some with both data and bibliographic information; you may use a few to perform calculations. Service is organized around the Structure and Nomenclature Search System (SANSS), a chemical dictionary-type file. SANSS allows for searching by chemical structure, nomenclature, molecular formula, and molecular weight. The database is small compared to those of CAS ONLINE and Questel and consists of about 225,000 chemicals selected from 73 data sources important to the federal government, academia, and industry.

Some of the most popular CIS databases are Oil and Hazardous Materials Technical Assistance Data System (OHMTADS), Federal Register Search System (FRSS) based on the U.S. government *Federal Register*, Clinical Toxicology of Commercial Products (CTCP) based on the standard textbook of the same name, and Registry of Toxic Effects of Chemical Substances, which is analogous to the list (of the same name) published annually by the National Institute of Occupational Safety and Health. Other NIH/EPA databases contain spectral data, nucleic acid sequences, NMR data, information on crystal structures, and other physical and chemical properties of substances. The Chemical Modelling Laboratory Database (CHEMLAB) provides for estimation of chemical properties such as boiling point and solubility based on conformational analysis, while the Mathematical Modelling System (MATHLAB) can be used for statistical calculations such as form-fitting and non-linear regression. The CIS system also has an electronic mail capability.

SYSTEM PROTOCOLS:

When you search CIS for bibliographic information, commands are similar to those found on the large bibliographic systems already described. Commands for special CIS capabilities such as building a structure to be searched, looking for substances for a particular structure, and searching for spectral peaks are unique to the different CIS databases. Probably because search requirements are so varied, each CIS database has its own manual.

CASE STUDY:

A scientist in the research and development department of a major chemical company wants descriptions of commercial insecticides that have compounds containing a trichloromethyl group. The searcher decides to use the Clinical Toxicology of Commercial Products (CTCP) database in the NIH/EPA system. The first step is to build the structure fragment in SANSS. See Listing 6–5. The CHAIN 1 command creates a single carbon atom. AGR (Add a Group) CCl3 adds this unit to the atom. After verification of correctness of the structure, the searcher keys in the FPROBE command to search the SANSS database for compounds containing the fragment.

In the second phase, the searcher switches to the CTCP database (GO CTCP) and looks for insecticides coded for Manufacturer's Authorized Use (MAU). The third step is to combine the insecticides with the substances containing the trichloromethyl group—thus, five substances are found to satisfy both conditions. This is File 3.

Then, the SSHOW command, used to display one of the five records, prints, in addition to the CAS registry number, the structure, extensive nomenclature, and names of the other CIS databases having information about the compound. The final two search statements are required to complete the search and to find the products containing the specified insecticides. The very last step is to print the names and ingredients of the insecticides.

LISTING 6-5

SEARCH OF CLINICAL TOXICOLOGY OF COMMERCIAL PRODUCTS DATABASE ON NIH/EPA CIS FOR COMMERCIAL INSECTICIDES HAVING A COMPOUND WITH A TRICHLOROMETHAL GROUP

```
NIH-EPA CIS (Version 3.26)     12:35    18-Mar-83


          Latest news for CIS    . . .
            27 Feb 83; CHEMLAW Component Now Available For Use
Enter SANSS →Component Mnemonic? (H for HELP): SANSS
 Database
          Structure and Nomenclature Search System
          (Version 3.41/5.2) October, 1981 ($85/hr)


          Latest news for SANSS   . . .
            25 Oct 81; Substantial Update Made To SANSS Data Base

          Complete data base selected.
Create a Chain with→Option? CHAIN 1
 One Carbon Group
             →Option? AGR CCL3 AT 1
Add a CCl₃ Group
              3CL
               *
               *
               *
  Unspecified    2C***1$
   Position     **
              *  *
              4CL 5CL

          [All bonds are 'chain' (acyclic)]

Find Compounds →Option? FPROBE 2
  Containing the
      Fragment   Type E to exit from all searches,
                 T to proceed to next fragment search.

          Fragment:
                         1C
                          *
                          *
                          *
                    3CL****2C*****4CL
                          *
                          *
                          *
                         5CL

          Required occurrences for hit :  1
          This fragment occurs in   446 compounds

          File = 1,   446 compounds contain this fragment

Enter Clinical →Option? GO CTCP
 Toxicology of
  Commercial
Products (CTCP)   CTCP Search System (Version 3.01/3.0 - June, 1982) ($85/Hr.)
    Database
          Latest news for CTCP    . . .
            30 Jan 83; Major New Types of Information Included in CTCP
          Copyrighted by the Trustees of Dartmouth College

          The authors of the CTCP data base have made diligent (but not
          exhaustive) efforts to ensure the accuracy of the data. The nature and
          scope of the information, however, are such that errors of fact,
          omission and judgment cannot be completely excluded. Suggestions are
          welcome; type "HELP AUTHORS" for more information.
```

LISTING 6-5 (continued)

Search for Products Authorized for Use as Insecticides
→Option? **MAU/INSECTICIDE**
File: 2 Total number of products found: 1887
Number of current products: 1848

Combine Concepts →Option? **#1 AND #2**

The mixed files you requested to be processed were:
File   Type   Component

  1   Pure CAS Registry Numbers
  2   Local Identifiers   CTCP
Continue with processing (Y/N/Help)(Y)? Y

File   2 is being converted to CAS Registry Numbers.
Conversion complete.   2653 related references
consisting of   178 unique CAS Registry Numbers were found.

File: 3 Count: 5

Display Record →Option? **SSHOW 3**

How many (E to Exit)? **1**

Type E to terminate display.

Entry   1   CAS RN 50-29-3
CIS Sources Of Information

    2 - CIS, EI Mass Spectrometry
    5 - EPA/CIS, OHM/TADS: 7216510
    6 - CIS, Cambridge X-Ray Crystallography: CPTCET10
   32 - NIOSH/CIS, RTECS: KJ3325000

23 Non-CIS References Available

C14H9Cl5O

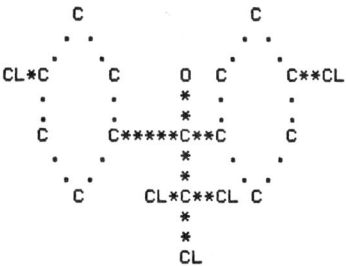

Benzene, 1,1'-(2,2,2-trichloroethylidene)bis[4-chloro- (9CI)
.alpha.-Bis(p-chlorophenyl).beta.,.beta.,.beta.-trichloroethane
.alpha..,.alpha.-Bis(p-chlorophenyl)-.beta.,.beta.,.beta.-trichlor
    ethane
p,p'-Dichlorodiphenyltrichloroethane
  107 more names available

How many (E to Exit)? **E**

Search CTCP for Registry Numbers from File 3
→Option? **CAS/#3**
File: 4 Total number of products found: 309
Number of current products: 295

LISTING 6-5 (continued)

Limit File 4 to → Option? **#2 AND 4**
Insecticides   File: 5 Total number of products found: 180
                        Number of current products: 178

Print Three Records → Option? **TYPE 5/2/1-3**

```
                         File  5; Entry    1; Accession No.      119
          ACME BAGWORM SPRAY
            Insecticide
            BAGWORM/INSECTICIDE
            (PBI/Gordon/ 105/)
                                    Activity Record: 11-76;11-80;
                                    Book edition:    V
Rating            Ingredient Name           CAS RN    Loc. #   Toxicity   Amount
                  ------------------------------------------------------------
                  Toxaphene*................  8001-35-2  27650     4       20.00%
                  Kelthane*.................  115-32-2   27180     3        3.60%
                  Xylene*...................  1330-20-7   5330     4       68.50%

                  --------------------

                         File  5; Entry    2; Accession No.      122
          ACME PESTROY 25% METHOXYCHLOR
            Insecticide
            INSECTICIDE
            (PBI/Gordon/ 105/)
                                    Activity Record: 11-76;11-80;
                                    Book edition:    V
                  Ingredient Name           CAS RN    Loc. #   Toxicity   Amount
                  ------------------------------------------------------------
                  Methoxychlor*.............  72-43-5    27190     3       25.00%
                  Xylene*...................  1330-20-7   5330     4

                  --------------------

                         File  5; Entry    3; Accession No.      157
          AGWAY METHOXYCHLOR 2-E
            Insecticide
            INSECTICIDE
            (Agway/ 118/)
                                    Activity Record: 07-76;03-80;
                                    Book edition:    V
                  Ingredient Name           CAS RN    Loc. #   Toxicity   Amount
                  ------------------------------------------------------------
                  Methoxychlor(technical)...  72-43-5    27190     3       24.0%
                  Xylene*...................  1330-20-7   5330     4       69.0%

                  --------------------
```

CAS ONLINE

NAME: CAS ONLINE
Chemical Abstracts Service
2540 Olentangy River Road
P.O. Box 3012
Columbus, OH 43210

TELEPHONE: (800) 848-6533
(614) 421-3698

NUMBER OF DATABASES:
2

HOURS: *Service:* Sunday 7PM to Friday 8PM EST (except Tuesday, Thursday 6PM–8PM)
Hotline: Monday–Friday 8:30AM–5PM EST

COST: (January 1, 1983)

Service initiation fee: $50

$35 per connect hour, between $.10 and $1 per record displayed on-line or offline, and the following search charges:

Full-file substructure search $80
Sample substructure search $ 5 (Free if preceding a full-file search)
Family substance search $12
Exact substance search $12

There is an academic discount plan whereby the students, faculty, and staff of colleges and universities may have unlimited access for $500 per month during non-peak hours—anytime except from 8AM–2PM EST. Only offline prints will be charged.

No minimums.

Communications charges are not included. They are:

TYMNET: $10/hour
TELENET: $10/hour
Direct Dial: No charge
Billing is monthly.

SUBSCRIPTION INFORMATION:
Subscribing involves returning an order form.

USER AIDS: CAS ONLINE Workbook $20   (contains Guide to Commands)
Guide to Commands $10
CAS ONLINE Screen Dictionary $20
Graphic Structure Input Manual $20   (self-instruction)
CAS ONLINE News

COMMUNICATIONS:
TYMNET, TELENET, and Direct Dial

300 and 1200 baud

TRAINING: Introductory Workshop: $200 (fee redeemable in online charges)

Training is held regularly at CAS in Columbus, Ohio and at locations throughout the country, usually in conjunction with professional meetings.

DESCRIPTION: CAS ONLINE provides access via structure and substructure searching to the entire file of over seven million compounds entered into the registry system since 1965. Using this system, you can search for chemical substance information on the basis of specific structural information *only,* thus bypassing all the very difficult problems associated with determining appropriate chemical nomenclature. Introduction of CAS ONLINE and the Questel system (described next) in late 1980 represented a true breakthrough in the ability to retrieve chemical information.

There are two CAS ONLINE databases. One is the full database of substances and structures, and the other is a sample file of about 300,000 items that you use to test a search strategy prior to incurring the considerable cost of a full-file substructure search.

You can display or print the full text of CA abstracts and index entries by keying in CA numbers. CA plans to add a direct link to the full bibliographic CA Search database by the end of 1983.

SYSTEM PROTOCOLS:

The basic search procedure is to build a structure online, either through graphic structure input or text structure input, to search the database, and to display answers either online or offline. The structure may be complete (for an exact substance search), or it may have an unspecified position (a substructure search). A third type of search is a family search, which retrieves an exact substance and a multicomponent substance, e.g., a salt. There are two methods of structure input.

Graphics Structure Input:

Graphics structure input on the CAS system requires use of the Hewlett-Packard 2647A or 2647F graphics terminal (which costs approximately $18,000 when modem, tablet, stylus, and printer are included). After entering a STRUCTURE command, you can draw a two-dimensional structure on the screen and select items from a menu through use of a tablet with a stylus or the cursor. With the Hewlett-Packard terminals, you may display online the structures of the substances retrieved in the search.

Text Structure Input:

This input method is used to build structures or substructures online by using commands similar to those on the NIH/EPA system. If you use a terminal or personal computer with graphics output capability—equipment compatible with Tektronix 4010 (Plot 10) graphics, which costs approximately $5000—you can display structures of the retrieved substances online.

The least costly (equipment costs about $1000) and still quite satisfactory method of searching is to use text structure input on an ordinary ASCII terminal or microcomputer with an ASCII terminal emulator program and modem. You can then retrieve textual answers online and have the structures printed offline at CAS and mailed to you. Contact CAS for information on equipment needed to use the system.

General: CAS ONLINE is a very powerful system. The database is updated weekly. It now allows for searches in which one or more positions are unspecified or are specified in terms of limited alternate possibilities (such as a halogen). Information displayed or printed (in addition to the structure) for each substance is registry number, collective index names, molecular formula, and up to 10 recent references from the Chemical Abstracts bibliographic file. When the full bibliographic database is searchable (by the end of 1983), it will be possible to use output from the structure search to search the full Chemical Abstracts database for references and to modify searches on the basis of bibliographic fields—i.e., to limit a structure search to only substances covered in the English language literature or to articles describing a synthesis. Of course, at present you can use the registry number retrieved in a structure search to find all references to the substance in the CA Search database on Dialog, SDC, BRS, and other services.

Most of CAS ONLINE's commands are similar to Dialog's. To build structures, you can recall a previous structure, add bonds, create rings and chains, and specify charges and valences. While the system is not difficult for a chemist to learn, the high cost of errors warrants training for people who want to make full use of CAS ONLINE search capabilities.

QUESTEL

NAME: Questel, Inc.
Suite 818
1625 I Street, N.W.
Washington, DC 20006

TELEPHONE: (800) 424-9600 (Hotline)
(202) 296-1604 (Washington, DC)

INTERNATIONAL OFFICE:
Questel
40, rue du Cherche-Midi
75006 Paris, France
Tel: (1)544.38.13

NUMBER OF DATABASES:
44

HOURS: *Service:* Monday 1AM to Friday 6:30 EST (except 6:30PM-8:30PM EST)
Hotline: Monday-Friday 8:30AM-5:30PM EST

COST: (February 1, 1983)

No registration fee.

For bibliographic databases, from $36 to $130 per connect hour.
For DARC structure and data files, $60 per hour for inputting a search request, $100 per hour when Chemical Abstract Service files are being accessed, and from $.14 to $.20 per substance to display or print answers.

Search fees are:

Registry number	$ 1
Substructure	$72
Sample file	$11
Exact match	$ 8 (includes families such as salts)
Batch substructure	$36 (permits 20,000 answers)
Mass spectra	$20
UPCAS (monthly update)	$20

No minimums.

Education and government research departments are entitled to a 10-percent discount (excluding communications). Volume discounts and deposit accounts are available.

Communications charges are not included. They are:

TYMNET: $10/hour plus $12 per kilosegment (64K) transmitted
TELENET: $10/hour plus $12 per kilosegment (64K) transmitted

Billing is monthly.

SUBSCRIPTION INFORMATION:
To subscribe, an individual or responsible person within an organization needs to sign a contract. Training is recommended but not required. The $100 training fee can be applied against connect time.

USER AIDS:
Questel User Manual $10
Questel Workshop Manual $10
DARC User Manual $10
DARC Workshop Manual $10
Questel-a-gram Newsletter
Other specialized manuals and guides

One set of manuals is sent free with each new password.

COMMUNICATIONS:
TYMNET, TELENET, UNINET

Transmission to the computer in Dalbonne, France is via satellite through Western Union, ITT, or RCA

300 and 1200 baud

TRAINING:
Chemistry I: Two days $100 (introductory)
Chemistry II: 1½ days $100 (advanced)
Chemistry III: One day $100 (abbreviated introductory)
TITUS: One day $70
Refresher sessions

Questel has training sessions in the Washington, D.C. office and on-site throughout the country and abroad. Training fees are returned as free time to be used after workshops.

DESCRIPTION: Questel, Inc., a subsidiary of the French company, Telesystemes, has 38 bibliographic databases in a full range of subject areas—from the sciences to business to the humanities—but those that have been most emphasized in the United States are the DARC chemical files. DARC is a chemical structure search system very similar to CAS ONLINE. It utilizes exactly the same Chemical Abstracts database as CAS ONLINE, with the minor difference that CAS is updated weekly while DARC is updated monthly.

SYSTEM PROTOCOLS:

DARC is similar to CAS ONLINE in another respect: It provides a sample file that you can use to test a strategy prior to a full-file search. Otherwise, DARC works with the same type of commands for building structures and has similar capabilities for searching exact structures and substructures and for displaying and printing output. Major advantages of DARC are interactive Boolean logic, which allows for cost-effective searching, and a direct link to the Chemical Abstracts bibliographic database for subject searching and for using retrieval from a structure query to perform a search for a complete bibliography. You can use registry numbers as the starting point for building a structure.

Equipment required for graphic input is less costly for DARC than for CAS ONLINE. You can use the Tektronix 4112 series at about $5500 ($1500 additional for the tablet), the Apple microcomputers with the Teksim chip and communications (although this arrangement has some resolution problems), or te DEC VT 100 intelligent terminal with a retrographics board at $2500 for both graphic input and output. A real bargain is the Lear Seigler Dumb Terminal at $500 plus a $500 retrographics board that will give graphic output. Of course, any ASCII-compatible terminal can be used for text input and text output.

GTE TELENET MEDICAL INFORMATION NETWORK

NAME: GTE Telenet Medical Information Network
8229 Boone Boulevard
Vienna, VA 22180

TELEPHONE: (703) 442-2500

NUMBER OF DATABASES:
5

HOURS: *Service:* 24 hours every day
Hotline: Monday–Friday 6AM-6PM EST

COST: (January 1, 1983)

One time subscription fee: $100 per organization

User registration: $25 each

For AMA/NET information services, the connect time charges are from $25/hour to $27/hour.

MED/MAIL communications services are $16/hour in prime time and $7/hour in non-prime time. Prime time is 7AM to 6PM Monday–Friday.

There are a few other relatively small miscellaneous charges.

A substantial monthly minimum is charged based on the number of registered users within the subscriber organization:

First user $45
Second through 11th user $25 each
Eleven or more users $295 per organization

Communications charges are included.

Billing is monthly.

SUBSCRIPTION INFORMATION:
Subscribers must sign a contract and pay the subscription and registration fees.

USER AIDS: One self-pace manual included with initial subscription; $15 for each additional copy

COMMUNICATIONS:
TELENET

300 or 1200 baud

TRAINING: Self-pace manual

DESCRIPTION: GTE Telenet Medical Information Network is a joint venture of GTE TELENET Communication Corporation and the American Medical Association (AMA). It features AMA/NET, a medical information service based on four AMA publications and MED/MAIL, an electronic messaging system, and has plans for considerable expansion to include services such as drug alerts, adverse drug reaction reporting, diagnostic assistance, poison control information, and paperless insurance claims.

Probably the most important information service at present is the Drug Information Base, an electronic version of *AMA Drug Evaluations*. By January 1983, this database contained critical evaluations of 1200 drugs marketed under about 4000 trade names. An important advantage of the database is that one-twelfth of it will be updated monthly, making the online version much more current than the

SCIENTIFIC, TECHNICAL, AND MEDICAL VENDORS AND DATABASES

printed version. Critical revisions and additions can be made immediately.

Other AMA/NET databases are counterparts of *Current Medical Information and Terminology,* which contains brief descriptions of diseases, disorders, and conditions, *Physicians' Current Procedural Terminology,* and *Socioeconomic Research Resources,* a database covering articles on the non-clinical aspects of health care.

MED/MAIL is an electronic messaging system that can be used to send messages to other subscribers. You can also use it to order documents from the AMA library and to post and read messages of general interest on bulletin boards. You can locate information on AMA meetings and continuing medical education activities via bulletin boards.

Plans are to add in the near future the computer-assisted instruction programs from Massachusetts General Hospital (see Chapter 10 for description), drug alerting services from the Food and Drug Administration, and information from the Center for Disease Control.

SYSTEM PROTOCOLS:

Methods for selecting and changing databases are menu-driven, while searching is partly menu-driven and partly command-driven. After retrieving a set of records, you may display the "titles" record, select a record from the title menu, and then display only the part of the record that is of interest. For example, after a search of a disease-related database for *appendicitis,* you can decide to look only at "Signs and Symptoms."

CASE STUDY:

A physician treating several patients for hypertension wants to look at the interactions of several hypertensive drugs. See Listing 6–6. Using Drug Information Base in response to the COMMAND prompt, she requests records of drugs prescribed for hypertension. After receiving a partial list, she selects *propranolol* and then asks that the interactions of propranolol be displayed. Note that the convention for finding drugs used for a condition is USE=.

L I S T I N G   6–6

SEARCH OF THE DRUG INFORMATION DATABASE ON THE AMA/GTE SYSTEM FOR INFORMATION ON INTERACTIONS OF HYPERTENSIVE DRUGS, PARTICULARLY PROPRANOLOL

```
GTE
TELENET
MEDICAL INFORMATION NETWORK

SELECTIONS:
```

Beginning Menu {
```
   1   AMA/NET INFORMATION BASES
   2   MED/MAIl
```
}

```
------------------
```

LISTING 6-6 (continued)

```
        ? INFORMATION AND ASSISTANCE

        BYE TO LEAVE MEDICAL INFORMATION NETWORK

        PLEASE ENTER YOUR SELECTION: 1
```
Select Information Databases →
```
        110.1 GTE TELENET CORPORATION

            YOUR REQUEST TO USE MEDICAL INFORMATION BASES IS NOW BEING
        PROCESSED.  WAIT A FEW MOMENTS, PLEASE.

                      AMERICAN MEDICAL ASSOCIATION
                      AMA/NET INFORMATION BASES

        SELECTIONS:

            1.  DRUG INFORMATION BASE
            2.  DISEASE INFORMATION BASE
            3.  MEDICAL PROCEDURE AND SERVICE INFORMATION BASE
            4.  SOCIO/ECONOMIC BIBLIOGRAPHIC INFORMATION BASE
            5.  RECOVER YOUR MOST RECENT INFORMATION BASE SEARCH RESULTS

        ------------------------------------------------------------------
```
Enter Drug Information Database →
```
        ?   INFORMATION AND ASSISTANCE ON THESE SELECTIONS

        BYE  RETURN TO THE MEDICAL INFORMATION NETWORK SELECTION
             PAGE TO SELECT OTHER SERVICES OR EXIT THE SYSTEM
```
Find Drugs Used for Treating Hypertension →
```
        PLEASE ENTER YOUR SELECTION: 1

              AMA/NET    DRUG INFORMATION BASE
        COPYRIGHT 1982                      American Medical Association

        Command?  find use=hypertension

        Search 1: 76 drug(s) found.

        Do you want to see a list of durgs? (YES)
```
Carriage Return to Browse Record Titles →
```
        Number          Drug Name
           1       ALSEROXYLON
           2       AMILORIDE HYDROCHLORIDE  AND HYDROCHLOROTHIAZIDE
           3       AMILORIDE HYSROCHLORIDE
           4       ATENOLOL
                      .
                      .
                      .
```
View Record →
```
          58       PREDNISONE
          59       PROPRANOLOL

        Please SELECT number to display: (MORE) 59

        Please enter the topics you wish to display: (?)  INT
```
Code to See Drug Interactions Field →
```
        Display Number 1

        TOPIC - INTERACTIONS: PROPRANOLOL   (0011)
           SELECTED DRUG TO DRUG:

        CIMETIDINE
                May increase bioavailability.

        CLONIDINE
                Hypertension (rare);  has occurred during combined therapy
                and after withdrawal of clonidine.

        DIURETICS, THIAZIDE
                Propranolol enhances the effect  of thiazides on serum
                triglyceride and urate levels.
                      .
                      .
```

COLLEAGUE

NAME: BRS COLLEAGUE
1200 Route 7
Latham, NY 12110

TELEPHONE: (800) 833-4707
(800) 555-5566 (New York state)
(518) 783-7251

NUMBER OF DATABASES:
3 (biomedical)
70 (total)

HOURS: *Service:* Monday-Saturday 6AM-4AM EST
Sunday 6AM-2PM and 7PM-4AM EST
Hotline: Monday-Friday 8AM-1AM EST
Saturday 8AM-5PM EST
Sunday 8AM-2PM EST

COST: (June 1, 1983)

COLLEAGUE has three pricing structures for subscriptions to the Biomedical Bibliographic Library.

INDIVIDUAL HOURLY
One-time registration fee $50
$47/hour MEDLINE.

Other BRS databases at standard rates.

$43/hour for the other two biomedical bibliographic library databases.

One password.

Credit card only.

INDIVIDUAL MONTHLY
One-time registration fee $50

$50 per month with three-month minimum.

Includes two hours use of biomedical databases per month (with additional time at $22/hr) and access to all other BRS databases at standard rates.

One password

GROUP ANNUAL
One-time registration fee for one password $50

Pre-paid subscription fee per password $550. Includes 25 hours use of biomedical databases per password (with additional time at $22/hr) and access to all other BRS databases at standard rates.

Telecommunications charges are included.

NOTE: As of this writing, prices for other COLLEAGUE libraries were not available.

SUBSCRIPTION INFORMATION:
Subscribers fill out agreement forms and pay the registration and subscription fees.

USER AIDS: Manual   gratis with each password

COMMUNICATIONS:
TYMNET, TELENET, and UNINET

TRAINING: Users may utilize regular BRS training or teach themselves using the manual. See information on BRS in Chapter 5 for training specifics.

DESCRIPTION: Plans are for COLLEAGUE to be organized into "libraries." The first, the Biomedical Bibliographic Library, contains MEDLINE from 1966 onward, Health Planning and Administration, produced by the National Library of Medicine, and Pre-Med, a database of literature from 109 core medical journals available within 10 days of their receipt by medical libraries.

The second library, covering critical care medicine, will consist primarily of textbooks from major medical publishers; the third, internal medicine, will contain major medical texts and the full text of articles from prime journals such as *The New England Journal of Medicine*. Projected implementation date is late 1983.

SYSTEM PROTOCOLS:
The COLLEAGUE command language is intermediate between that of the regular BRS system and BRS After Dark. It is partly menu-driven, but has more capabilities and greater flexibility than After Dark. A unique feature is "caps" which may be placed over the regular keyboard to act as function keys—to perform actions such as to print. The COLLEAGUE language is still under development.

OTHER SYSTEMS

The seven systems described above are—or, in the case of GTE/AMA Network and COLLEAGUE, are expected to be—the most popular specialized information services in science, technology, and medicine in the United States. It is worth noting that four of the six are less than three years old! "New" systems will come to our attention with regularity. Some are genuinely new, while others are local or foreign services expanding to new markets.

Systems discussed below deserve the attention of a user with the appropriate subject interests. That I do not cover them in more detail is not a quality judgment but reflects their relatively limited use in the United States at present.

Pergamon Infoline

Pergamon Infoline
Pergamon International Information Corporation
1340 Old Chain Bridge Road
McLean, VA 22101
(800) 336-7575
(703) 442-0900

This British service (see Appendix I for the address in England) with a U.S. division offers some of the same databases as Dialog, BRS, and SDC at competitive prices. Four valuable and unique Infoline files are Fine Chemicals Directory, an automated catalog of commercially available chemicals; PATSEARCH, a database of U.S. patents; PIRA, literature in the paper, board, printing, and packaging industries; and RAPRA, which covers rubber and plastic materials. You can access Infoline in the United States through TYMNET, TELENET, and UNINET.

EMIS

Electronic Materials Information Service (EMIS)
IEEE/INSPEC Service Center
445 Hoes Lane
Piscataway, NJ 08854
(201) 981-0060

EMIS is an online fact-retrieval and publications service developed by INSPEC, a division of the Institution of Electrical Engineers in England. Primary users are electrical engineers and researchers who process, use, and study solid-state electronics materials. Currently, EMIS contains approximately 7,000 records on silicon, gallium arsenide, indium phosphide, and lithium niobate and 400 records on other substances.

The two EMIS information databases are the Materials Properties File, which gives data on literally *hundreds* of properties (such as melting point, stopping power, and spin density), and the Materials Supply File, which has information on commercial suppliers of the materials.

INSPEC designed EMIS to serve as an electronic journal, a medium for rapid publication of research results. Each article entered by a subscriber may have up to 60 lines of text on one material topic, with date of publication, referees' comments, and author's replies appended.

Communication to EMIS is through the international GEISCO GE MkIII computer network and is limited to 300 baud. You search the system, which is partly menu-driven, by using codes given in the EMIS manual. EMIS is simple. You can probably learn it in less than an hour of studying and practice. Cost is $18 per connect hour plus charges for transmitted characters and used computer resources; cost is less with use guarantees.

Lithium Information Center

Lithium Information Center
Department of Psychiatry
University of Wisconsin-Madison
600 Highland Avenue
Madison, WI 53792
(608) 263-6171

The Lithium Information Center maintains a computerized database containing references to journal articles, meeting abstracts, books, and other publications on the uses of lithium in medicine. Established in 1975, the database now has about 10,000 references. You can access it directly by telephone and search by title, keyword, and other bibliographic fields for $7.50 per hour.

Occupational Health Services

Occupational Health Services, Inc. (OHS)
515 Madison Avenue
New York, NY 10022
(800) 223-8978
(212) 752-4530

OHS databases are Environmental Health News, an electronic newsletter for environmental and occupational health professionals, and HAZARDLINE, an online databank with extensive information on over 500 hazardous workplace substances. HAZARDLINE contains OSHA standards, chemical names, descriptions, physical and chemical properties, protective clothing standards, symptoms, first aid procedures, approved methods for large-quantity disposal—over 27 different types of information in all. The only cost is $120 per connect hour, including communications. Access is through TYMNET or the STSC networks at 300 or 1200 baud. The search language is partly menu-driven, with extensive HELP commands and many codes. With the manual's help, you can learn OHS in a matter of minutes.

Infrared Information System

Infrared Information System (IRIS)
Sadtler Research Laboratories
3316 Spring Garden Street
Philadelphia, PA 19104
(215) 382-7800

IRIS is a system for identifying unknown compounds using spectra produced by Sadtler. The database contains approximately 110,000 spectra. You search it by coding for peaks in a manner similar to that involved in searching the printed Sadtler indexes. Since there is only one type of search, this system should be relatively easy to learn for a chemist who has used spectra manually. Costs are a quarterly fee of $75 to $200 (depending on use volume), per search charges ranging from $4 to $18, and some minor housekeeping charges.

CHAPTER 7

Business and Economic Vendors and Databases

While there are valuable bibliographic databases in the business, economic, and legal areas, source databases—one-stop information sources—tend to be even more important. Business people, lawyers, economists, and others seeking news can now all have online access to a vast array of corporate data, complete news stories, full text of laws and legal decisions, stock quotes, and business and economic statistics. Some of these databases—for example, the economic time series—even support data manipulation and calculations so that you can rearrange and display the data in a variety of formats.

DATABASES

The three major vendors—Dialog, SDC, and BRS—as well as The Source and CompuServe, all provide access to a wide spectrum of databases in business and economics. See Table 7–1.

As in science fields, characteristics of a particular database can vary over systems. The number of years online or the searchable fields, for example, may differ.

TABLE 7–1

AVAILABILITY OF MAJOR BUSINESS, ECONOMIC, NEWS, GOVERNMENT, AND LEGAL DATABASES THROUGH NON-SPECIALIZED VENDORS

DATABASE	DIALOG	KI*	BRS	DARK**	SDC	SOURCE	COMPUS***
ABI/INFORM	X	X	X	X	X		
Commerce Business Daily	X						
Congressional Information Serv.	X						
Disclosure	X						X
News (various)	X	X			X	X	X
Predicasts	X						
Stock quotes (various sources)						X	X
Value Line					X		

*Knowledge Index
**BRS After Dark
***CompuServe Information Service

103

Each of the systems mentioned above has other databases covering business, economics, news, law, and government. These are smaller or more specialized than the databases listed in Table 7-1. Less obvious, but important, is the need to be aware that business, economic, and legal information is included in technical and social science databases. MEDLINE, for example, covers articles on the management of a medical practice, and PSYCINFO has articles on the legal issues in psychiatric care.

Management

Management Contents and ABI/Inform are the two databases with broad coverage of management literature. Chemical Industry Notes, Pharmaceutical News Index, AGLINE (agriculture), ACCOUNTANTS, P/E News (petroleum/energy), and LABORDOC are valuable sources of information in their respective industries. ADTRACT covers "literature" ignored by all other database producers—advertisements appearing in about 150 major U.S. consumer magazines.

Harvard Business Review, a key management publication, is the first scholarly journal to be publicly available in full-text format.

Corporate

People looking for corporate data have their choice of several good directory/data-type databases. Disclosure on Dialog, Dow Jones, and other services provides extracts of reports of approximately 8,000 publicly owned companies filed with the U.S. Securities and Exchange Commission. Much larger is DUN's Market Identifiers, with product, marketing, and financial data on more than one million U.S. public and private businesses. Similar files are EIS Industrial Plants, EIS Nonmanufacturing Establishments, Media General Financial Services, Million Dollar Directory, and Value Line.

Listing 7-1, a search of Value Line on CompuServe for data on National Medical Enterprises, illustrates the kind of detailed corporate data that you can find in these databases: revenues, debts, capital expenditures, and key values (such as return on equity, book value, and price/earnings ratio) that serious investors like to see. This type of search is rarely more complex to perform than the one shown, which simply required putting in the ticker symbol and responding to a few questions.

Avid users of the printed Value Line publication will note three popular features missing from the online report: the timeliness value and the safety and industry ranks.

News

By far, the most comprehensive source of news is the New York Times Infobank, now on the Mead system with LEXIS and NEXIS. See SPECIALIZED SERVICES below. The full database, dating from 1969, is not available elsewhere. National Newspaper Index (NNI) on Dialog and Knowledge Index covers *The Times* (from 1979) in addition to *The Christian Science Monitor* and *The Wall Street Journal*.

Newsearch (Dialog) is a database for the current month only. It is updated daily by indexing from the three NNI newspapers and popular magazines. Month-old information is transferred from Newsearch to NNI and the Magazine Index database. Even more timely is wire service news, which you can obtain through The Source, CompuServe, Mead Data Central, Dow Jones, and several other services. Dow Jones, of

BUSINESS AND ECONOMIC VENDORS AND DATABASES

LISTING 7-1

SEARCH OF VALUE LINE IN COMPUSERVE FOR INFORMATION ON NATIONAL MEDICAL ENTERPRISES

```
VALUE LINE DATABASE
   UPDATED:  3/18/83

INSTRUCTIONS Y OR N:N

TICKER SYMBOL:NME
```
↑
NYSE Symbol for National Medical Enterprises

```
REPORTS AVAILABLE ARE:
1) INCOME STATEMENT
2) BALANCE SHEET
3) SOURCES AND USES OF FUNDS
4) KEY RATIOS
5) 3 TO 5 YR. FORCASTS
6) ALL

<CR> FOR NEW COMPANY
<EXIT> TO EXIT
? FOR HELP

KEY DIGIT OR DIGITS
SEPARATED BY COMMAS   !6
```
↑
Choose to View All Reports

```
             NATIONAL MED ENTERP.
```

Authorization to Pay for the Reports
```
THE REPORTS SELECTED
WILL COST $3.00

OK TO PROCEED Y OR N      !Y

--INCOME STATMENT-- 5/81     5/82
GROSS REVENUES    892.410  1167.070
COST OF GDS SD    738.210   957.700
SELL & ADM EXP      0.000     0.000
DEPREC, AMORT      24.980    38.020
TOTAL INTEREST     36.270    52.350
UNCONSLTD SUBS      0.000     0.000
OTHER INCOME        0.000     7.440
OTHER EXPENSES      0.000     0.000
MINOR INTEREST      0.000     0.000
PRETAX INCOME      96.250   133.240
TOTAL TAXES        44.450    58.000
SPECIAL ITEMS       0.000     0.000
NET INC BEF EX     51.800    75.240
EXTRAORD ITEMS      0.000     0.000
KEY <ENTER> FOR NEXT PAGE   !

--BALANCE SHEET--  5/81     5/82
CASH & EQUIVS     105.480   150.960
ACCTS RECEIVBL    172.130   219.130
INVENTORIES        30.560    44.370
OTH CURN ASSTS      4.630     8.480
TOT CURN ASSTS    312.800   422.930

GROSS PLANT       540.680   745.380
ACCUM DEPRECTN     56.970    88.900
NET PLANT         483.710   656.480
LNGTRM INVESTS     40.010    53.370
DEFERD CHARGES      4.420    25.070
INTANGBL ASSTS     26.570    45.350
OTH LGTM ASSTS      0.000     0.000
TOTAL ASSETS      867.500  1203.190
KEY <ENTER> FOR NEXT PAGE   !


NOTES PAYABLE       0.000     0.000
ACCTS PAYABLE      49.090    66.320
TAXES PAYABLE      21.250    21.780
```

Listing 7-1 (continued)

```
OTH CURNT LIAB    69.710    99.480
DEFERRED TAX      36.790    53.950
MINOR INTEREST     0.000     0.000
LONG TERM DEBT   299.350   495.880
OTH LNGTM LIAB    10.010     8.800
TOT LIABILIT'S   486.210   746.210
PREFERRD STOCK     5.140     5.140
COMMON STOCK       1.120     1.170
ADDT'L CAPITAL   282.520   305.180
RETAIND EARNGS    92.510   145.490
TOTAL EQUITY     381.290   456.980
KEY <ENTER> FOR NEXT PAGE   !


   --SOURCES & USES--  5/81    5/82
CASH FLOW         76.780   113.260
PROPERTY SALES     0.000     0.000
COMN FINANCNG    132.560    19.330
PRFRD FINANCNG     0.000     0.000
LT DEBT FINCNG   117.510   237.190
OTHER SOURCES     -3.990   -30.890
CAPITL SPENDNG   129.070   202.800
OTH INVESTMNTS     4.930    13.360
COMMON RETIRED     0.000     0.000
PREFRD RETIRED     0.000     0.000
DEBT RETIRED      94.390    45.590
COMMN DIVIDNDS    12.790    17.990
PRFRD DIVIDNDS     0.500     0.500
ADDTN TO W CPL    81.180    58.650
KEY <ENTER> FOR NEXT PAGE   !

   ----KEY RATIOS----  5/81    5/82
EARNGS PR SHAR      1.24     1.60
PRICE/EARN RAT     14.06    11.54
RETRN ON EQUIT     13.59    16.46
RETRN ON ASSTS      5.97     6.25
DIVS PER SHARE      0.30     0.39
DIVIDEND YIELD      1.72     2.11
SALES / ASSETS    102.87    97.00
MKT/BOOK VALUE      2.08     1.92
CURRENT RATIO     199.45   203.03
QUICK RATIO         1.80     1.82
TIMS INT EARND      3.65     3.55
BETA                 N/A     1.40
C SHRS OUTSTDG     44.81    46.93
NET IN AVAIL C     51.30    74.74
KEY <ENTER> FOR NEXT PAGE   !


   --3 TO 5 YR FORECASTS--
SHARES OUTSTANDING          54.00
SALES                      2400.3
EARNINGS PER SHARE           3.05
DIVIDENDS PER SHARE          0.80
BOOK VALUE PER SHARE        18.50
HIGH TARGET PRICE           65.00
LOW TARGET PRICE            40.00
% APPRECIATION HIGH        105.00
% APPRECIATION LOW          25.00

EST EPS FR 12 MO PERIOD
ENDING 6 MONTHS HENCE        2.05
EST DIV PER SHARE FOR
NEXT 12 MONTHS               0.50
KEY <ENTER> FOR NEXT PAGE   !
```

course, also provides access to *The Wall Street Journal* and *Barron's*. NDEX, an SDC database, covers nine major regional newspapers, such as *The Chicago Tribune* and *The Los Angeles Times,* and 10 black newspapers.

NEXIS, from Mead Data Central, is a very comprehensive international news service that indexes six newspapers, more than 25 magazines, eight wire services, and newsletters. Coverage dates start from 1975 on, depending on the publication. VU/TEXT Information Services from *The Philadelphia Inquirer,* the NewsNet electronic journals, and Info Globe—all described below—are other sources for news.

Law and Government

Legal Resource Index provides coverage of the key law journals and other legal monographs and government publications. LEXIS and WESTLAW, two powerful systems designed for lawyers, contain the full text of statutes, federal and state case law, and other legal research tools such as the widely used Shepard's Citations. See full descriptions in the next section.

Through the combination of the GPO Monthly Catalog and NTIS (National Technical Information Service), searchers can locate online references to non-serial government publications that are for sale. CIS, a database of the Congressional Information Service, comprehensively covers congressional working papers and other federal legislative activities. *The Federal Register* and *Commerce Business Daily* have online equivalents. For legal information in chemistry and on patents, you can turn to CHEMLAW, Chemical Regulations and Guidelines, and PATLAW.

Stocks

Dow Jones, Quick Quote on CompuServe, and UNISTOX on The Source all have current stock prices that are updated during trading hours and a range of other data on financial markets. Dow Jones and CompuServe also display stock histories.

Both The Source and CompuServe offer software that enables the investor to build and save an individual stock portfolio online, thereby eliminating the need to enter each symbol to search all the stocks in the portfolio. The CompuServe "PORTFOLIO" program will even calculate automatically the total value of the portfolio. Dow Jones has similar offline software—described in Chapter 9—for evaluation and analysis of stocks.

Economics

Economics Abstracts International on Dialog provides coverage of about 1800 publications on markets, industries, and research in economic science and management. Coverage is international and includes industry- and country-specific data, and information about investment climates, import regulations, and distribution channels.

Also on Dialog are forecasts and time series from Predicasts and Business International Corporation. The largest organization providing economic and financial databases is Data Resources, Inc. (DRI) of Lexington, Massachusetts. Founded in 1969 by world-renowned Harvard economist Otto Eckstein, DRI offers over 100 million data series and sophisticated software that allows clients to build models and to perform other operations. See below for further information on DRI. Just a few of the other organizations offering similar services are Wharton Econometric Forecasting Associates, Inc., Standard & Poor's Compustat Services, Inc., and I.P. Sharp Associates in Canada.

The value of online economic data is enhanced by software that enables a user to produce customized displays such as charts and graphs and, in some services, to build forecasting models. The search in Listing 7–2 is a very simple example of this capability. It is a search of the BIDATA database from Business International on the I.P. Sharp system. BIDATA contains 20,000 time series of 315 annual national account, demo-

---

LISTING 7–2

SEARCH OF BIDATA ON THE I.P. SHARP SYSTEM FOR ECONOMIC TIME SERIES RELATING TO BRAZIL

```
        BIDATA
        TYPE 'HELP' IN RESPONSE TO ANY PROMPT IF YOU NEED AN EXPLANATION
            OF THAT PROMPT.  TO LEAVE THIS PROGRAM, TYPE 'QUIT' OR 'EXIT'
            FOR BIDATA FORECAST REPORTS.  LEAVE THIS PROGRAM AND TYPE
            'BIFORECAST'.

        ENTER TIME FRAME (E.G. '75 TO 80' OR '65  75'):
                                                            78 TO 80
        ENTER VARIABLE CODE(S) SEPARATED BY COMMAS:
                                                      GDPC,IMUS,CPI,EXAV
        ENTER COUNTRY CODE(S) SEPARATED BY COMMAS:
                                                      BRA
        CURRENCY, BASE YEAR, OR PER CAPITA CONVERSION (Y/N)?
                                                              Y
        ENTER COUNTRY CODE FOR CURRENCY CONVERSION (OR SPACE):
                                                                USA
        ENTER BASE YEAR FOR CONVERSION TO CONSTANT PRICE DATA (OR SPACE):
                                                                           75
        ENTER EITHER 'PC' FOR PER CAPITA (OR SPACE):
                                                      PC
        GROUP THE DATA BY (C)OUNTRY OR (V)ARIABLE:
                                                     C
        CALCULATE RATE OF GROWTH FOR EACH ITEM (Y/N)?
                                                        Y
        ENTER A TITLE (Y/N)?
                              Y
        TITLE (SPACE OR CR WHEN DONE):
Report Title ──▶ SELECTED ECONOMIC INDICATORS
        SOURCE: THE BI/DATA DATABASE
        REDO THE TITLE (Y/N)?
                               N
        ENTER PRINT WIDTH:
                           80
        PRINT THE COST OF THIS REPORT (Y/N)?
                                              N
        PRINT THE OUTPUT AS (T)ABLE OR (D)ISPLAY:
                                                   D
        TO PRINT OUT YOUR REPORT, PRESS THE CARRIAGE RETURN AFTER THE
            NEXT PAUSE.  YOU MAY WANT TO ALIGN THE PAPER TO THE TOP
            OF THE PAGE.
```

LISTING 7–2 (continued)

```
                    SELECTED ECONOMIC INDICATORS
                    SOURCE: THE BI/DATA DATABASE
------------------------------------------------------------------

                                         1978      1979      1980
------------------------------------------------------------------
(C) = 1975
US DOLLARS
PER CAPITA

BRAZIL
    GROSS DOMESTIC PRODUCT (C)           1,313     1,362     1,438
        RATE OF GROWTH                              3.72      5.55
    IMPORTS FROM THE US (US$)            26.64     29.53     36.67
        RATE OF GROWTH                             10.88     24.16
    CONSUMER PRICE INDEX                   283       432       790
        RATE OF GROWTH                             52.67     82.83
    YEAR AVGE EXCHNG RATE ; US$          18.07     26.94     52.71
        RATE OF GROWTH                             49.11     95.64
```

graphic, price, production, balance of payment, and trade indicators for 131 countries. This search is for selected economic data on Brazil from 1978 through 1980. You are led by menus to make all the necessary decisions. The list of codes can be obtained from either I.P. Sharp or from Business International. Most interactions are self-explanatory. One that is not—CURRENCY, BASE YEAR, or PER CAPITA CONVERSION—makes possible more meaningful cross-country comparisons by allowing you to convert price data to a uniform currency. You can also convert the time series to a uniform base year and to a per-capita basis. You can then display data by country or by variable and select a title for the report.

DOW JONES

NAME: Dow Jones News/Retrieval
Dow Jones & Company, Inc.
P.O. Box 300
Princeton, NJ 08540

TELEPHONE: (800) 257-5114 (Hotline)
(609) 452-1511 (New Jersey)
(800) 223-2274 (Marketing)

NUMBER OF DATABASES:
19

HOURS: *Service:* Daily 6AM–4AM EST
Hotline: Monday–Friday 8AM–11PM EST
Saturday 9AM–5PM EST

INFORMATION ONLINE

COST: (January 1, 1983)

*Registration fee:** $50

	WEEKDAYS 6AM–6PM	EVENINGS, WEEKENDS, HOLIDAYS
Dow Jones News	$1.20	$.20
Stock Quotes	$ .90	$.15
Financial & Investment Services	$1.20	$.90
General News & Information	$ .60	$.30

*May be waived for purchasers of an authorized Dow Jones Software package.

Per-minute connect time charges:
   The rates are for 300 baud. 1200 baud is 1.7 times higher. Smaller per-minute rates available for people willing to pay annual or monthly fees. See additional information under Subscription Information.

Communication charges included.

Billing is monthly and direct. No credit cards.

SUBSCRIPTION INFORMATION:
You sign an agreement that is available directly from Dow Jones. For the standard subscription, there is a one-time start-up fee of $50. Other memberships are "Blue Chip," which entitles you to a one-third discount on non-prime usage (evenings and weekends) in return for the $50 start-up fee and $75 per year, and "Executive," which gives you a one-third discount on all use in return for a $50 per-month subscription fee per location.
   The $50 registration fee is waived for purchasers of an authorized Dow Jones software package. Several packages are for analysis of downloaded data and are described in Chapter 9. Another package is the Dow Jones Connector (for $49.95), which contains the operating guide and directory and entitles you to one hour of free time. You can purchase the packages at computer stores.
   A limited amount of free time on Dow Jones comes with purchase of some other communications software and hardware such as the CompuServe start-up kits.

USER AIDS: Fact Finder $10 (included with subscription)
Directory of Symbols   (comes with Fact Finder)
An Introduction to Free Text Search of the Dow Jones News Database   gratis
Dowline magazine   gratis

COMMUNICATIONS:
TYMNET, TELENET, DATAPAC

300 or 1200 baud

TRAINING: Formal training is not required. You can learn the relatively few simple commands quickly by reading the user aids.

DESCRIPTION: Service has expanded beyond the stock market information that is most closely associated with the Dow Jones name.

Business and Economic News: News comes from *The Wall Street Journal, Barron's,* and the Dow Jones News Service and dates back to June 1979. The news database is updated continually during business hours. You can search it with stock symbols (for information on specific companies) or with a command language resembling that of BRS.

Stock Prices: Through Dow Jones, you can access (with a required minimum 15-minute delay) current prices of stocks, options, bonds, mutual funds, U.S. treasury issues, and other government securities. Historical stock quotes and Dow Jones averages are also on this service.

Financial and Investment Services: Major databases in this area are Disclosure II and Media General Services, which provide access to corporate financial data such as revenues, earnings, P/E ratios, and stock performance. Other services are economic forecasts by brokerage firm analysts, key economic news, and money market forecasts.

General News and Information Services: In this area, Dow Jones has weather and sports news, the full 20-volume text of the *Academic American Encyclopedia,* UPI news, movie reviews, the Comp-U-Store electronic shop-at-home service, and the full transcripts of Louis Rukeyser's *Wall Street Week* television show.

Electronic Mail: You can tap into the electronic mail system of MCI Communications (the telephone company) through News/Retrieval. MCI centers throughout the country take mail from the network, print it by laser, and deliver it in four hours, overnight, or by next-day federal service, depending on how much you are willing to pay.

Dow-A-Lert: Dow-A-Lert is a current-awareness service that covers all wire services and Dow Jones publications. Equipment is a small programmable radio that you set with codes for subjects of interest. Whenever news on your code is added to the system, the radio turns on and broadcasts a brief bulletin. Stock quotes are broadcast for selected Fortune 500 companies when the stock moves one point or more. You can tape the broadcast if you will not be available or if you do not wish to be interrupted. Cost is $150 for installation and $73 per month for service. Call the separate Dow-A-Lert hotline (800) 352-5378 for further information.

SYSTEM PROTOCOLS: The system has both menu- and command-driven modes. In menu mode, you can readily obtain instructions by either selecting the appropriate menu item or typing the HELP command. The system commands used most are simple; they consist of punctuation marks followed by stock exchange symbols or other codes that you can find easily in the user aids. For example, to receive the latest Tandy stock price, you enter ",TAN". Retrieving text requires commands that resemble closely those of the BRS system.

CASE STUDY: An investor interested in purchasing stock in National Medical Enterprises wants information on the company. She decides to search Dow Jones to see how the stock has performed over the past few years, obtain basic performance data, and look for recent news stories that might help her make a decision. See Listing 7–3.

The investor first checks the News Retrieval Directory for the stock symbol and the exchange on which it is traded. Bypassing the menus, she enters directly the ";" command followed by "1" for the New York exchange, the symbol, and "P1" for the most recent two-week time period, and retrieves prices and volumes. She then retrieves this same information back to the beginning of 1981. Next, she gains access to Media General Financial Services for the performance data ($NME/F) and, in the last step, prints a recent pertinent news article.

LISTING 7–3

SEARCH OF DOW JONES FOR INFORMATION ON NATIONAL MEDICAL ENTERPRISES

```
       DOW JONES NEWS/RETRIEVAL
          COPYRIGHT (C) 1983
       DOW JONES & COMPANY, INC.
          ALL RIGHTS RESERVED.

30 FREE MINUTES OF //SPORTS IN
MARCH FOR BLUE CHIP, EXECUTIVE
MEMBERS. TYPE //MENU FOR A LIST
OF DATA BASES.
ENTER QUERY
```

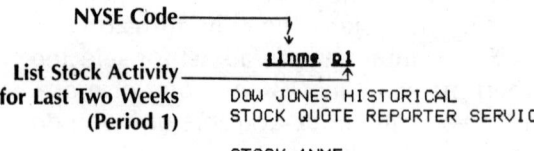

List Stock Activity for Last Two Weeks (Period 1) — NYSE Code

```
DOW JONES HISTORICAL
STOCK QUOTE REPORTER SERVICE

STOCK 1NME
```

BUSINESS AND ECONOMIC VENDORS AND DATABASES   113

LISTING 7-3 (continued)

```
DATE       HIGH      LOW       CLOSE     VOL(100/S)
03/02/83   31 1/2    30 3/4    30 7/8    1552
03/03/83   31 3/4    30 3/4    31 1/4    3589
03/04/83   31 1/2    30 7/8    31 1/2    1850
03/07/83   32        31        31 5/8    1699
03/08/83   31 7/8    30 1/2    30 1/2    1279
03/09/83   31 3/4    30 1/2    31 5/8    1385
03/10/83   32 1/8    31 3/8    31 1/2    1912
03/11/83   32        31 1/8    32        2433
03/14/83   32        31 1/8    31 3/8    3707
03/15/83   31 3/4    31 1/8    31 5/8     759
03/16/83   32 3/8    31 3/4    32 1/8    1102
03/17/83   31 7/8    31 1/2    31 5/8    1185
```

List Activity for → **llnme p2**
Previous Two
Weeks (Period 2)   DOW JONES HISTORICAL
                   STOCK QUOTE REPORTER SERVICE

                   STOCK 1NME

```
DATE       HIGH      LOW       CLOSE     VOL(100/S)
02/11/83   30 1/4    29 1/4    29 1/2    2964
02/14/83   30 3/8    29 1/4    30 1/8    1368
02/15/83   30 3/8    29 7/8    30        1374
02/16/83   30 1/8    29 5/8    29 5/8    1091
02/17/83   29 1/2    28 7/8    29 3/8     834
02/18/83   29 5/8    28 7/8    29         778
02/22/83   29 1/2    29 1/8    29 1/8     990
02/23/83   29 3/8    28 1/2    28 3/4    1155
02/24/83   29 7/8    28 7/8    29 7/8    1365
02/25/83   30 1/8    29 3/8    29 3/4    2088
02/28/83   30 3/8    29 3/4    30 1/8    2294
03/01/83   31 1/4    30 1/8    31 1/4    2456
```

List Monthly Data → **llnme 83 m**
for 1983
                   DOW JONES HISTORICAL
                   STOCK QUOTE REPORTER SERVICE

                   STOCK 1NME

```
   1983    MONTHLY SUMMARY
DATE       HIGH      LOW       CLOSE     VOL(100/S)
01/83      29 5/8    26 1/2    28 1/4    42349
02/83      30 3/8    27 1/4    30 1/8    28127
03/83      32 3/8    30 1/8    31 5/8    24908
```

           lnme 82 q

           DOW JONES HISTORICAL
           STOCK QUOTE REPORTER SERVICE

           STOCK NME

Quarterly Data for → 1982 QUARTERLY SUMMARY
1982
```
           HIGH      LOW       CLOSE     VOL(100/S)
FIRST      18 5/8    12 1/4    13 7/8     76634
SECOND     17        13        14 1/2     57438
THIRD      21 3/8    13 5/8    19 3/4    119223
FOURTH     29 3/4    19 5/8    29        168483
```

* COMPOSITE QUOTES BEGIN WITH THE 4TH QUARTER OF 1981
           llnme 91 q

           DOW JONES HISTORICAL
           STOCK QUOTE REPORTER SERVICE

LISTING 7-3 (continued)

STOCK 1NME

Quarterly Data for 1981 → 1981 QUARTERLY SUMMARY

```
              HIGH      LOW      CLOSE    VOL(100/S)
FIRST         44 1/2    32 5/8   43 1/2   39314
SECOND        28 3/4    21 1/2   23 1/2   37648
THIRD         24 3/8    15 5/8   18       59669
FOURTH        21 3/4    16 1/8   17 3/8   76978
```

* THE ABOVE FIGURES REFLECT A NEW ISSUE AS OF 04/30/81

Obtain Fundamental Data on NME → $nme/f

```
         MEDIA GENERAL-FINANCIAL
              SERVICES, INC.
      MARKET AND FUNDAMENTAL DATA
      COMMON STOCKS AND RELATED

      SUMMARY MATERIAL ON INDUSTRY
      GROUPS, COPYRIGHT (C) 1983.

      TO CONTINUE, TYPE THE PAGE
      NUMBER YOU WISH AND PRESS
      RETURN
```

Page 1 → **1**

```
NATIONAL MEDICAL ENTPRS
-FUNDMNTL DATA- 03/11/83   (552)
REVENUE         (1)
-LAST 12 MOS $1,731 MIL
-LAST FISCAL YEAR $1,167 MIL
-PCT CHANGE LAST QTR 62.6%
-PCT CHANGE YR TO DATE 55.4%
EARNGS 12MOS $78.85 MIL
EARNINGS PER SHARE
-LAST 12 MONTHS $1.65
-LAST FISCAL YEAR $1.48
-PCT CHANGE LAST QTR 25.0%
-PCT CHANGE FY TO DATE 24.6%
-PCT CHANGE LAST 12MOS 18.7%
-FIVE YR GROWTH RATE 37.0%
```

Page 2 → **2**

```
DIVIDENDS       (2)
-CURRENT RATE $0.50
-CURRENT RATE YIELD 1.6%
-5 YR GROWTH RATE 35.8%
-PAYOUT LAST FY 26%
-PAYOUT LAST 5 YEARS 24%
-LAST X-DVD DATE 02-18-83
RATIOS
-PROFIT MARGIN 4.6%
-RETURN ON COMMON EQUITY 16.1%
-RETURN ON TOTAL ASSETS 6.5%
-REVENUE TO ASSETS 144%
-DEBT TO EQUITY 105%
-INTEREST COVERAGE 3.7
-CURRENT RATIO 2.0
```

Page 3 → **3**

```
SHAREHOLDINGS   (3)
-MARKET VALUE $1,504 MIL
-LTST SHR OUTSTND 47,000,000
-INSIDER NET TRADING -229,000
-SHORT INTEREST RATIO 2.1 DYS
-FISCAL YEAR ENDS 5 MOS
```

Find News about NME → .nme

```
N  NME       01/02 AL 1/1
   /NME   UHSIB            /           /
```

LISTING 7–3 *(continued)*

```
            03/11 HEARD ON STREET:MEDICARE MOVE
         (WJ) DOESN'T HURT HOSPITAL STOCKS
         STORY UNDER ABOVE HEADLINE MAY BE
         FOUND VIA COMPANY SYMBOL HCA
```

Print Story ──────▶ **.hca**
Containing News
Relating to NME

```
         N   HCA          01/02 AO 1/5
         /AMI    HUM    HCA    LMK   /STK PHA/CNG
            03/11 HEARD ON STREET:MEDICARE MOVE
         (WJ) DOESN'T HURT HOSPITALS -2-
            THE BILL PASSED BY THE HOUSE WOULD
         SET FIXED MEDICARE PAYMENTS TO
         HOSPITALS FOR 467 CATEGORIES OF
         TREATMENT.  UNDER THE CURRENT SYSTEM
         HOSPITALS RECEIVE REIMBURSEMENT FOR
         COSTS   PLUS A REGULATED RETURN ON
         EQUITY CURRENTLY ABOUT 7% TO 8% ON AN
         AFTER-TAX BASIS.
            BEFORE ALL ASPECTS OF THE HOUSE'S
         PROPOSED LEGISLATION WERE CLEAR   SOME
         HAD FEARED THAT THE NEW 'PROSPECTIVE
         PAYMENTS' PLAN WOULD MEAN THAT
         HOSPITALS OPERATED FOR PROFIT WOULDN'T
         MAKE ANY PROFIT WHEN DISPENSING
         SERVICES UNDER MEDICARE  AN AID PROGRAM
         FOR THE ELDERLY.  WHAT SEEMS TO HAVE
         DAWNED ON INVESTORS LATELY IS THAT THE
         PAYMENTS SYSTEM WILL ENABLE HOSPITALS
         TO POCKET THE DIFFERENCE IF THEY CAN
         PROVIDE SERVICES AT LESS THAN THE FIXED
         PAYMENTS.
            THE PAYMENT SCHEDULES ARE EXPECTED
         TO BE GUIDED BY THE AVERAGE COSTS FOR
         PROVIDING SERVICES OF ALL HOSPITALS
         WITHIN NINE GEOGRAPHICAL REGIONS
         ESTABLISHED BY THE BILL. JOHN HINDELONG
         HEALTH-CARE ANALYST AND DIRECTOR OF
         RESEARCH AT A.G. BECKER   BELIEVES THAT
         FOR-PROFIT HOSPITALS ARE SO MUCH MORE
         EFFICIENT IN PROVIDING SERVICES THAN
         NONPROFIT HOSPITALS   THAT THEY WILL BE
         ABLE TO IMPROVE THEIR PROFIT MARGINS IN
         MEDICARE AS A RESULT OF THE NEW SYSTEM.
            HINDELONG HASN'T CHANGED HIS
         EARNINGS FORECASTS FOR THE COMPANIES
            •
            •
            •
         MEDICAL ALSO ON AN AUGUST FISCAL YEAR
         $2 UP FROM $1.60 AND NATIONAL MEDICAL
```

DATA RESOURCES, INC. (DRI)

NAME: Data Resources, Inc.
24 Hartwell Avenue
Lexington, MA 02173

TELEPHONE: (617) 863-5100

INTERNATIONAL OFFICES:
Toronto, Canada   Tel: (416) 961-9323
Brussels, Belgium   Tel: (322) 648-5445

London, England   Tel: (441) 222-9571
Paris, France   Tel: (331) 267-3641

NUMBER OF DATABASES:
Over 100 million data series

HOURS: Service: During business hours
Consultation: 24 hours per day

COST: Clients of DRI are large corporations that pay fees that are tailored to the services they require.

USER AIDS: Online documentation
Retrieval codes
Reference and tutorial manuals

COMMUNICATIONS:
DRINET (in five countries and 18 cities in North America and Europe), TYMNET, and WATS

300 and 1200 baud

TRAINING: Each year DRI offers hundreds of courses at 20 worldwide locations. In addition to training in information system use, DRI education covers theory and application of econometrics, data manipulation, and model building.

DESCRIPTION: One of the keys to DRI's success is its staff of nearly 300 consultants (located in 16 cities), who help clients in day-to-day use of the system. Assistance given by these consultants goes far beyond that provided by other vendors' hotlines. They adapt services to clients' needs and familiarize new customers with the system's capabilities. They also provide links to large staffs of industry experts and economists, computer and software analysts, and data specialists who also help clients and prepare analyses and reports.

DRI offers a vast array of online economic and financial databases. The over-100 million data series contain historic and predictive information that ranges from broad economic indicators to very detailed statistics on specific industries or geographic locations. For example, the U.S. Regional database contains 53,000 time series of economic activity in state, regional, and metropolitan areas. U.S. Regional might be used to answer the question: What is the average personal income of Chicago residents by age, sex, and race?

The Energy database tracks costs, prices, production, imports, exports, consumption, reserves, and other economic aspects of the petroleum and natural gas industries. The DRI system contains data from Value Line and Standard and Poor's as well as its own proprietary data.

Retrieved data can be used directly in system software packages for graphics, analysis, report preparation, database management, and modeling. The principal analytical software package offered by DRI is its own proprietary language, EPS. You can use EPS online, or, through a new service called MicroEPS, you can download data in the popular VisiCalc format. These files are immediately readable by VisiCalc or other electronic spreadsheets that accept VisiCalc files. MicroEPS is available only to DRI subscribers.

Another joint product with VisiCorp, the developers of VisiCalc, is VisiLink, a terminal software package that enables microcomputer users to work with selected sets of DRI information called Datakits on a fixed-cost basis. You need not be a DRI client to purchase VisiLink. See Chapter 9 for a description.

The most widely used model is the macroeconomic model of the U.S. economy. You can use this to forecast about 1,000 different measures of economic activity. DRI has also developed specific-industry and cross-industrial models.

SYSTEM PROTOCOLS:

DRI protocols vary with the particular database and need. Some are menu-driven, and some are commmand-driven. Users keep abreast of system changes by taking advantage of the system HELP component, AID. Additional AID services are economic newsletters and file management and text services.

AGRISTAR

NAME: AgriData Resources, Inc.
205 West Highland Avenue
Milwaukee, WI 53203

TELEPHONE: (800) 558-9044
(800) 242-6001 (Wisconsin)

NUMBER OF DATABASES:
6

HOURS: *Service:* 24 hours per day, every day
Hotline: 24 hours per day, every day

COST: (March 1, 1983)

Registration fee: $199 for the first six months or $399 for the first year.

There is a basic charge of $39 per month or $433 per year thereafter.

Online connect time is $25 per hour for 300 baud and $30 per hour for 1200 baud including communications.

There is a small additional charge (average $.20) for displayed or printed reports.

Billing is monthly.

SUBSCRIPTION INFORMATION:

AgriStar is marketed through Radio Shack Computer stores near farm communities and through direct purchase. The initial package includes a manual and other user aids.

118   INFORMATION ONLINE

USER AIDS: AgriStar User Manual included in initial fee
Quarterly AgriStar System Index included in initial fee
Biweekly AgriStar Review
Monthly Farm Futures Magazine

COMMUNICATIONS:
UNINET or WATS

300 or 1200 baud

TRAINING: The system is self-instructional.

DESCRIPTION: AgriStar is designed to be the total business information service for the farmer. The core is AgriScan, a database of over 10,000 pages of continuously updated business, financial, marketing, weather, and price information including analyses by reporters, economists, researchers, and meteorologists throughout the world. For example, a farmer using AgriScan might find that Russia just purchased two million tons of wheat, and therefore, the price of wheat may go up the next day.

StarGram, an electronic mail and communications service, allows "person-to-person" communication and electronic messaging. AgriCompute contains a set of modeling, analysis, and forecasting software programs that can be accessed for downloading. The other three databases are AgriTech, a how-to library of production information; AgriMart, an electronic listing of products and services for the farmer; and AgriGuide, an agricultural business encyclopedia.

SYSTEM PROTOCOLS:
AgriStar is basically menu-driven but offers keyword searching for people who prefer to retrieve information directly. A useful feature of keyword searching is the automatic creation of a menu that lists report numbers and titles once the search has been narrowed to a reasonable number of items. AgriStar also incorporates a "setup"-type feature whereby the farmer can program function keys to produce a personalized list of reports. Called CODEFILE, this capability greatly simplifies use of routine requests that must be placed day after day.

WESTLAW

NAME: WESTLAW
West Publishing Company
50 West Kellogg Boulevard
P.O. Box 3526
St. Paul, MN 55165

TELEPHONE: (800)   328-9833
(612)   228-2500   (Minnesota)

NUMBER OF DATABASES:
22

HOURS: *Service:* Weekdays 7AM–11PM EST
Saturday and Sunday 7AM–8PM EST
Hotline: Weekdays 7AM–11PM EST
Saturday and Sunday 8:30AM–5PM EST

COST: (January 1, 1983)

Start-up charges are $280 for one day's training for eight trainees and $70 per trainee for additional trainees (there is, however, a limit on the number of trainees per class).

Training is required for personnel who will use WESTLAW.

Subscribers receive two free hours of use above the minimum for each trainee. These hours must be used during the first 30 days of service.

OPTION 1
Monthly subscription charges are $100 for the first terminal in each organization and $50 for additional terminals.

Connect charges depend on the number of hours used each month. They range from $105 per hour for the first three hours to $45 per hour for more than 100 hours.

Monthly minimum is $345 for three hours. Unused minimum hours may be carried over for a limited time but cannot be credited against minimums.

OPTION 2
Monthly subscription charges of $150 per terminal with a flat usage rate of $150 per hour.

Communications charges are included.

Billing is monthly.

SUBSCRIPTION INFORMATION:
Subscribers must sign a contract and undergo training at the rates outlined above under COST.

USER AIDS: WESTLAW Reference Manual $10 (provided with the subscription)
User Manual $2 (given to all trainees)
User Guide   gratis

COMMUNICATIONS:
TYMNET or TELENET

1200 baud only

TRAINING: Westlaw requires on-site training for new users at $280 (for up to eight users) and $70 for each additional trainee to a maximum of

$2100. WESTLAW then credits each account for two hours of free time per trainee in the first 30-day period. West also gives refresher courses.

DESCRIPTION: WESTLAW and LEXIS, described next, are the two major systems for practicing lawyers. The product of a renowned, long-term publisher of legal research books, WESTLAW contains the full text of codes, regulations, court cases, and other documents important to legal research and goes back in some instances as far as the 1920s. In addition to covering federal courts, WESTLAW has subject-specific databases such as The Federal Tax Library and Delaware Corporation Law. It also deals with antitrust and business regulations and patents.

The West service includes case law from all 50 states, a set of state law libraries for some courts, and attorney general opinions dating back to 1977 for eight states. Black's Law Dictionary and the popular Shepard's Citations, which can be used to find out which cases have cited a particular case, are also on WESTLAW.

SYSTEM PROTOCOLS:

WESTLAW works with certain terminals or microcomputer/software combinations. You may purchase outright ($4,220) or on the installment plan ($387/month for one year) or you may lease ($245/month) an appropriate terminal-printer-modem combination from WESTLAW or select one from a list of certified compatible equipment. Familiar microcomputers on the list are models of the TRS-80, DEC, IBM PC, Northstar, and Xerox. Typical software costs are about $350.

WESTLAW promotion strongly makes the point that their databases are full text *plus*. The *plus* items are synopses, headnotes containing important conceptual terms that may not appear in the court opinion, and classifications according to the West System of Digest Topics and Key Numbers. The system allows you the option of searching by words or by classification codes. You can run searches on codes in addition to keywords and phrases, names of judges and lawyers, specific courts, citation of cases or statutes, and time periods. It is basically command-driven.

CASE STUDY: A lawyer with a client whose employee was injured by a punch press is looking for cases relating to liability of the press seller or manufacturer in similar situations. See Listing 7–4.

He enters on WESTLAW a search that asks for cases in which some form of the terms *product* or *strict* appear in the same sentence as *liability* and elsewhere in the case *punch* appears in the same sentence as some form of the word stem *press*. The printout example shows the title and synopsis of a case responding to the query. The user could also print the headnote or full text.

LISTING 7-4

SEARCH ON WESTLAW FOR PRODUCT LIABILITY CASES

```
                    COPR. (C) WEST 1983 NO CLAIM TO ORIG. U.S. GOVT. WORKS
              THE CURRENT DATABASE IS FS
              YOUR QUERY:
Search Statement ──→ PRODUCT* STRICT/S LIABILITY & PUNCH /S PRESS*
              YOUR SEARCH IS PROCEEDING.

         ENTER X IF YOU WISH TO CANCEL YOUR SEARCH.


                    COPR. (C) WEST 1983 NO CLAIM TO ORIG. U.S. GOVT. WORKS
         Citation         Rank(R)      Page(P)       Database     Mode
         536 F.Supp. 84   R 1 OF 14    P 1 OF 25     FS           T
                          George BAILEY, Plaintiff,
                                       v.
Title ──────────→ ITT GRINNELL CORPORATION, et. al., Defendants.
                          Civ. A. No. C81-232
                  United States District Court, N.D. Ohio, E. D.
                                  Feb. 5, 1982
Synopsis ──→ In employee's products liability action for personal injuries
         suffered while operating punch press which his employer had
         purchased from defendant, defendant moved for partial summary
         judgment. The District Court, Krupansky, J., held that Ohio case
         law of strict tort liability and Ohio's warranty in tort theory
         were inapplicable since defendant was, at most,"occasional seller"
         of its used machines.
         Motion granted.
```

MEAD DATA CENTRAL

NAME: Mead Data Central
P.O. Box 933
9333 Springboro Pike
Dayton, OH 45401

TELEPHONE: (800) 227-4908 (Marketing)
(800) 543-6862 (Hotline)
(800) 762-6626 (Ohio)

INTERNATIONAL OFFICES:
London, England Tel: (01) 405-6679
Paris, France Tel: 011-33-1-320-1560

NUMBER OF DATABASES:
19

HOURS: *Service:* Weekdays 3AM–2AM EST
Saturday and Sunday 7:30AM–10PM
(available 365 days per year)
Hotline: Same as service hours

COST: (January 1, 1983)

Registration fee: $100 plus $10 per professional user for the first 20 users and $4 each for the next 60.

Reduced charges for additional locations within an organization.

INFORMATION ONLINE

Initial instruction is $75 per professional, to a maximum of $2,250, with one free hour rebated for each person trained.

One-time terminal installation costs are $200 or $400, depending on the terminal, and $200 per stand-alone printer.

Monthly equipment charges are $55 or $150 per terminal, with the higher cost for a deluxe terminal, and $150 for the stand-alone printer.

Additional equipment is available at reduced charges; the equipment charges cover communications, modem maintenance and repair, and paper and ink for the printer.

NEXIS-only basic pricing is $50 for a subscription without training; no monthly equipment charges.

Connect time during prime hours is from $90 per hour for the first five hours to $30 for each hour over 100.

Non-prime rate is $45 per hour or the prime rate, whichever is less.

Prime time is from 7:30AM to 7:30PM, local time.

Additional surcharges are based on volume of information processed in a search and on offline printing charges.

No minimums.

Communications charges are included.

Billing is monthly.

SUBSCRIPTION INFORMATION:
Subscribers must pay the initial fee of $100, plus charges per professional user, terminal and printer installation charges, and training fees.

USER AIDS: LEXIS handbook   gratis
NEXIS Primer   gratis
Online tutorials
LEXPAT Primer

COMMUNICATIONS:
MDC

1200 baud only

TRAINING: Three-hour course.

No charge to subscribers.

Subscribers may be trained on-site or in major cities. Law schools use simulators developed by Mead. Mead provides free follow-up training.

DESCRIPTION: The three major Mead databases are LEXIS, NEXIS, and the New York Times Information Bank. LEXIS is a full-text legal database (very similar to that of WESTLAW) covering federal, state, and special-area law. Auto-Cite is a special LEXIS database for checking the status of virtually any cited case. Shepard's is also available through LEXIS.

NEXIS is a full-text news database. Coverage is based on six newspapers including *The Christian Science Monitor* and *The Washington Post*; about 50 industry magazines and newsletters such as *Business Week, Inc.*, and *Byte*; and major national and international wire services. Retrospective information for most publications begins in the mid-1970s or later.

The first and still the premier news database, The Information Bank of the New York Times, was transferred to the Mead Service in 1983. With abstracts of over two million items from *The New York Times* and dozens of other publications from 1969, the Information Bank is one of the most valuable news databases available. New York Times On-line, the full text of every substantive article appearing in *The Times* from June 1, 1980 to the present, supplements the Infobank.

Other databases on the service are The Advertising & Marketing Intelligence Data Base, Deadline Data on World Affairs (geopolitical data such as population statistics and names of leaders in the countries of the world), TODAY (daily summaries of the most important general and business news).

Mead also has *The Encyclopedia Brittanica*, and current editions of Brittanica yearbooks, *The Federal Register*, Disclosure (an accounting library), and more.

SYSTEM PROTOCOLS:
You can search the Mead databases only with special terminals that have been designed specifically for the system. The keyboard contains many preprogrammed function keys labeled in plain English such as NEW SEARCH (for starting a new search) and NEXT PAGE (to look at the next page of a case). The combination of these keys with menus makes the Mead system one of the simplest to learn and to use. It is almost universally searched by lawyers directly.

Mead subscribers can "pass through" Mead to Dialog using the special terminals and a few of the function keys. But, the search language, which is still the basic Dialog language, works more efficiently on ordinary terminals. One advantage of using Dialog through a Mead subscription is that the communications costs are slightly less.

Mead is currrently evaluating the possibility of providing access to its databases with ordinary telecommunication equipment such as that described in the next chapter.

OTHER SYSTEMS

I.P. Sharp

I.P. Sharp Associates Limited
Suite 1900 Exchange Tower
2 First Canadian Place
Toronto, Ontario
Canada M5X 1E3
(416) 364-5361

I.P. Sharp is an international time-sharing company with a large collection of publicly accessible numeric databases—over 30 million time series in 80 different databases. Subject areas are currency rates, demographics, U.S. and international economics, securities, government, energy, insurance, transportation, and aviation. The software allows users to manipulate data and display them in a variety of formats including multicolor graphics and to perform analyses and forecasting.

Wharton Econometrics

Wharton Econometric Forecasting Associates, Inc.
3624 Science Center
Philadelphia, PA 19104
(215) 386-9000

Founded by Nobel Prize-winning economist Lawrence R. Klein of the Wharton School of the University of Pennsylvania and now owned by the Ziff-Davis Publishing Company, Wharton provides data, forecasting, modeling, and consulting services similar to DRI and I.P. Sharp. Online time series contain both national and international data with the World Economic Model, a major analytical tool, being a major product.

NewsNet

NewsNet
945 Haverford Road
Bryn Mawr, PA 19010
(215) 527-8030 (Pennsylvania)
(800) 345-1301

NewsNet offers online access to the full text of nearly 100 electronic newsletters in a full range of subjects from advertising to energy to politics to telecommunications. Telecommunications coverage is particularly strong. Starting date for most of the newsletters is 1982. Basic service at 300 baud is $24 per hour with a $15 monthly minimum. You can access online HELP commands and choose between menus and commands. NewsNet has a current awareness counterpart, NewsFlash, a kind of electronic clipping service that is delivered either to an online "mailbox" or to a special printer in the subscriber's office.

VU/TEXT

VU/TEXT Information Services
P.O. Box 8558
Philadelphia, PA 19101
(215) 854-8297

A product of the *Philadelphia Inquirer,* VU/TEXT contains full text of the *Inquirer* from January 1981, the *Philadelphia Daily News* from January 1980, the *Lexington (KY) Herald-Leader* from January 1983, the *Wall Street Transcript* from July 1981, the *Academic American Encyclopedia,* and The Pennsylvania Legislative Database (which contains all bills introduced in the current session of the legislature). Cost is from $60 to $90 per hour, depending on whether the user is willing to guarantee a minimum. VU/TEXT is command-driven.

Info Globe

Info Globe
444 Front Street West
Toronto, Ontario
Canada MSV 2S9
(416) 598-5250

Info Globe maintains a complete electronic file, updated daily, of articles in the national Canadian newspaper, *The Globe and Mail.* The other database on Info Globe is Marketscan, a stock quotation database for the Toronto, Montreal, Alberta, and Vancouver exchanges as well as for the New York and American exchanges. Costs are $150 per connect hour, plus some print fees.

SPECIALIZED SERVICES

There are numerous other business and economic online information services for special audiences. Federal agencies and government contractors use JURIS (Justice Retrieval and Inquiry System). The GTE Financial System One provides real-time trading data on the financial markets for investment professionals. MultiList/McGraw-Hill gives real estate brokers online access to properties listed for sale in certain areas. Bloodstock Research Information Services, Inc. produces a database of pedigree racing information primarily for horse farms, breeders, trainers, and insurers. Radio station programmers have Billboard, which gives statistics on record title playing, and photographers have PhotoNet. For a small fee, you can seek a job in a high-technology firm through Connexions and receive a refund if you are hired. Additional financial, statistical, and corporate data can be found in Standard and Poor's Compustat Services through selected timesharing vendors or in the World and Passport databases of National CSS Inc., a subsidiary of Dun & Bradstreet. Appendix I contains the addresses and telephone numbers of these organizations.

CHAPTER 8
Equipment and Communications Software

The simplest piece of equipment you can use for online communications with a remote computer is a *dumb* terminal. A dumb terminal only communicates. Even without a printer, these terminals cost a minimum of about $400, and, as communicating is their only function, they are generally purchased only for business applications in which the volume of online use is high enough to justify equipment dedicated to this one purpose. Even in this situation, users may prefer the additional capabilities of communicating word processors or microcomputers.

You need three items to make a microcomputer function as a dumb terminal does: a communications interface, a modem, and communications software. Most microcomputers now come equipped with an interface; you can obtain a modem for under $200. Moreover, you can use your micro to perform communications functions that *dumb* terminals are not equipped to handle, such as dialing automatically, transferring files, and "talking" with other microcomputers. Communicating word processors, *smart* terminals, and *intelligent* terminals have some of these capabilities but, of course, cannot perform many of the other functions of microcomputers.

TERMINALS

The two basic types of terminals are print (characters are typed on paper) and CRT (characters are displayed on a cathode ray tube). Because a CRT terminal with a printer is more expensive than a print terminal alone, and because a printed copy of output is usually needed in information retrieval, print terminals are by far the most common type for this application.

In appearance, print terminals resemble typewriters. See Fig. 8–1. Terminals range widely in cost and other features. The least expensive set-up tends to be a 300-baud (almost equivalent to 30 cps) portable terminal with a built-in acoustic coupler (into which the telephone handset is placed) and a thermal printer. Disadvantages of the thermal printer are that it uses heat sensitive paper (relatively expensive, less pleasant to use than "regular" paper, and deteriorates over time) and that images on heat sensitive paper are less sharp than those produced by a typewriter. On the positive side, thermal printing is quiet.

Print quality of impact-printing terminals, such as the one with a separate acoustic coupler shown in the photograph, is much better than that of thermal-type terminals, and the paper is standard. But they are noisier, more expensive, and larger. Another major factor that influences terminal cost is speed. Most online systems de-

FIGURE 8-1

Print terminal with acoustic computer

scribed in this book can be accessed at either 300 baud or 1200 baud (120 cps). Faster terminals, which are more costly and require more expensive modems, are rapidly becoming the standard in business. Three-hundred-baud thermal print terminals start at $1,000, while the price of low-end, 1200-baud impact printing terminals is approximately $2,000.

Other equipment is on the market that, in terms of cost and capabilities, bridges the gap between terminals and microcomputers. *Smart* terminals offer functions such as parameter definition and the ability to edit or format data prior to entry. *Intelligent* or *user-programmable* terminals feature software support such as an operating system, programming languages, one or two applications like text processing, and sometimes a built-in dialing function.

A recent trend is toward very small portable terminals. One type, exemplified by Radio Shack's TRS-80 Videotex and RCA's VP-3501, has a built-in modem and attaches to a television set for display. Both cost about $400. Dimensions are 14-3/4 inches long by 13-3/4 inches wide by 3-1/2 inches high for the Radio Shack. Even smaller (7-1/4 inches wide by 4-1/4 inches high by 4-3/4 inches deep) is the iXO Telecomputer, which has a one-line 16-character screen. The iXO price is around $500.

Modems must be purchased for terminals that do not have them built in. See the section below on microcomputers for a discussion of types of modems and their cost.

You will find names and addresses of selected terminal manufacturers in Appendix III. *ONLINE Terminal Microcomputer Guide and Directory* and two Datapro guides listed in the bibliography under DIRECTORIES-Equipment contain very complete information on terminal characteristics and availability.

MICROCOMPUTER COMMUNICATIONS

As mentioned above, your computer requires three items to communicate:

- A communications interface
- A modem
- A communications software package

To complete the set-up, you also need a cable (for connecting the interface to the modem), a telephone outlet (but not necessarily a telephone), and a telephone cord (if the modem is the direct-connect type). The variety in modems and communications software compares to that of other computer peripherals and software. The means for obtaining the interface, if it is not already built into your micro, is closely tied to specific equipment, but even here you can have (or be required to make) choices. Since the interface, in terms of options, is the simplest of the items required for communication, we shall deal with it first.

Microcomputer Communications Interfaces

One of the few microcomputer standards, the RS232C, is the communications interface for all machines except early Commodore computers, including the popular VIC and 64, which use an interface that only works with a special Commodore modem. Commodore also sells for $150 a converter kit that changes its interface to the standard. The RS232C puts out *serial* data. One function of the communications card is to change *parallel* data, which is transmitted at least eight bits at a time, to *serial* data, which is transmitted one bit at a time. Remote communications must take place serially because telephone lines transfer only one bit of data at a time.

Fortunately, RS232C ports are rapidly becoming a standard microcomputer feature. Even more fortunate is that built-in modems may not follow far behind. However, right now you may be faced with purchasing an interface board for your machine. The card will plug into one of the expansion slots. If you happen to run short of expansion slots you may be able to buy a multipurpose board that includes communications as one of the functions; examples are the boards made by Quadram. See Appendix III for the address. Multiple-function boards list for about $600, while the cost of single-purpose boards is closer to $150.

Modems

Your dealer should supply a cable for connecting your RS232C outlet plug to your modem plug. You must be careful to obtain the proper male/female combinations on the ends of the cable, and wiring to the pins must be correct. Crossover wiring of pins may be required to make the particular modem-computer combination work, and this is a job for a technical expert.

The modem sits between the micro and the telephone communications network. The jobs of the modem are to convert voltage signals put out by your computer into sound signals that can be transmitted over telephone lines and to convert the returning telephone signals back into computer-understandable voltage signals. This process is called *mo*dulation *dem*odulation, hence the term "modem."

Direct-Connect Versus Acoustic Couplers—Figure 8-2 depicts a typical *direct-connect* configuration. Using a cord with the newer type small plastic modular plug on the end, the modem connects directly to the telephone outlet; the computer keyboard is used for the dialing function. Another type of modem connects to the telephone and to your machine—you use the telephone for dialing and simply "hang up" after the computer-to-telecommunications network link is established. The third kind of modem is the *acoustic coupler;* connection is made by manually dialing the phone number and—after the other computer "answers"—placing the telephone receiver into the rubber cups of the coupler. See Fig. 8-3 for schematics of these three possibilities.

Since acoustic couplers were the least expensive modems in the past, they were very popular. As the cost of other types of modems has come down, however, there is now no particular advantage to the acoustic coupler. You can use couplers with any kind of telephone outlet, but you can do the same with direct-connect modems if you purchase an inexpensive adapter plug to convert an old-fashioned outlet to receive the modular jack.

FIGURE 8-2

Microcomputer with direct-connect modem

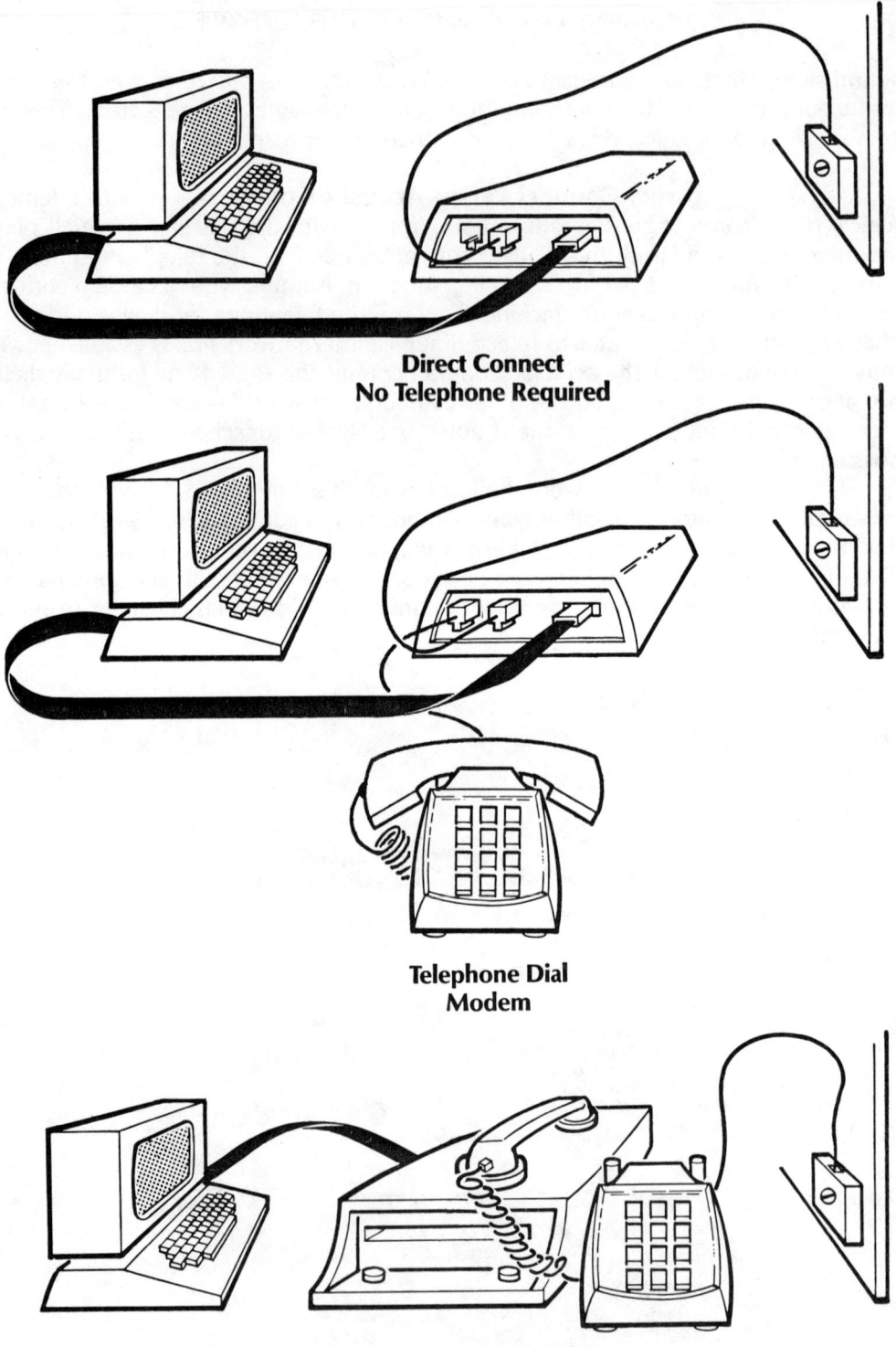

FIGURE 8-3

The disadvantage of acoustic couplers is that they are more sensitive to interference. The handset may loosen, allowing in noise from the room, or the modem may pick up extraneous noise for no discernible reason. Also, the microphone in the handset may begin to cause distortion after extended, continuous use; this is because it uses carbon granules, which compact under the duress of high-pitched data transmission tones. You will have to either rap the receiver occasionally to loosen the granules or purchase a special high-quality element to eliminate the problem. Few manufacturers produce acoustic couplers that transmit at 1200 baud.

The problems are substantially reduced with direct-connect modems because impulses are sent directly to the telephone lines. So, unless someone offers you a special deal on an acoustic coupler, you may as well purchase a direct-connect.

Speed—The basic choice in modems is between 300 and 1200 baud. The considerations that apply are the same as those described above under terminals. With a 1200-baud modem, you can send and receive information approximately four times faster than with 300-baud equipment. However, this does not necessarily mean that the entire online transaction will be four times faster or one-fourth the cost. Some services charge a premium on connect time for high-speed access. Moreover, the amount of human and computer "thinking" and keying time remains the same. So, if your applications require that you do considerable analysis and responding while online or that the computer makes a large number of time-consuming calculations, time differences between the two transmission speeds will not necessarily be appreciable. However, if you also upload or download large files, or if your major application is transferring large files, then 1200 baud makes a lot of sense.

In the online applications described in Chapters 4 through 7, primary file transfer takes place at the point of downloading the final bibliography or other information, so your estimate of the amount of information you expect to download combined with the connect-time rate for services you will use are factors in choosing between a 300- and 1200-baud modem. Bibliographies of 30 to 40 references or less, which do not contain abstracts, can comfortably be displayed and downloaded at 300 baud. You will become impatient downloading larger bibliographies, more than a few references with abstracts, or full text at 300 baud. But 1200 baud can sometimes even be a disadvantage—as is the case when you read online directions on CompuServe or The Source. Unless you are a successful graduate of a speed-reading course, you will have trouble reading at 1200 baud; text may scroll off the top of the screen before you have a chance to comprehend it.

Another consideration is that some services, CompuServe and The Source for example, charge more for 1200-baud use. This, of course, decreases potential cost savings for connect time. Another factor, which in the future will have a substantial effect on potential savings in using the higher speed, is the trend toward charging on the basis of non-connect-time factors such as actual retrieved information (i.e., displayed, printed, or downloaded items).

Most 1200-baud modems are designed to function at 300 baud as well. The reverse is not true. Similarly, there is a difference in network nodes in that most that accept 1200 baud also work at 300 baud. There are additional TYMNET and TELENET nodes at 300 baud only and a few 1200-only nodes in large cities that also have the dual type. This presents no particular problems. The difficulty occurs when you have access only to a 300-baud node, as in some of the relatively small urban areas. Someone in this situation has to pay fairly steep extra-telecommunications or long-distance-telephone charges, which would probably more than offset any potential savings from transmitting at 1200 baud. If you do not live in a major metropolitan area, determine which services you anticipate using and check out the speeds of your local access nodes before purchasing a modem.

The 1200-baud modems have other disadvantages. They are more sensitive to *line noise*—outside interference due to electrical storms and other environmental conditions—than their 300-baud counterparts are. Special conditioned lines solve this problem, but they add expense and are usually not needed by microcomputer users accessing remote databases.

You may hear of modems that transmit at speeds of 4800, 9600, or even higher baud. These require special conditions, will not work over voice-grade telephone lines, and generally are not supported by the timesharing services described previously.

Costs—There is a price to be paid for higher speed. The 1200-baud modems, even at a discount, cost about $400, while you can purchase 300-baud equipment for as little as $100. Added features, of course, increase the cost.

Specifications—There are a large number of stand-alone modems designed to work with any micro having a standard RS232C interface. Others, such as the VicModem for the Commodore, the Radio Shack Direct Connect Modem I, and several modems for the Atari, allow for connections to special interfaces in the respective machines. Modems-on-a-card, which fit inside the computer—e.g., the Hayes Micromodem II for the Apple, and Microperipheral's PConnection for the IBM PC—are necessarily machine-specific.

If possible, you should select a modem in conjunction with communications software. The software is machine-dependent, and the modem and software are interdependent, factors that may limit your choice of modems.

There are several modem characteristics either required or strongly recommended to ease simple communication with remote computers. Even though most modems marketed for use with terminals or microcomputers have these options, it is good to be aware of them before buying.

Interface compatible with your terminal—In almost all cases, this will be the RS232C standard discussed above.

Bell system compatibility—This refers mainly to frequency and length of tone standards established by Bell.

      Bell 103 compatible with 300 baud
      Bell 212A or Racal-Vadic (VA3400) compatible with 1200 baud

The 212A is versatile in that it communicates at both 300 and 1200 baud and in both full and half duplex. We prefer the 212A over the Bell 202, which can only operate at 1200 baud and half duplex. Another undesirable standard is the Bell 113, which works at 300 baud, but only in the originate mode. Most commercial online services accept all these standards.

EQUIPMENT AND COMMUNICATIONS SOFTWARE

Duplex switching: Full duplex—is a transmission mode in which you simultaneously send and receive data over communications lines. Most online services specify full duplex, although they can usually be made to work in *half duplex* by using special commands at log-on time to tell the system that you are operating in half duplex. The half-duplex mode permits transmission in either direction, but not at the same time.

Originate and answer modes—Communication between computers requires that one be in *originate mode* and the other in *answer mode*. It does not really matter which is which, but since the commercial online services are in answer mode, your computer must be set to originate. You will want both modes, most likely, if you want to communicate with other microcomputers.

Asynchronous operation—Data from a disk-or tape-storage device can be transferred efficiently in a continuous stream—*synchronous* communication. However, data entered irregularly, with stops and starts (as when a human being is punching a keyboard) must be handled *asynchronously*.

Certification—The telephone company requires direct-connect modems to be certified by the Federal Communications Commission (FCC). This is the responsibility of the manufacturer; you should find a notice of certification in the user's manual. You have an analogous responsibility to let your local telephone company know that you are using the modem. Your user's manual should give you directions for doing this.

Added Features—We have just discussed the essential features you should look for in any modem. Below is a list of added features that you may find attractive and worth the added cost, which may be considerable. For example, some programmable modems with built-in clocks cost over $1,000.

Auto dialing—dialing directly from the keyboard using a directory of stored telephone numbers. This is a frequently found enhancement that requires an appropriate hardware-software combination. Some combinations also provide for automatic re-dialing when the computer called is "busy." This is very useful for tapping into local bulletin boards that have a restricted number of access ports. This "luxury" will seem to be a necessity after you have used it for a while.

Delayed auto transmission—using a clock to set the computer to dial, log on, transmit, and log off at a specified time. This is often done to take advantage of low off-hour rates or in response to a busy signal.

Touch-tone dialing—providing signals that correspond to touch-tone dialing in addition to those put out by the older, rotary-type telephones.

Auto answer—capability to be turned on in answer mode to receive incoming calls.

Built-in speaker—giving an audible answer so that the operator or person dialing in will know that the computer is responding.

On/off light—indicating when a connection is in effect.

Storage—storing offline files such as directories, forms, and messages that are received and sent.

Auto notification of message receipt—lets user know that a message is waiting.

TWX compatibility—giving capability for using the microcomputer as a teletype to send messages to other TWX-compatible machines or to send telegrams.

LCD time display—built-in clock.

Multiple interfaces—additional interfaces that permit more than one micro to share a modem or have a direct connection to a printer.

Internal buffer—useful if the printer is on during transmission and if it operates at a speed slower than the modem's.

Fit within the micro—designed to fit inside the computer.

Alternate voice/data feature—allows you to interrupt transmission but not disconnect in order to talk to someone with whom you are in online communication.

Upgradable—upgrading from 300 to 1200 baud without purchasing an entirely new modem.

9600 baud—for local communications.

Error correcting—provision for automatic error correcting.

Self-test—for determining whether cables have been properly hooked up and whether components are functioning.

Some modems are really specialized microcomputers. They have substantial memory and built-in software for, say, editing, and they are programmable.

Software

As mentioned, unlike modems, which are almost always machine-independent, the programs for making microcomputers behave like terminals—and do much more—are written for specific computers. They are frequently referred to as *communications packages* or *terminal programs* and, not surprisingly, come in basic and deluxe versions with corresponding price tags.

EQUIPMENT AND COMMUNICATIONS SOFTWARE

All software packages perform the basic function of turning your computer into a dumb terminal that sends and receives messages in ASCII code, and all provide for some ability to set communications protocols. The most important additional capability is *downloading*—capturing data in the computer memory buffer and then transferring it to tape or disk—but there are many, many additional features that make searching and other operations associated with online access much easier and less expensive.

In reviewing various software features listed below, you should keep in mind that it is not only the presence or absence of a feature that matters, but how easy it is to use. Differences in ease of use can be substantial. And, the software may be either menu- or command-driven, or some combination of both, and may have the advantages and disadvantages generally associated with these two approaches.

Protocols—The minimum protocols that online vendors specify are baud rate, duplex, parity, word length, and number of stop bits. You may have limited yourself to 300 baud in your choice of software. If not, you should be able to set the baud rate and at least these other parameters. You may find your default package set at the following configuration, which works with most bulletin boards and, through TYMNET and TELENET, with many of the online services.

Baud rate: 300
Duplex: full
Parity: even
Word length: 7
Stop bits: 1

When in doubt or when you cannot obtain a recommended setting, try this one.

As previously discussed, baud rate refers to transmission speed, and duplex refers to whether you can send and receive messages simultaneously. Other protocols are:

Parity—a binary digit added to a set of bits to detect single-bit errors in a bit string. The parity bit makes the sum of the digits either always odd or always even. Systems may specify "none" for parity, in which case they generally will work with even sums.

Word length—a confusing piece of terminology; each "word" is really a character (letter, number, or punctuation symbol), and the length is the number of bits needed to define a character. In telecommunications, most characters are made up of 10 bits: the start bit, the data bits, the parity bit, and the stop bit.

Stop bits—in asynchronous communication, the last bit of every character.

Synchronous/asynchronous—In synchronous communication, there is a constant time between transmission of bits. Because of the stops and starts, the type of online communications discussed here are asynchronous.

"Handshaking" options—These are conventions used to tell one computer to pause, as the other one is temporarily busy. This is useful, for example, when a buffer is full and the computer needs to transfer data to disk. The most common convention is XON/XOFF. Note that if you have this switch on, you still cannot be sure that the remote computer will recognize it. Dialog and BRS do not. However, you can tell TELENET (with an @ENAB TFLOW at log-on) to control data flow with XON/XOFF.

Control character screen—Turning this feature on will screen out control characters sent by certain timesharing systems. These characters may overwrite, scramble, or clear your screen or otherwise interfere with smooth transmission.

Enhancements—The number of extra software features is quite overwhelming. Some are so useful that they seem more like requirements than enhancements. As usual, you will pay a price for extras and you will not be able to find one software package that has them all.

To simplify matters, we have tried to list features in decreasing order of importance to the "typical" home-computer user who is accessing remote databases for a combination of personal and business reasons. Related capabilities are grouped within this framework. This list is not exhaustive.

Downloading—The ability to transfer files from remote computers to your storage medium is by far the most important additional capability. This gives you the opportunity to view information at your leisure; to edit, manipulate, and reformat it; to reproduce and print it. The alternative, trying to copy from a screen while using up valuable online time, is expensive and unpleasant. And, while the option of printing everything that appears on the screen while you are online seems attractive, it is often more difficult to achieve than downloading and offers less flexibility in what you can do later with the data. The best programs allow you to download selected parts of a session and will automatically dump downloaded data from the RAM buffer to the disk when the buffer is full. If this is not automatic you should be able to determine the buffer status and perform the dump yourself. It is also useful to be able to view the buffer contents and to clear the buffer if you change your mind about wanting to save information.

Uploading—the reverse of downloading. You create files locally and send them to other computers. This allows you time to review and to edit the information before transmission and also saves time (as even 300-baud transmission is much faster than the speed at which people can type). Some common applications of uploading are sending messages, creating public or private online files, and adding to a conference or bulletin board. Specialized applications that may be supported specifically are automatic log-on or auto-log-on plus command transmission. A useful uploading feature, not always included, is having characters displayed on the screen as they are sent.

Auto log-on—provision for storage of log-on protocols for systems used frequently. This saves the inevitable, irritating log-on errors that are so easy to make and means that you do not have to keep log-on instructions, user names, and security passwords handy.

Direct dial—ability to dial directly through your keyboard. This requires a modem that also has direct-dial capability.

Telephone number directory—With the directory, you can store frequently dialed numbers (e.g., your local network nodes and bulletin boards) and dial by hitting one key.

Auto re-dial—automatically re-dials a busy number until a connection is made.

Word processor compatibility—lets you read and edit a downloaded file through use of your computer's word processor. A less common alternative is a text-editing function built into the communications program.

Slow printer buffer—Few printers are fast enough to keep up with even 300-baud modems, so either the computer stops while printing—thereby substantially increasing connect time—or it loses print characters. The buffer stores output and thus allows the printer to "catch up" while you pause to consider what to do next.

Printer toggle—ability to turn printer on and off at will while you are online.

Break or interrupt function—allows you to interrupt transmission from any system without otherwise interfering with the transaction.

Prestel access—Provides access to the videotex system that is popular in Great Britain and Europe and that is beginning to make an impact in the United States.

Storage of protocols—lets you store protocols for the services you use so that you do not have to set them each time you go online.

Answer mode—lets you respond to incoming calls from another microcomputer; this is the opposite of the originate mode used to communicate with remote computers.

Status line—shows you what parameters are in effect.

Access to DOS commands—lets you stop transmission, perform functions locally, and return without breaking communications.

Screen formatting—ability to set a convenient screen width.

Protocol change—option to change protocols without breaking transmission; useful when you do not know the protocol and want to test changes.

Help screen—a display, while online, of your software commands.

Scrambler—enables you to convert incoming or outgoing data into something else, usually for security reasons.

Error detection and corrections—automatically corrects and re-sends data..

Programmable keys—lets you send ASCII characters (such as square brackets) that may not be on your keyboard.

Costs—Software costs vary from nothing (e.g., Modem7 and other programs which are in the public domain) to about $400. Most are in the $50 to $150 range. Differences are attributable to the special features available and various indeterminate factors.

Purchasing Modems and Software—You can purchase modems from the same sources that sell microcomputer equipment—primarily in computer stores or by mail. Appendix III contains a selected list of manufacturers to contact for names of local outlets; the Datapro report list in the bibliography in the equipment section under DIRECTORIES is a particularly good source of specific information.

Appendix III also contains names and addresses of selected suppliers of communications software, as well as names of software packages and computers on which they run. We have yet to see a comparison of software for any but a few of the enhancements described above, but there is a limited feature-by-feature breakdown in the Benson, Thé and Rhodes articles and a comprehensive list of communications software for microcomputers in the CLASS report, all in the bibliography to this chapter.

Most microcomputer manufacturers have modems and communications software as part of their peripheral lines. In some cases, they market a modem-terminal package—e.g., the Osborne Comm-Pac. Although this may not be the least expensive way to go, it has the advantage of safety. You know you will have all the right cables and that the features will work together. There is some chance that people with experience with the configuration will be around to offer advice. Most important, if something doesn't work, one organization is accountable.

Nearly the same result may be achieved by purchasing a system like the popular Hayes Micromodem II for the Apple II, which is a complete package consisting of communications board, coupler, and terminal program. A comparable system is Ven-Tel's PC modem, which includes plug-in card, cable, and Crosstalk, a sophisticated program customized for the IBM PC. Know the warranty period and test your modem thoroughly during that time.

The basic problem is to find a modem-program combination that has the features you want and that utilizes all the features of each. You'll simply waste money if you buy a Cadillac software program and a Volkswagen modem. There is no point, for example, in paying for software with an online directory from which you can auto-dial if your modem does not have the dialing capability.

If you frequently need a special application, you might consider communications packages and hardware-software combinations designed to facilitate the application. For a specific application, they are easier to use than a general package is, and in some cases they are the only possibility for fulfilling the specific purpose. Examples are Western Union's EasyLink (for sending messages through the TELEX network), the Chat II Message Processor from Chat Communications, the British firm Zycor Ltd.'s Teledek TI (for giving terminal owners videotex capability), Microcom's MICROCourier electronic mail program for the Apple with a Hayes Micromodem, and the Teksim Tektronix Simulator (for graphics).

Online vendors are a source of information regarding communications equipment and software. Dialog publishes a free, one-sheet handout called "Making the DIALOG Connection with a Personal Computer," which is essentially repeated as part of the Knowledge Index guide, and The Source produces a sheet called "Source Equipment Compatibility Requirements," which lists equipment needs for the most popular microcomputer brands. Most manuals give the basic protocol settings for baud rate, duplex, parity, and code and stop bits. You can ask technical questions of persons staffing the hotlines and get varying degrees of success with answers. Other good sources of information are articles and reviews in microcomputer magazines, which can be found by using the Microcomputer Index or the International Software Directory databases on Knowledge Index and on other systems. Some software vendors allow you to purchase documentation—a very important feature by itself—independently of the software so that you can make an informed evaluation.

CHAPTER

9

Transferring Files, Search Aids, and Offline Software

INTRODUCTION

One of the most exciting new aspects of microcomputer communications is the development of support software that either makes the process easier or less expensive or adds to the usefulness of downloaded data. This is an infant field; to see where it is heading, let's consider two scenarios.

Scenario 1: Bibliographic Research

You are doing a long-term research project on substance abuse among high school students and have developed an extensive collection of articles on the topic. References to the articles are contained in a database created with your micro using a database management package. Right now you need information on the psychological factors that lead to heavy use of alcohol among teenage girls, and so, you decide to search your database. Finding only a couple articles, you want to extend your inquiry to the large online databases. Since you do not perform searches often, you are not quite sure which vendor or database to use and would have to do some brushing up to use the system commands and even to log on.

Instead of going to the library for help or spending a lot of time poring over manuals to reeducate yourself, load into your micro a communications package that selects an appropriate vendor and a database and logs you on in the novice mode. Enter your request in natural English, and the retrieved references are downloaded to a disk file in the format of your local database. Review the references offline and add the ones you want to your database.

Dreaming? Not entirely. The Sci-Mate system of the Institute for Scientific Information provides most of the capabilities just described.

Scenario 2: Stock Market Analysis

A small investor who "plays the market" a little, you decide after dinner to see how your investments performed today. You are slightly concerned because you heard on the radio that the overall market was down nearly 10 points. You load your communications software, which logs on to the Dow Jones System, and with one command retrieve the closing prices of all the stocks in your portfolio. After logging off, you then display a line graph that compares the performance of your securities for the recent time period to the Dow Jones Industrial Average. Today's prices are included automatically.

There is nothing futuristic about this scenario. Everything described is possible today using the Dow Jones Market Analyzer with an IBM PC or Apple microcomputer.

Discussion

The key features of the software packages just discussed are that they both facilitate the retrieval process and make the retrieved information more useful. They do this in the following ways:

- By providing an easy-to-use ("friendly") interface
- By taking care of the "housekeeping" procedures (e.g., logging on)
- By allowing you to create local files that store often used search keys (e.g., symbols for your stocks)
- By downloading the information in a format that is suitable for use by other programs

The purpose of this chapter is to describe software packages that support information retrieval in these ways. But first, let's look at the file transfer process itself and some of the reasons for using it.

TRANSFERRING FILES

With most commercial software packages, uploading (transferring files to) or downloading (transferring files from) large online services is a relatively simple procedure. Once connected to the service, you simply give a command to start and another command to stop. If you are downloading, you have to specify the name of the file to which you are downloading either before or during the process.

The major difficulty you are likely to encounter during the online session itself is running out of memory space, and this is only a problem if you do not have a package that allows you to write the memory data to disk during the session. If you are transferring so much data that one disk is insufficient, your software should have a provision for stopping to change disks.

You are likely to encounter more problems as you transfer files between two microcomputers. In order to accomplish this successfully, one computer must be set in originate mode, the other in answer. Then, speed and other protocols mentioned in Chapter 8 should match. You do not have to worry about compatibility of disk formats, which need not be the same. Indeed, a primary purpose of file transfer using communications is to move a program or some data from one machine to another when respective disks cannot be read directly.

Occasionally, after transmission from a remote timesharing computer or from another micro, you may find that information does not appear as expected. Often this is due to control character incompatibility, indicated by odd characters in the text or by odd spacing. The solution is either to turn the screen switch on during transmission to screen out control characters or to reconfigure the downloaded data in some manner. You should find instructions for these procedures in your manuals.

There are probably as many reasons for wanting to transfer files as there are for sending and receiving any type of information. You will want to download bibliographies, electronic mail, and other information from an online vendor to examine it later at your leisure and to have a permanent record. You may want to send a manuscript to a publisher, a co-author, or a reviewer, or you may want to create electronic mail messages offline for online transmission. It is becoming more common to send text online to commercial printers who can use it without re-keying. ASCII communications systems are a great format equalizer. One of the prime functions of the hobbyist bulletin boards described in the next chapter is making public domain software available for downloading, and the Telephone Software Connection (see Appendix I for address) is in the business of selling software by offering it for downloading. You dial up and pay a fee for the software you request.

Copyright must be taken into account when you download information copyrighted by publishers. So far, no universal guidelines have been developed to tell you what you may do with downloaded data, but most would agree that you may at least edit it to remove unwanted material and improve the appearance. After that, there is no agreement on whether the downloaded data can be retained, even for local use, or can be searched repetitively. Some publishers expressly forbid copying the database; those that do deal with the question prohibit delivery or use by third parties. Many publishers simply have not addressed this question yet and merely state that their databases are copyrighted.

INTEGRATED COMMUNICATIONS AND OFFLINE SOFTWARE

Sci-Mate and the Dow Jones Market Analyzer are multifunction search aids in that they perform several search facilitation functions—they assist the search process and manipulate downloaded data. Some of the other packages discussed here are more limited.

Sci-Mate

Institute for Scientific Information
3501 Market Street
Philadelphia, PA 19104
(800) 523-1850

Sci-Mate is available on disks that can be read directly by the following computers:

    Vector 3 or 4
    IBM PC (with CP/M 86 operating system only)
    Apple II (with Z80 card, CP/M, 16K RAM card, and 80-column card)
    TRS-80 Model II (with CP/M)
    CP/M-80 system with standard 8" drive

With the INSTALL utility program provided as part of the package, Sci-Mate can be adapted to run on most Z-80, CP/M micros.

Program	Cost
Sci-Mate Universal Online Searcher	$440
Sci-Mate Personal Data Manager	$540
Both	$880

Sci-Mate consists of two linked programs, the Universal Online Searcher and the Personal Data Manager. You can use these programs independently, but you will gain the greatest advantage if you use them together. This is because the Searcher makes it possible for you to download in the format of the Data Manager and, thus, automatically create a local database. *To our knowledge, Sci-Mate is the only commercially available software for accomplishing this very useful task with a microcomputer.* You can also download to a database management system with the Star system of Cuadra Associates, but Star comes packaged with a 16-bit micro and extensive peripheral equipment and is considerably more expensive.

Sci-Mate is menu-driven. You can use the Universal Searcher on Dialog, BRS, SDC, Medline, and the ISI Search Network in either the menu-driven mode or in their original languages. Sci-Mate also works as a simple terminal program for accessing other systems. With a direct-dial modem, Sci-Mate will dial, log you on automatically, and present you with an initial menu listing a choice of modes. The menu-driven language is easy to use. For the ISI Search Network, it offers the user prompts for commands and searchable fields; for other services, the language is menu-driven for the commands only.

Listings 9–1 through 9–4 show a ISI/BIOMED system search using the Universal Searcher in menu-driven mode. The search also illustrates citation indexing, a powerful capability of the ISI databases. Citation indexing is based on the premise that there is a subject link between a paper and papers listed in its bibliography (cited papers). ISI databases like SCISEARCH and Social SCISEARCH record these relationships. In the example, we searched for articles citing the Peter Doherty paper titled "Development and Loss of Virus-Specific Thymic Competence in Bone-Marrow Radiation Chimeras and Normal Mice" in volume 58 of *Immunological Reviews* in 1981.

You see the WELCOME menu after you load Sci-Mate into your micro. In Listing 9–1, the user first decides to use the Universal Online Searcher, next to search an ISI

LISTING 9–1

SCI-MATE INITIAL MENU AND UNIVERSAL ONLINE SEARCHER MENU

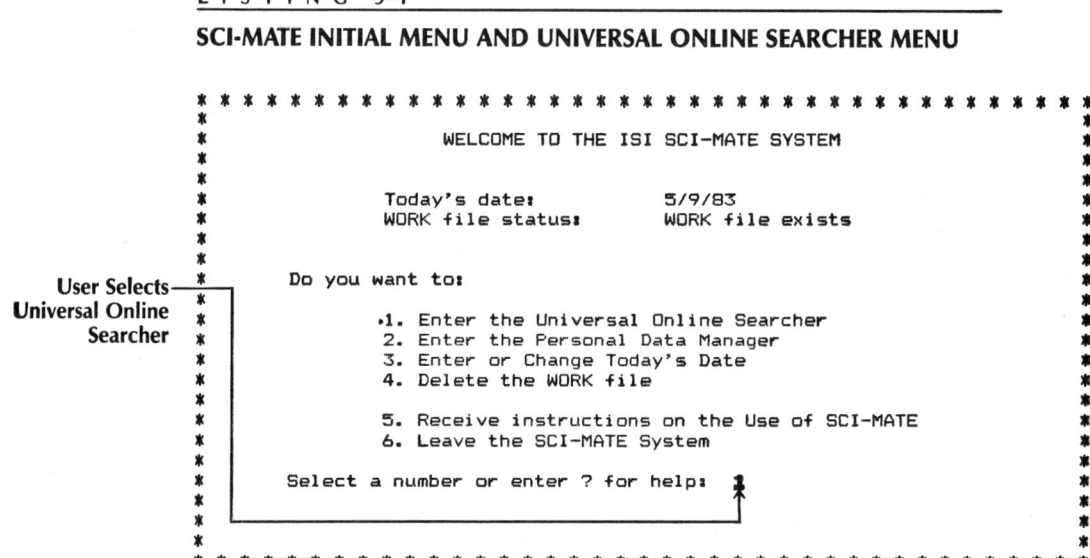

LISTING 9-1 (continued)

```
ONLINE MENU
-----------------------------------------------------------------------

Welcome to the SCI-MATE Universal Online Searcher!

Do you wish to:

        1. Search an ISI data base:     SCISEARCH 1981-DATE
              ISI/BIOMED                SCISEARCH 1978-1980
              ISI/COMPUMATH             SCISEARCH 1974-1977
              ISI/GEOSCITECH            SOCIAL SCISEARCH 1972-DATE

        2. Search any data base on selected hosts
              DIALOG        NLM         BRS         ORBIT(SDC)

        3. Enter the Passive Terminal Mode

        4. Leave the Universal Online Searcher

        5. Receive instructions in the basics of Online Searching

Select a Number:  1
```
User Selects ISI Service → (line 1)

LISTING 9-2

INITIATING A SEARCH OF THE ISI/BIOMED DATABASE THROUGH SCI-MATE

```
ONLINE SEARCH
----------------------------------------------------------------- $$ ---

You are connected to the ISI/BIOMED data base.

The WORK file exists.

Search modes available are:

        1. SCI-MATE Search Mode (menu-driven)
        2. Native Search Mode   (ISI command language)
        3. Delete the WORK file
        4. Leave the ISI/BIOMED data base (return to Online menu)

Select a Number:  1

SCI-MATE SEARCH MENU                    No sets have been created
----------------------------------------------------------------- $$ ---

Do you want to:

        1. BROWSE the Search term index
        2. SEARCH and retrieve

        3. Use the SAVE STRATEGY subsystem
        4. Set current awareness parameters (SDI)

        5. Return to the Online Search menu

Select a Number:  2
```
User Selects Menu-Driven Search Mode → (options 1–4)

User Opts to Search for References → (option 5 / Select line)

database, and then (not shown) selects the ISI/BIOMED database. Just after this point, the Universal Online Searcher logs on to the system and the BIOMED database, eliminating the need for the user to dial and go through log-on procedures.

Next (in Listing 9-2) the user selects the Sci-Mate menu-driven mode (as opposed to the Native Search mode, which utilizes ISI's command-driven language) to perform a search (option 2 at the bottom of Listing 9-2).

TRANSFERRING FILES, SEARCH AIDS, AND OFFLINE SOFTWARE 145

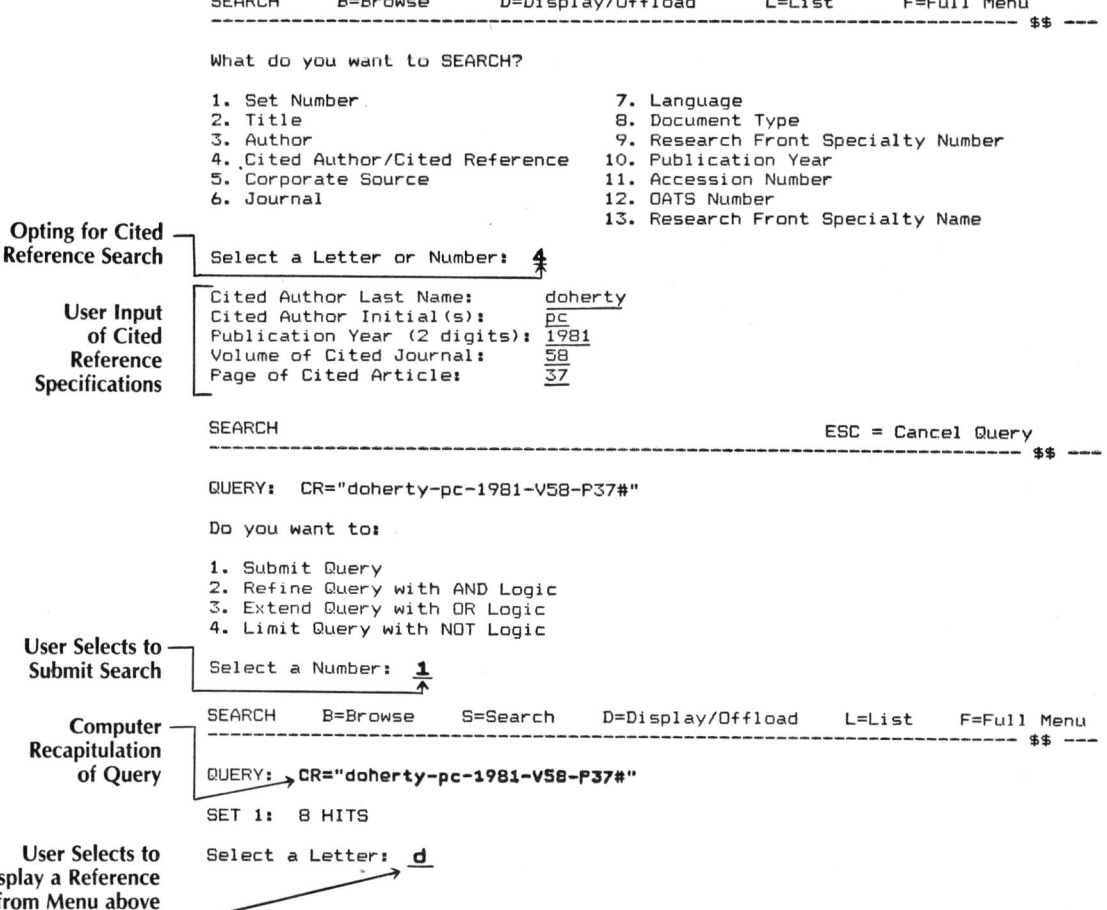

LISTING 9-3

SEARCH USING SCI-MATE FOR ARTICLES CITING A 1981 ARTICLE BY PC DOHERTY

In Listing 9–3, the user chooses to perform a Cited Author/Cited Reference search from the menu of 13 search-type options and then is prompted to enter specific information relating to the cited reference. Four prompts request the cited author's last name and initials, the year of publication, and the volume and page of the cited journal.

Searching without the benefit of Sci-Mate, a user would be required to enter a command in a precise format with exact punctuation. See the command in the example in the middle of Listing 9–3, after the phrase QUERY: CR="DOHERTY-PC-1981-V58-P37#. Most people cannot remember these formats unless they use them often, and so Sci-Mate saves a lot of pre-search research time and frustration. But the menu format takes longer to step through online, and so the Universal Online Searcher in menu-driven mode is likely to be more expensive to use than the original command-driven format.

INFORMATION ONLINE

LISTING 9-4

DISPLAY OF RECORDS USING SCI-MATE

```
DISPLAY/OFFLOAD       B=Browse        S=Search         L=List        F=Full Menu
------------------------------------------------------------------------ $$ ---

Set to be Displayed:  1           8 Hits
QUERY:    CR="doherty-pc-1981-V58-P37#"

Options In Effect:     SET TO BE DISPLAYED is      1
                       PRINT FORMAT is             1
                       OFFLOAD RECORD OPTION is    all
                       WORK FILE STATUS            does not exist

Choose one of the following actions:
    1.   Change SET TO BE DISPLAYED
    2.   Change PRINT FORMAT
    3.   Change OFFLOAD RECORD OPTION/DELETE WORK FILE
    <CR> Start display of records

Enter a Number, Letter or <CR>:
```

User Hits Carriage Return

```
1
AN  BD1121446
TI  DIFFERENCES IN THE MHC-RESTRICTED SELF-RECOGNITION REPERTOIRE
    OF INTRA-THYMIC AND EXTRA-THYMIC CYTO-TOXIC LYMPHOCYTE-T
    PRECURSORS
LA  ENGLISH
DT  ARTICLE
AU  KRUISBEEK AM; SHARROW SO; SINGER A
CS  NCI,IMMUNOL BRANCH,BETHESDA, MD,20205
SO  JOURNAL OF IMMUNOLOGY 130(3):1027-1032
YR  83
RF  25
ON  QC721
SP  81-0312; 81-0675; 81-0788; 81-2781
```

LISTING 9-5

SCI-MATE INITIAL MENU AND PERSONAL DATA MANAGER MENU

```
*********************************************
*                                                                   *
*              WELCOME TO THE ISI SCI-MATE SYSTEM                   *
*                                                                   *
*                                                                   *
*        Today's date:          5/9/83                              *
*        WORK file status:      WORK file exists                    *
*                                                                   *
*                                                                   *
*     Do you want to:                                               *
*                                                                   *
*            1. Enter the Universal Online Searcher                 *
*            2. Enter the Personal Data Manager                     *
*            3. Enter or Change Today's Date                        *
*            4. Delete the WORK file                                *
*                                                                   *
*            5. Receive instructions on the Use of SCI-MATE         *
*            6. Leave the SCI-MATE System                           *
*                                                                   *
*     Select a number or enter ? for help:  2                       *
*                                                                   *
*                                                                   *
*********************************************
```

User Selects Personal Data Manager

TRANSFERRING FILES, SEARCH AIDS, AND OFFLINE SOFTWARE

LISTING 9–5 *(continued)*

```
OFFLINE                         Current USER File : ISRAEL
----------------------------------------------------------------
You May:

        1. Search the USER File
        2. Enter a New Record
        3. Display/Copy WORK File Records
        4. Select/Create Another USER File

        5. Create and Update Templates
        6. Generate Document Request Status Report
        7. Generate Columnar Report

        8. Return to the SCI-MATE Menu

Select a number: 3
```

In the final steps of the search procedure, the user submits the simple query (rather than refining it with Boolean logic, as would be usual with subject word searching) and is given options to change the set to be displayed, to change the print format, and to change the offload record option. He decides to accept the defaults currently in effect and prints the references, which are simultaneously and automatically downloaded.

The user might then proceed to step back through the menus to perform another search on BIOMED or on another database, to log on to another system through Sci-Mate, or to go to the Personal Data Manager. In the illustration, we skip some steps that return the user to the WELCOME menu (Listing 9–5).

Listings 9–5 through 9–9 show what can be done with downloaded data using the Personal Data Manager, a sophisticated data management and retrieval program. From the WELCOME menu, the user selects the Personal Data Manager (number 2) and then copies the downloaded references from the work file to the user file called ISRAEL (Listing 9–6). Each record is examined before being entered into the user file. Eight records are added (top of Listing 9–7), and the user decides to keep the work file. He is then shown the work file menu and asks for the OFFLINE menu in order to perform a search.

LISTING 9–6

SCI-MATE PROCEDURES FOR COPYING WORK FILE TO USER FILE

```
WORK FILE SUBSYSTEM              Current USER File : ISRAEL
----------------------------------------------------------------
WORK File Status :   WORK File Exists

Do you want to:

        1. Copy the WORK File to the USER File
        2. Display the WORK file
        3. Sort the WORK file
        4. Erase the WORK file
        5. Create a Text File

        6. Return to the OFFLINE Menu

Select a number: 1
                 ↑
```

Opting to Copy References to User File

                    COPY WORK FILE TO USER FILE

                    Would you like to:

                        1. Examine and Copy One Record at a Time
                        2. Copy All Records from WORK File to USER File

 Choosing to
 Examine
 Records Entering
 User File   3. Return to the WORK FILE SUBSYSTEM Menu

                    Select a number: **1**
                                      ↑

                    WORK FILE TO USER FILE 1   C=copy record   D=do not copy   T=apply templat
                    Date: 5/9/83   F=set flags   P=print   S=stop copy
                    Source: IS   Template: 1   ENTER COMMAND:

                    Database ISI/BIOMED
                    Title   DIFFERENCES IN THE MHC-RESTRICTED SELF-RECOGNITION REPERTOIRE
                              OF INTRA-THYMIC AND EXTRA-THYMIC CYTO-TOXIC LYMPHOCYTE-T
                              PRECURSORS
                    Author   KRUISBEEK AM; SHARROW SO; SINGER A
                    Res Spec 81-0312; 81-0675; 81-0788; 81-2781
                    Citation JOURNAL OF IMMUNOLOGY 130(3):1027-1032
                    Acc No.   BD1121446
                    Address   NCI,IMMUNOL BRANCH,BETHESDA,MD,20205
                    Language ENGLISH
                    Year   83
                    No. Refs 25
                    OATS No. QC721
                    Refs
                    Doc Type ARTICLE
                    Notes

LISTING 9-7

PROCEEDING IN SCI-MATE PERSONAL DATA MANAGER FROM ENTERING RECORDS TO SEARCHING

                    COPY WORK FILE TO USER FILE

                    Number of Records Copied : 8

                    Accession Numbers Added to the USER File: 49 TO 56
 Opting
 to Keep
 Work File   Do You Want to Erase the WORK File? (Y/N) **N**
                                                                ↑
                    WORK FILE SUBSYSTEM   Current USER File : ISRAEL

                    WORK File Status :   WORK File Exists

                    Do you want to:

                        1. Copy the WORK File to the USER File
                        2. Display the WORK file
                        3. Sort the WORK file
                        4. Erase the WORK file
                        5. Create a Text File

                        6. Return to the OFFLINE Menu

 Return to
 Initial Offline Menu Select a number: **6**
                                             ↑
                    OFFLINE   Current USER File : ISRAEL

                    You May:

                        1. Search the USER File
                        2. Enter a New Record

TRANSFERRING FILES, SEARCH AIDS, AND OFFLINE SOFTWARE   149

```
                    3. Display/Copy WORK File Records
                    4. Select/Create Another USER File

                    5. Create and Update Templates
                    6. Generate Document Request Status Report
                    7. Generate Columnar Report

                    8. Return to the SCI-MATE Menu
```

Selecting to Search ──── Select a number: **1**

LISTING 9-8

SEARCH OF ISRAEL DATABASE FOR ARTICLES MENTIONING "SPLEEN" USING THE SCI-MATE PERSONAL DATA MANAGER

```
            SEARCH                       Current USER File : ISRAEL
            ----------------------------------------------------------------

            Would you like to:

                    1. Search by Accession Number
                    2. Search Text : Find Total Hits Before Display
                    3. Search Text : Display Hits as Retrieved

                    4. Return to the OFFLINE Menu
```

Selecting Hits Display Option ──── Select a number: **2**

```
            TEXT SEARCH                           <ESC> = Return to Previous Menu
            ----------------------------------------------------------------
```

Entering Search Term → Enter a Search Statement
spleen

```
            SEARCH                       Current USER File : ISRAEL
            ----------------------------------------------------------------

            Records searched :    56
            Records retrieved :    1

            Would you like to:

                    1. Display and Edit Hits
                    2. Sort Hits
                    3. Copy Hits to WORK File
                    4. Generate a Columnar Report for the Hits

                    5. Begin A New Search
                    6. Return to the OFFLINE Menu
```

Choosing to Display Hits ──── Select a number: **1**

Listing 9-8 shows the steps involved in performing a simple keyword search on the term *spleen*, and the single retrieved reference is displayed in Listing 9-9. The user could then modify this record by adding a note, for example, to include it in the bibliography of a paper he is currently writing or to have a certain graduate student read it.

We show only a small sample of the capabilities of the Personal Data Manager. You can display the "template" of fields just as shown in Listing 9-9 or modify it to enter your own records and generate reports to your specifications. For example, you might create an author index to a local-subject database.

> **LISTING 9-9**
>
> **DISPLAY OF RETRIEVED RECORD ON SCI-MATE PERSONAL DATA MANAGER**
>
> ```
> SEARCH AN 56              N=Next    E=Edit     L=Delete Hit/List    S=Stop
> Date 5/9/83  Hit: 1       B=Back    P=Print    D=Delete/File
> Source: IS   Template: 1  ENTER COMMAND:
>
> Database ISI/BIOMED
> Title    VIRUS-IMMUNE AND ALLOREACTIVE RESPONSE CHARACTERISTICS OF
>          THYMOCYTES AND SPLEEN-CELLS FROM YOUNG MICE
> Author   SCHWARTZ DH; DOHERTY PC
> Res·Spec 81-0506
> Citation JOURNAL OF IMMUNOLOGY 127(4):1411-1414
> Acc No.  BD0705231
> Address  WISTAR INST ANAT & BIOL,36TH ST SPRUCE,PHILADELPHIA, PA,19104
> Language ENGLISH
> Year     81
> No. Refs 20
> OATS No. MG716
> Refs
> Doc Type ARTICLE
> Notes
> ```

Dow Jones Software

Dow Jones & Company, Inc.
P. O. Box 300
Princeton, NJ 08540
(800) 257-5114 (Hotline)
(800) 223-2274 (Marketing)
(609) 452-1151 (New Jersey)

Program	Cost	Computer
Dow Jones Market Analyzer	$350	Apple IBM PC
Dow Jones Market Microscope	$700	Apple IBM PC
Dow Jones Market Manager	$300	Apple
News and Quotes Reporter	$130	Apple
Dow Jones Reporter	$100	IBM PC

Dow Jones produces only the first three programs and authorizes the others. Similar packages are also available for the Atari and Commodore computers. Prospective purchasers should consider that packages have special hardware requirements such as minimum RAM, specific modems, and two disk drives.

The Apple and IBM Reporters are basically enhanced communications packages with special features that facilitate use of the Dow Jones service. The Dow Jones packages give the analyst power to compute and to generate reports directly from downloaded information. The popular Market Analyzer is a general purpose stock-charting and graphing package for people interested in technical analyses of the stock market. With the Market Analyzer, you can automatically update your files with daily data and construct a myriad of charts including price/volume indicators, trend lines, and automatic comparisons with standard indicators.

The Dow Jones Market Microscope is a fundamental stock market indicator for professional money managers. The two primary functions are: creating ranked lists of stocks selected by the user according to indicators he or she considers critical; and notification when stocks reach critical buy and critical sell points that the user predetermines. The Market Manager and Commodore's Portfolio Manager are portfolio management programs with analyses and accounting functions.

microDISCLOSURE

Disclosure, Inc.
5161 River Road
Bethesda, MD 20816
(800) 638-8076
(301) 951-1300 (Maryland)

Program	Cost	Computer
microDISCLOSURE	$250	IBM PC Apple (projected)

Technical specifications for the IBM are (at least) 64K of memory, two disk drives, an asynchronous communications adapter, and an 80-column monitor display. MicroDISCLOSURE performs functions similar to the Dow Jones analyses packages for the Disclosure II database of company records on Dialog. The program is menu-driven from the moment you load the diskette. If you have an auto-dial modem, microDISCLOSURE will dial, log you on, and ask you which companies or search criteria you desire. You need not know Dialog commands. Retrieved financial information can be downloaded to disk and can be manipulated and displayed offline. MicroDISCLOSURE lets you compute common financial ratios (e.g., debt to equity) and create specialized reports (such as balance sheets) on companies.

VisiLink

VisiCorp
2895 Zanker Road
San Jose, CA 95134
(408) 946-9000

Program	Cost	Computer
VisiLink	$250	IBM PC Apple

Technical specifications for the Apple are 48K RAM, 16-sector diskette, Applesoft BASIC, two disk drives, 40-column display, and one of the following modems—Hayes Micromodem II, Novation Apple-Cat II, Novation 212 Apple-Cat II. The IBM user needs 128K RAM, PC DOS 1.1 or 2.0, two double-sided disk drives, 80-column display, and one of a number of popular modems.

VisiLink is a joint product of VisiCorp, the VisiCalc company, and Data Resources, Inc. (DRI), which provides online access to large business and economic databases. Refer to Chapter 7 for a description of DRI. VisiLink is a communications program for accessing a subset of the DRI database, preformatted DataKits. From the electronic catalog residing in your microcomputer, you choose one or more of the DataKits, which are then immediately downloaded in the form of preformatted VisiCalc worksheets. You may integrate private information with downloaded data to do a wide range of analyses.

You are *not* charged for connect time when using VisiLink. You simply pay for the downloaded DataKits according to a price schedule that is part of the electronic catalog. Prices vary from $10 plus a variable cost based on units ordered (e.g., portfolio risk analysis is $3 plus $1 per company) to $125 for the Health Care Planner. Most are in the $25 to $40 range and cover primarily major industries, the stock market, money markets, and national and international economic data.

Video Patsearch

Pergamon International Information Corporation
1340 Old Chain Bridge Road
McLean, VA 22101
(800) 336-7575
(703) 442-0900 (Virginia)

Video Patsearch is an integrated microcomputer/videodisk system. The hardware acts as a terminal; it can be used to search the PATSEARCH database on Infoline and also to access other vendors. The offline videodisk stores full text of patents, which can then be displayed online.

Searching takes place in the language of the supplier. Full text of stored patents may be displayed easily using search keys retrieved during the search. Video Patsearch works well with bibliographic chemical databases and, because it can emulate the graphics capabilities of Tektronix terminals, can be used for searching CAS ONLINE and Questel. The cost of Patsearch is $6,000 per year plus an additional $1,500 for the Tektronix graphics option. Rates include one and a half hours of free time on Infoline.

OFFLINE PACKAGES

You can now purchase current subject-related portions of one database, ERIC, on disk, and BIOSIS should be available in a similar form in the near future. Other development work at the University of Virginia is aimed at implementing a local search system on the IBM PC for the highly regarded drug and poison information services, Drugdex and Poisindex.

MICROsearch (ERIC)

ERIC Clearinghouse on Information Resources
School of Education
Syracuse University
Syracuse, NY 13210
(315) 423-3640

Program	Cost	Computer
MICROsearch	$6/disk	Apple II plus

The Apple must have 48K RAM and an Apple DOS 3.3 operating system. For $11 (including postage and handling), you can obtain a demonstration kit (from the Clearinghouse) that contains all search software, a sample database disk, and the user manual.

MICROsearch is a current awareness service that issues two to three disks quarterly in two subject areas, educational technology and library/information science. Each disk contains 200 to 300 records, and the menu-driven software is very simple. You can search by title words, indexing fields, and authors using logical operators and right-hand truncation. A re-execute feature, which runs a strategy on subsequent disks, helps offset the inconvenience of having the database divided. Retrieved items may be displayed or printed.

Further development will allow users to build their own databases for searching using the MICROsearch software and will expand the types of equipment on which the software runs.

B–I–T–S
Biosciences Information Service
2100 Arch Street
Philadelphia, PA 19103
(215) 587-4800 (Pennsylvania)
(800) 523-4806 (Hotline)

Program	Cost*	Computer
B-I-T-S	$.40/record (with abstracts) $.20/record (no abstracts)	any CP/M based 8-bit micro, plus IBM PC and clones under PCDOS (MDOS)

*Lower rate for more than 10,000 abstracts per year. 500 record minimum

B–I–T–S is a selective dissemination of information service delivered on floppies. Each month B–I–T–S provides references based on a search of your interest profile, which is stored in the BIOSIS computer. B–I–T–S comes formatted for a specified, limited set of computers and retrieval packages. Because of its relatively low cost (about $200), ease of use, and capacity to handle variable length records (which saves a great deal of disk space), most test users use an adaptation of the FYI Superfile retrieval program. That adaptation is called BioSuperfile and is available from BIOSIS.

ONLINE SEARCH AIDS

Dubbed "front ends," search aids are software packages that function between the user and the search system. They are used primarily to make online information retrieval easier. Integrated packages discussed above all have search-aid components. Since many organizations have an interest in making the online search process so easy that anyone can do it, there is much development in this area right now.

Orbit SearchMaster
SDC Information Services
2500 Colorado Avenue
Santa Monica, CA 90406
(800) 421-7229

Still in the development stage, the SearchMaster communications software package for the Orbit system will dial and log you on automatically, upload preset search strategies, and execute searches unattended. A menu-driven system, the SearchMaster will also lead you through strategy development, "pass through" to other search systems, store a library of search strategies preformulated by experts, and allow editing of search results.

Search Helper
Information Access Company
404 Sixth Avenue
Menlo Park, CA 94025
(800) 227-8431
(415) 367-7171 (California)

Search Helper is a program for searching the Information Access databases, primarily Magazine Index, Newsearch, National Newspaper Index, and Legal Resources Index on the Dialog system. It runs on the Apple II or Vic Commodore and costs $1,700 per year including 15 hours of connect time. Using Search Helper menus, you build a strategy formulation offline, although once online, you may interact with the service. When you are ready, Search Helper will log you on to the service, execute your search, and log you off—all while you have a cup of coffee. This sort of procedure is efficient though contrary to the interactive nature of online.

UserLink
UserLink Systems, Ltd.
9 Brabyns Brow
Marple, Stockport,
Cheshire, SK6 7DA
England
061-427 5976
    or
C. Olsen and Associates
977 Redmond Avenue
San Jose, CA 95120
(408) 268-4586

UserLink is actually a modem with built-in software. Primarily, it simplifies and speeds up the initial search steps. Its main goal is to save money. Offline message preparation, storage, and editing allow you to log on, send a message, or begin an initial search strategy with only a few keystrokes. You can download data, store it, and then re-use it in another system. There is a chemical substructure access system option that emulates the graphics characteristics of the Tektronix 4010 and that can also be used for teletext access. UserLink comes in standard ($1,740) and extended versions ($2,490).

CSIN

Computer Corporation of America
675 Massachusetts Avenue
Cambridge, MA 02139
(617) 492-8860
   or
CSIN Network Administrator
Council on Environmental Quality
722 Jackson Place NW
Washington, DC 20006
(202) 395-7285

The Chemical Substance Information Network (CSIN) is a mini-processor-based system that simplifies searching for one information question in multiple online services and databases. Now functioning with an operational prototype (VAX 11/780 using the UNIX language), CSIN is used by nearly 100 organizations; operations are subsidized by the federal government with the expectation that fees will be instituted in 1984. CSIN should become more widely available in the next few years.

CSIN connects to CAS ONLINE, NIH/EPA CIS, NLM, DIALOG, SDC, the EPA's Chemicals in Commerce Information System, and the Coast Guard's Hazard Assessment Chemical System. First, you call up CSIN. It will log you on, upload, download, and automatically transform information downloaded from one vendor into the format of another. CSIN translates downloaded data from one database into a form searchable in another. Probably even more useful to novice searchers is the menu-driven search-formulation software that enables the user to create search questions called "scripts," which CSIN changes into the search language of the individual service. To use these menus you need not understand the search language. CSIN offline software also stores synonym lists, which will automatically be used to augment most search terms.

microCAMBRIDGE

Cambridge Scientific Abstracts
5161 River Road
Bethesda, MD 20816
(301) 951-1400

Announced for late 1983, microCAMBRIDGE is a menu-driven communications package for searching (through Dialog) the six databases produced by *Cambridge Scientific Abstracts*. The databases are *Aquatic Sciences and Fisheries Abstracts*, *Conference Papers Index*, *ISMEC (Information Service in Mechanical Engineering)*, *Life Sciences Collection*, *Oceanic Abstracts*, and *Pollution Abstracts*.

MicroCAMBRIDGE will auto-dial, log you on, display menus to guide you through your search, translate your responses into Dialog commands, and download your bibliography. It runs on an IBM PC or Apple with at least 64K of memory.

CHAPTER 10
Computer-Mediated Communication and Other Online Applications

Almost anything that computers can do can be done online through commercial services. But there are, of course, innumerable circumstances in which local processing makes more sense. Organizations with large data processing volumes and with needs for security and control over their own information prefer to develop their own computer centers. And, for many individual and small business applications (e.g., word processing and standard accounting) local programs are simply more economical. The principal advantage of online systems is that they can facilitate communication with and provide access to large databases and sophisticated programs that are not used enough to justify the expense of acquiring and maintaining them locally.

Chapters 4 through 7 describe most of the popular applications of online services, with an emphasis on retrieval of information. There are, however, many organizations from which you can obtain online services similar to those provided by information utilities such as electronic mail. My purpose here is to make you aware of additional possibilities by describing the other main classes of online services and by mentioning a few key organizations. Refer to the publications listed in the bibliography for this chapter and in DIRECTORIES for further information.

COMPUTER-MEDIATED COMMUNICATION

All of the information utilities and several other online information services support electronic mail and some also provide other types of electronic message transmission, namely, online conversations, bulletin boards, and computer conferencing. TYMNET, TELENET, and Dialcom also support popular message transmission networks. But before describing specific services, I will define the major types of messages sent and received online.

- *Electronic Mail:* Electronic mail is analogous to ordinary mail delivery. You can send a message to the private, password-protected "mailbox" of one individual or to a group's mailboxes. On the receiving end, you may "check your mail" by scanning a list of senders' names with sending dates (sometimes addresses); you may read your mail, respond to it, save it, or "throw it away" by deleting it from the system. One improvement over ordinary mail is that you can find out if the recipient has read your message. Some other common features of well-developed electronic mail systems are:

Online editing
Print delivery
Maintenance of online distribution lists
Online directory of users (who wish to be listed)
Message classification by Urgent or by Private (can only be read by intended recipient although others may use the password)
Delivery during a specified time period
Notification that the message has been read

- *Online Discussion:* Online discussions are direct, interactive conversations, one-to-one or in a group. CHAT on The Source and CB on CompuServe are examples.

- *Computer Conferencing:* Conferencing is an ongoing discussion over time. It permits participants to exchange information and ideas. Conferences have been compared to panels, forums, debates, and round tables. They are public or private (only certain individuals are invited to join the conference). All focus on a particular topic although they may branch out to subtopics. The two best known fee-based conference systems are PARTICIPATE on The Source and on Dialcom and EIES (described below), but you may also join conferences on free systems supported by hobbyists.

- *Electronic Bulletin Boards:* Bulletin boards allow you to post messages to be read by anyone who has access to the system. The large ones are divided by topic, and some can even be searched by keyword. Usually, you can browse a directory of titles before reading an entire message. You will find bulletin boards on all major utilities and on several other services. See POST on The Source and BULLET on CompuServe. A major online phenomenon is the hobbyist bulletin board, which is different enough from other services described in this book—it's free!—to warrant the separate discussion that follows.

OnTyme

Tymshare, Inc.
20705 Valley Green Drive, VG3
Cupertino, CA 95014
(800) 227-6185
(408) 446-6000

Accessible from TYMNET nodes in nearly 300 major metropolitan areas and more than two dozen foreign countries, OnTyme is an easy-to-use electronic mail system. For terminals with auto-answer, OnTyme offers an out-dial feature. You can store received messages in a multilevel electronic "filing cabinet." Basic charges are $200 per month subscription fee, $3 per hour of connect time, and $.25 per 1,000 characters of input or output. Minimum billing after three months is $500.

Telemail

GTE Telenet Communications Corporation
8229 Boone Boulevard
Vienna, VA 22180
(800) 336-0437
(800) 572-0408 (Virginia)

Telemail, on the TELENET telecommunications network, was one of the first electronic mail services. Telemail has many sophisticated options such as filing of received messages, delivery through telex or TWX, extra security, distribution lists, and online directory information. The Telemail monthly account charge is $140, with connect time rates of $14 per hour, plus $.05 per 1,000 transmitted characters. This service also has a monthly billing minimum of $500.

Dialcom

Dialcom
1109 Spring Street, Suite 400
Silver Spring, MD 20910
(301) 588-1572

A pioneer, Dialcom now claims to be the most widely used electronic mail system in the world. It has 22,000 customers. Focusing on top-level management, Dialcom provides other advanced office automation products, including the full spectrum of electronic messaging (PARTICIPATE for computer conferencing, an electronic bulletin board, and online interactive "talking"). Also available through Dialcom are several information products: UPI news, stock market data, electronic publishing, the ABI/INFORM bibliographic database of management information, the Official Airline Guide, and a "gateway" link to the major information vendors such as Dialog, BRS, and SDC.

Costs are $15 per connect hour, including TYMNET and TELENET network charges with a $100 monthly minimum. Surcharges are in effect for the proprietary information services.

EIES (Electronic Information Exchange System)

Computerized Conferencing and Communications Center
New Jersey Institute of Technology
323 High Street
Newark, NJ 07102
(201) 645-5211

Primarily known for its pioneering computer-conferencing system, EIES is now a highly developed, comprehensive service including electronic mail, notebooks, and word, text, and document processing. The electronic *notebook* is a kind of personal file, a private electronic space for gathering thoughts and organizing materials. Word, text, and document processing allow individuals and groups to compose and distribute reports and papers. There is also a possibility for custom programming that will aid a particular communication process (project monitoring, for example).

You can learn to use EIES in less than an hour. Users have access to five levels of interface language; thus, as they become more experienced, they move from menus to commands. HELP commands and online consultants assist new users, who join a community of 700 individuals and more than 50 groups. Some examples of EIES uses are: building a database that synthesizes current knowledge about viral hepatitis; developing social and intellectual networks for handicapped children; planning a national conference on library and information services. Within the formal structure, there is an informal personal and social network wherein computer hobbyists trade horror stories, amateur poets "publish," flirters trade lines, and users obtain support at times of personal difficulty (as during a tenure battle). Often accused of playing a dehumanizing role, the computer seems to have fostered a new kind of communications in which some of the usual barriers are minimized.

Based at a university, EIES is a self-supporting not-for-profit network that was started with a grant from the National Science Foundation. In addition to providing a reliable, state-of-the-art service to users, EIES has the goal of continuing to "develop and evaluate new features . . . and to advance the state of the art and our understanding of user behavior in this new medium of communication." EIES is still a laboratory. Nevertheless, membership is open to everyone.

Class one membership is $75 per month plus telecommunications charges. Class two membership, which has some restrictions, is $8 per hour plus telecommunications with a $15 initiation fee and $25 per month minimum. There is also a membership option for groups of six or more and additional storage charges and special fees. The developers encourage the use of EIES for research.

COMPUTER-ASSISTED INSTRUCTION (CAI)

People training in the health sciences may access *computer-assisted instruction* programs through the Health Education Network, which has programs at Ohio State University and Massachusetts General Hospital. The other major source of online CAI is Edunet, through which you can connect to major university computers throughout the country to access programs in many different disciplines. See the discussion of Edunet below under OTHER TIMESHARING SERVICES.

Computer-assisted instruction programs are essentially tutorials in which the student responds to questions from the online program. The computer's responses vary from encouraging comments like "very good" to explanations of why the student's response was wrong and which answer is correct. Programs "branch out"—according to student input—in order to give practice in students' weak areas and to challenge (or at least not to waste the time of) good students.

Health Education Network (OSU)
OSU Network Coordinator
The Ohio State University
College of Medicine
076 Health Sciences Library
Columbus, OH 43210
(614) 422-6192

Begun in 1972 with funding from the Lister Hill National Center for Biomedical Communications, the network is now an incorporated, non-profit organization. OSU has slightly more than 100 programs for students in several health professions and even makes some programs available to patients. In level of difficulty, they range from "Patient Management of Diabetes" (for patients) to "Anticoagulation Medications" (for physicians). Rates are from $10 to $12 per hour depending on the monthly commitment, with a minimum commitment of $60 per month.

Health Education Network (MGH)

MGH Network Coordinator
Massachusetts General Hospital
Laboratory of Computer Science
Boston, MA 02114
(617) 726-3950

MGH has 25 programs aimed primarily at medical students in the clinical phase of training and practicing physicians who desire continuing education. The case study approach is used most often. For example, the "Cardiac Arrhythmias" program simulates patients with a variety of common rhythm disturbances. All institutional users are required to make a minimum monthly commitment of at least $150 for which the hourly rate is $15. The hourly rate drops to $11 for a commitment of $1,100, and individuals may join at the $15 per-hour rate with a $60 monthly minimum.

COMPUTER BULLETIN BOARD SYSTEMS (CBBS)

Although some computer stores and software producers maintain bulletin boards to serve their special interests, most CBBS are run by individuals simply for fun and service. And, while there are boards dedicated to special interests, the majority serve the primary function of providing a means for exchanging information and public-domain software among microcomputer owners. Many are dedicated to one microcomputer type and nearly all are free.

The first CBBS system went online in Chicago in February 1978, a time when information about microcomputers was scarce. It was a big hit from the first day and remains very popular. Since then the bulletin board movement has swept the country to the point where there are now more than 800. They can be addictive: You will find a compelling friendliness and sense of camaraderie in the board communications. Whether this will change as the personal computer movement grows and users have access to alternative sources of information about micros (and feel less pioneering) is hard to know. Meanwhile, a fascinating "underground," bulletin boards may well be *the most important* trend in computer-mediated communications today.

Accessing CBBS

To use a board, you dial the number and, after receiving the connect signal, enter one or two carriage returns. That's it—there is no complex log-on procedure; the bulletin board will take you from there. To start, you might want to try the original Chicago board at (312) 545-8086. See Listing 10-1, which shows a typical bulletin board interaction and which is largely self-explanatory. This is a fairly large system in Allentown, Pennsylvania; it has four disk drives. Some boards have fewer drives, others a hard disk. The friendliness of the greeting and other messages is typical, as are the online directions and the HELP command. "Bill" is known, in bulletin board jargon, as the SYSOP (for SYStem OPerator), and the ability to call him on the phone for "voice" communication is another common bulletin board feature.

COMPUTER-MEDIATED COMMUNICATION 161

LISTING 10–1
COMPUTER BULLETIN BOARD IN ALLENTOWN, PA

```
                      (Updated 10/24/82 - type ctl-C to skip this message)
Welcome Message →  Welcome to the Remote CP/M and Bulletin Board System
                   of Allentown, Pennsylvania, using the PMMI modem
                   with baud rates of 110, 300, 450, and 600.

                   This system has 4 drives (A thru D), with open user areas
                   0 thru 9. Feel free to "explore" the system.

                   Most public-domain software distributed by both CPMUG and SIG/M
                   (the two major CP/M-compatible software libraries) is available
                   on request. Leave a note for SYSOP telling which files you want
                   and they'll be there as soon as possible.

                   The message facility is accessed by the  A0>MINIRBBS cmd.

                   Some specialized user areas are: Atari files on D9, RCPM files
                   on D2, Modem programs on D3, Smartmodem on D4, "C" on B5 & B6
                   as well as others.

                   Documentation files on A0, plus the "HELP" and "CPMINFO" commands
                   are to help you get the most use from your call.

                   Booting system..
                   Allentown, Pa. RCPM System..Ver. 2.6M

System Operator →  Problems? Call Bill at 215-398-1634 for voice.
                   If the recorder answers, remember the 20 second limit

User Identification → What is your FIRST name ?carol
                   What is your LAST name ?fenichel
                   Checking user file...
                   Where (City,State) are you calling from ?philadephia, pa
                   Hello CAROL FENICHEL from PHILADEPHIA, PA
                   Is any of this misspelled ?no
                   This checking is only done the first time you call.

                   Pleased to meet you !

                   To learn more about this system, type "HELP".

                   To learn the CP/M commands, type "CPMINFO".

System Information → Control Characters
                   -------  ----------
                   ctl-C    Aborts most system functions.
                   ctl-K    Alternate abort (MINIRBBS functions only).
                   ctl-S    Pauses printout; any character continues
                   ctl-H    Backspace and delete character (for CRT)
                   DEL      Echo and delete character (for hardcopy terminals)
                   ctl-X    Erase (cancel) line (for CRT)
                   ctl-U    Cancel line (for hardcopy)
                   ctl-R    Retype current line (CP/M only)


                   This is a rather large system, with over 800
                   files in more than 30 areas. The next item can
                   save you considerable time over just looking at
                   all the directories.

                   To locate files, TYPE the file INDEX.DOC or use
                   the utility: FILEFIND filename.typ

                   The notation "C/R" means the RETURN (enter) key.

                   Note that filenames consist of 2 parts, which should be
                   separated by a period in commands.
                   Logging CAROL FENICHEL to disk...
```

INFORMATION ONLINE

LISTING 10-1 *(continued)*

```
You are caller # :   19310
Next msg. nr. is :   522

** BULLETINS **

05/01/83 The SYSOP will be unavailable from 5/6 thru
         5/16. Hopefully the system will stay up, and
         requests will be caught up on 5/17 or after.

04/01/83 LBR.DOC on A0 to explain .LBR utilities.

User cmd. accepts both user nr. and drive letter.

Please limit your system usage to 1 hour per day.

Entering CP/M...
```

Help Command → `A0>help`
```
CTL-S pauses,CTL-C aborts
          INFORMATION ON THIS SYSTEM AND ITS PROGRAMS
                        Updated 01/30/83
```

Help Directions
```
         Welcome to my remote Z-80 CP/M system. On this system
you are now the CONSOLE.

     Some basic commands for this system are:

'DIR' to show the directory of the current disk.

'USER n' to switch from one user level to another (n=0 to 9)

'x:' to change drives (x=A to D)

'TYPE' filname.typ to display a readable file.
       (non-text files will be rejected)


     For more information on how this system is configured
and where various files are kept, enter:

A0>TYPE THIS-SYS.DOC
   or
A0>TYPE INDEX.DOC

     Other .DOC files (mostly on A0), explain other details
of the system and its utilities.

     If you would like a description of how CP/M (the DOS
you are now using) operates, or details on the command
structure of the system, enter:

xn>CPMINFO

     There are 2 classes of files on this system, those with
a .COM suffix, and all the others. The .COM files are commands
or executable programs, and like the DIR, USER, and TYPE com-
mands, are invoked WITHOUT the suffix being used. All other
files may be used as parameters to commands such as TYPE, but
just the name without a command will get you nowhere.

     File transfer on this system is normally via the XMODEM
command. Look at file XMODEM.DOC on drive A0 if you are not
familiar with the procedure.

     You may read and enter messages by calling the utility:

xn>MINIRBBS

     This program has a menu of options. Your messages are
automatically saved on disk. Please kill messages addressed
to you after you have read them.
```

COMPUTER-MEDIATED COMMUNICATION

LISTING 10-1 *(continued)*

```
                Have fun!   When you are done, do this:
        xn>BYE
                The system will automatically terminate upon loss of
        carrier.  If you have any problems with the system, you can
        reset it by hanging up and calling back again.
```

System Operator ──────────────▶ Bill Earnest, SYSOP (K3WPU)
```
                        RD 1, Box 830
                        Orefield, PA 18069
                        (215) 398-1634 (voice)
        done
```

Disk A Directory ─────
```
        A0>dir
                       ─▶Directory (1.6L) for Drive A0:
        BULLETIN.       1K     LBR      .DOC    3K    SQ/USQ   .DOC    2K
        BYE      .COM   2K     LCRCK    .COM    6K    SYSTEM   .DIR   22K
        CAT      .DOC   2K     LDIR     .COM    7K    THIS-SYS .DOC    2K
        CHANGES  .DOC   7K     LMODEM   .COM    9K    TIME     .COM    1K
        CHAT     .COM   1K     LTYPE    .COM    9K    TOS      .COM    1K
        CHEK     .COM   3K     MINIRBBS .COM   18K    TYPE     .DOC    1K
        CPMCAT   .COM   1K     NEWBAUD  .COM    1K    TYPE     .OBJ    9K
        CPMINFO  .COM   6K     NEWCOM   .        1K    WHATSNEW.COM    2K
        CRCK     .COM   2K     OTHERSYS .FQB   20K    XFER     .DOC    8K
        FILEFIND .COM   1K     RCPM-036 .LQT   17K    XMODEM   .COM   14K
        FLIP     .COM   1K     RCPMDATA .1Q     8K    XMODEM   .DOC    3K
        HELP     .COM   3K     SD       .COM    2K    XTYPE    .OBJ    9K
        INDEX    .DOC   2K     SIGCAT   .COM    1K
                        38 Files      208K Displayed    406K Left
```

Xmodem Documentation ─────
```
        A0>type xmodem.doc
        Ctrl-S pauses, Ctrl-C Aborts.

        TYPEing file XMODEM.DOC (200 lines MAX)

                        XMODEM for Allentown RCPM           05/01/83

            XMODEM  is a special version of MODEM which is used at the RCPM
        location and is commanded by the distant caller. It does not
        disturb  the baud rate or other modem conditions,  and works in
        conjunction with your MODEM program.
            In general, start XMODEM with:

                    A>XMODEM S filename.typ ;To send yourself a file
                                    or
                    A>XMODEM R filename.typ ;To send a file to this
                                                system

            If you forget the format, just type XMODEM and it will give a
        quick command summary.

            To  use it,  you must have MODEM or an equivalent program  at
        your  end for compatible handshaking.  After XMODEM  signs  on,
        execute  MODEM at your end in the opposite mode,  and the  file
        will be transferred.
            .
            .
            Those  that  are interested in the technical details can  find
        the  protocol  description in file XFER.DOC here on A0  and  in
        MODMPROT.OQ1 on drive D0.
```

Accessing the Message System ─────
```
        A0>minirbbs
        Allentown, Pa. Message System.

        Next msg # will be: 522

        Active message count: 121
```

LISTING 10-1 *(continued)*

Message System Directions →
```
Function (E,R,S,K,C,G,P,X,Q,T (or '?' if not known)??
Functions supported
    S--> Scan messages      R--> Retrieve message
    E--> Enter message      K--> Kill message
    P--> Prompt (bel) togl  X--> eXpert user mode
    T--> connect Time disp  C--> Comment before exit to CP/M
    Q--> Quick msg.summary  G--> Goodbye-direct exit to CP/M
Commands may be strung together with semicolons.
For example, 'R;123' retrieves message # 123.
For forward sequential retrieval, use '+' after Msg. #.
```

Command to Scan Entries → `Function (E,R,S,K,C,G,P,X,Q,T (or '?' if not known)?S`

Message Number → `Msg Nr. ( 1 - 521 ) to start (C/R to end)?1`

```
Ctl-S to Pause,Repeat Ctl-K's to Abort.

Nr. 81 = 4 lines, dated 1/4/83 From: JIM LAWLOR
To: ALL  Re: 16KZ BOARD AVAILABLE

Nr. 87 = 9 lines, dated 1/5/83 From: BEN GREENE
To: ALL  Re: ATARI STUFF WANTED
    .
    .
Nr. 155 = 16 lines, dated 1/30/83 From: STEVEN BROWN
To: ALL  Re: M!CROMODEM II

Nr. 186 = 3 lines, dated 2/10/83 From: TOM SMITH
To: ALL  Re: DBASE ON OSBORNE
```

Command to Read an Entry →
```
***** End of summary *****

Function (E,R,S,K,C,G,P,X,Q,T (or '?' if not known)?R
```

Number of Entry to Read → `MSG Nr.( 1 - 521 ) to retrieve (C/R to end)?155`

```
Ctl-S to Pause,Repeat Ctl-K's to Abort.

Msg Nr. 155  Date entered: 1/30/83  From: STEVEN BROWN
To: ALL  Re: MICROMODEM II

I WOULD LIKE TO KNOW HOW,WHEN USING
THE TERMINAL SOFTWARE PROVIDED BY
HAYES...CAN I BOOT MY APPLE II+ INTO
CPM WITHOUT DISCONNECTING THE MODEM?
    .
    .
THANKS FROM:STEVE BROWN
```

Quit Message System →
```
Function (E,R,S,K,C,G,P,X,Q,T (or '?' if not known)?Q
Entering CP/M...
```

Exit CBBS →
```
A0>bye
Connect Time was 16 Mins.
Good Bye, Call again
```

In Listing 10-1, after identifying myself, receiving directions for new users, and learning that I am caller number 19,310—an indication of the popularity of boards although this is a relatively big one—I decide to type the HELP command for additional directions. I then proceed to look at the directory for disk A and download documentation for the xmodem program. Next, entering the bulletin board section (MINI-RBBS), I scan some listings and print one, a very common plea for help with a specific microcomputer problem. A nice aspect of bulletin board use is that the time clock syndrome, the rushed feeling arising out of the cost of online time, is absent, and so you feel free to browse leisurely and to study the online instructions. Even so, it is probably more efficient to print out commands for the boards you use often.

For step-by-step directions for downloading software from CP/M systems such as this, see the article by Bove and Smith listed in the bibliography of Chapter 8. While any computer can communicate with any CBBS, you should be aware that to be of any value, software must be transferred from the same operating system as your computer. Moreover, to receive free software from a remote CP/M system, you must use the same communication protocols as the system; this usually means running a version of the public domain package, MODEM.

It is not as easy to gain access to bulletin boards as to the large online services, although many are amazingly reliable, considering they are managed by volunteers. Some boards are "up" 24 hours a day, while others function only during certain time periods. But the biggest problem is that they are often "busy," meaning that no access ports are open. At such times a direct-dial modem and communications software with an automatic re-dial function come in very handy. Another way to solve the "busy" problem is to use the systems at unpopular times such as late at night or before 8 A.M. Insomnia is an advantage here.

Finding CBBS

The best sources of local numbers are involved friends or members of your computer club. Some bulletin boards list numbers of other CBBSs; club newsletters sometimes print them. Or you may want to purchase the *Online Computer Telephone Directory Poster*. It contains a listing of about 450 bulletin board numbers that are verified regularly. Or, you may check the Derfler listing in the July 1982 issue of *Microcomputing*, the public user-published file, "Public Access Systems" on The Source or the user-published files on CompuServe under the Apple User Group. Both the poster and the Derfler article are listed in this chapter's bibliography; the Directory itself is a newsletter listed in the Journals and Newsletters section of the bibliography. To give you other places to start, we list a sampling of board numbers in Appendix IV.

Another problem with bulletin boards is that they come and go with some frequency. Thus, it is not always possible to tell whether a system is busy, down temporarily, not scheduled to function at that time, or simply no longer operating. Once you finish checking some local boards, you will likely settle on a few to use regularly.

CBBS Software

After looking at many bulletin boards, you may begin to notice that they fall into categories. Boards that look alike are running the same software package. See Appendix III for a listing of some popular bulletin board software. The simplest are under $100, and a few even come as part of communications packages. Even the most elaborate cost less than $500, and you can purchase a fairly sophisticated system for $100 to $200.

So, with a relatively small incremental outlay, you could become a SYSOP! All it takes is a microcomputer (preferably with substantial mass storage), an auto-answer modem, and software.

One of the software packages listed in the appendix deserves special comment. This is Communitree, which is more than just a bulletin board. Communitree is a computer conferencing system similar to EIES and PARTICIPATE. See Listing 10-2 for a session on a Communitree system in New Jersey. As with the CBBS, interaction is largely self-explanatory. Presumably to maintain anonymity, users are not asked to identify themselves. The sample interaction shows the extensive online HELP commands and illustrates the package's purpose, which is clearly different from that of the regular CBBS. In the example, we display part of the Nuclear Arms conference to indicate the potential of conferencing for expressing feelings and carrying on meaningful dialogue. The last "branch" shows the kind of free-wheeling chiding that takes place in conferencing.

LISTING 10-2

CONFERENCE SESSION USING COMMUNITREE SOFTWARE

Indicates Acceptance of Lower Case → `LOWER CASE OK (C/R=YES)?y`

```
TYPE 'READ HELP' ANY TIME
OR 'READ CONFERENCES' TO START

'S' KEY TO PAUSE OR RESUME PRINTING

OPERATED BY STAN BECKERMAN IN DENVILLE,NJ. AFTER HELP
FILES TYPE "READ PURPOSE"
```

Entering Help Command → `COMMAND? read help`

Instructions →
```
*** HELP                    16-JUL-81
  PARENT=CONFERENCES               USAGE4067
'READ CONFERENCES' FOR CURRENT SUBJECTS.
'READ <NAME>' WHERE <NAME> IS ANY MESSAGE OR SUBMESSAGE.
'BROWSE CONFERENCES COMPLETE' TO SKIM.
'INDEX <NAME>' FOR INDEX OF SUBTREE.
COMMANDS AND OPTIONS MAY BE ABBREVIATED TO THEIR FIRST LETTERS.
PRESS 'S' KEY TO PAUSE OR RESUME PRINTING.
PRESS 'K' KEY TO STOP MESSAGE LISTING.
PRESS 'C' KEY TO KILL CURRENT COMMAND.
CONTROL-H OR DEL KEY FOR BACKSPACE.
TO LEAVE THE SYSTEM, JUST HANG UP!
'READ HELP-COMMANDS' FOR MORE FEATURES.
'READ HELP COMPLETE' FOR ALL HELP DOCUMENTATION.
     +++ SUBMESSAGES +++
    HELP-COMMANDS         16-JUL-81
    HELP-OPTIONS          16-JUL-81
    HELP-ADDTO            16-JUL-81
    MISC-HELP             16-JUL-81
    SYSTEM-PASSWORD       16-JUL-81
    QUICK-REFERENCE       10-OCT-82

COMMAND? read purpose
```

LISTING 10-2 *(continued)*

Purpose of Service

```
*** PURPOSE              27-FEB-83
  PARENT=CONFERENCES           USAGE=265
    THE  PURPOSE  OF  THIS  SYSTEM IS TO  FOSTER  THE  INTERACTIVE
SHARING OF IDEAS AND INFORMATION AMONG ITS USERS.
    TO   THIS  END,  SHORT CHATTY MESSAGES ARE  TO  BE  DISCOURAGED.
THERE ARE MANY EXCELLENT MESSAGE BOARDS OR MAIL BOARDS IN THE AREA
THAT ARE BETTER SUITED FOR THAT PURPOSE. THE UNIQUE TREE STRUCTURE
OF THIS SYSTEM LENDS ITSELF FAR MORE TO THE GENERATION OF CREATIVE
THINKING AND THE SHARING OF INFORMATION.
    HERE  ANY  TOPIC (CONTROVERSIAL OR OTHERWISE) CAN  BE  OPENLY
DISCUSSED  AND  NURTURED  ALONG  TO  ITS  CONCLUSION.  THOSE  USERS
DESIRING  ANONYMITY  WILL  FIND  NO  REQUIREMENT  TO  REVEAL  THERE
IDENTITY.  I  HOPE THE SYSTEM CAN EVOLVE INTO A TRUE  CONFERENCING
SYSTEM THROUGH THIS OPEN FORMAT.
    ALL USERS ARE URGED TO READ THOROUGHLY ALL OF THE HELP  FILES.
IF  YOU HAVE A PRINTER,  I SUGGEST YOU PRINT THEM OUT AND REFER TO
THEM WHEN USING THE SYSTEM. THERE ARE MANY FEATURES THAT FEW USERS
SEEM TO TAKE ADVANTAGE OF WHEN CALLING HERE. THEY ARE EXPLAINED IN
DETAIL UNDER THE 'HELP' BRANCH.

    THE SYSTEM CAN HOLD APPROXIMATELY 320 MESSAGES.  EACH MESSAGE
CAN  BE  A MAXIMUM OF 50 LINES OF 80 CHARACTERS  PER  LINE.  SHORT
MESSAGES  USE  JUST  AS MUCH STORAGE IN THE INDEX  AS  LONG  ONES.
THEREFORE  SHORT ONES ARE TO BE DISCOURAGED.  TO ACCOMPLISH  THIS,
'MAIL'  TYPE MESSAGES WILL BE LEFT ON-LINE ONLY FOR A VERY LIMITED
TIME  (VARYING FROM A FEW DAYS TO A WEEK).  AFTER THAT TIME  THEY
WILL  BE  EXILED AND SQUEEZED FROM THE DISK.  THE SYSTEM  WILL  BE
SQUEEZED AT LEAST ONCE A WEEK.  MORE IF NECESSARY.  THIS IS DUE TO
THE SPACE LIMITATIONS OF THIS TWO DRIVE APPLE SYSTEM.
    I HOPE WE CAN DEVELOP INTERESTING AND USEFUL DISCUSSION  HERE.
DURING   THE  UPCOMING  MONTHS  I  WILL  BE  LOOKING  FOR  SEVERAL
FAIRWITNESSES  TO AID IN THE CONTINUING EVOLUTION OF  THE  SYSTEM.
TYPE  'READ FAIRWITNESS' IF YOU HAVE NOT DONE SO PREVIOUSLY TO SEE
WHAT ONE DOES.
    I  BELIEVE  THIS CAN BE A TRULY INTERACTIVE SYSTEM IF  WE  ALL
WORK  TO MAKE IT SUCCESSFUL.  AS SYSTEM OPERATOR I CAN NOT  DO  IT
ALONE.  SO  PLEASE,  LET'S  GET SOME  REAL  DISCUSSIONS,  DEBATES,
REVIEWS, EDITORIALS, AND ARTICLES GOING HERE AND
SAVE THE 'MAIL' TYPE OF MESSAGES FOR THE BULLETIN BOARD SYSTEMS.
    YOUR  COOPERATION  IS APPRECIATED.  I ALSO ASK EVERYONE  TO
SPREAD  THE WORD.  LET THE WORLD KNOW WE'RE HERE.  WHEN YOU ACCESS
OTHER  SYSTEMS  LEAVE  A  MESSAGE WITH THE  PHONE  NUMBER  OF  THE
CONFERENCE TREE.

   --SYSTEM OPERATOR--
      +++ NO SUBMESSAGES +++

COMMAND?  read coferences
```

Active Conferences

```
*** CONFERENCES          0-JAN-80
  PARENT= NONE                 USAGE4336
CURRENT CONFERENCES ON THIS CONFERENCE TREE SYSTEM ARE:
      +++ SUBMESSAGES +++
    HELP                  16-JUL-81
    USERS                 16-JUL-81
    SYSTEM                16-JUL-81
    DEAR-SYSOP             2-APR-82
    SOFTWARE-REVIEWS       2-APR-82
    FINANCIAL-MARKETS      2-APR-82
    ALL-USERS              2-APR-82
    FLAGSHIP              20-APR-82
    MOVIE-REVIEWS         28-JUN-82
    COMPUTER-SYSTEMS       1-NOV-82
    PURPOSE               27-FEB-83
    FOR.SALE               7-MAR-83
    ABORTION?              9-MAR-83
    COME-ON-PEOPLE        20-MAR-83
    TI-99'ER-NEWS          5-APR-83
    IBMPC-TREE             6-APR-83
    SOFTWARE-WANTED        9-APR-83
    PASCAL-FORTRAN-PROGR  14-APR-83
    MAIL-ORDER-HOUSES     17-APR-83
    VIC-20-TREE           23-APR-83
```

INFORMATION ONLINE

LISTING 10–2 (continued)

```
TRADING              23-APR-83
BUSY-LINE            25-APR-83
NUCLEAR-ARMS         29-APR-83
JOB-HELP             29-APR-83
VIDEOTEX-HELP-NEEDED 30-APR-83
HEMINGWAYS            2-MAY-83
CHRISTIANITY          2-MAY-83
SF                    2-MAY-83
WANTED                5-MAY-83
ADVENTURE             5-MAY-83
GRAPHIC-PROGRAMS      8-MAY-83
CAR-CLUB              8-MAY-83
EPSON-VALDOCS        11-MAY-83
LIST-OF-BBS'S        13-MAY-83

COMMAND? read nuclear-arms
```

Browsing Nuclear Arms Conference →

```
*** NUCLEAR-ARMS           29-APR-83
    PARENT=CONFERENCES        USAGE= 29
TODAY, ONE OF THE MAJOR TOPICS ON PEOPLES MINDS IS THE QUESTION OF
NUCLEAR ARMAMENTS, NUCLEAR POWER PLANTS, AND OTHER USES OF NUCLEAR
SUBSTANCES LIKE: WHAT DO WE DO WITH THE WASTES?

     I WAS WONDERING WHAT OTHER PEOPLE'S OPINIONS ARE OF THIS  TOPIC.
PLEASE  FEEL FREE TO EXPRESS ANY VIEWS OR SHARE ANY FACTS YOU HAVE
ABOUT THESE TOPICS, HERE.
       +++ SUBMESSAGES +++
   NUCLEAR-WEAPONS         29-APR-83
   NUKES-VS-CONV-ARMS       3-MAY-83
   OPINION                  5-MAY-83
   NUKES                   10-MAY-83
   MILITARY-INDUSTRIAL-    13-MAY-83


COMMAND? read nuclear-weapons

*** NUCLEAR-WEAPONS        29-APR-83
    PARENT=NUCLEAR-ARMS       USAGE= 15
i think that nuclear arms aren't needed.  by 1987, the u.s. will
have perfected the 'particle accelerator beam weopens' which will
be  able  to  knock down any missile detected coming  at  us  from
russia.  even  with  the  scare  at 3 mile island, i'm pro-nuclear
power plants.  we  need  the cheap power  they  can  deliver  if
properly handled.
       +++ NO SUBMESSAGES +++


COMMAND? read nukes

*** NUKES                  10-MAY-83
    PARENT=NUCLEAR-ARMS       USAGE= 10
I KNOW ITS A SMALL SAMPLE SO FAR, BUT I FIND IT DISTURBING
THAT THE MESSAGES SO FAR SEEM GUNG-HO FOR NUCLEAR POWER.
DOES THIS INDICATE THAT COMPUTER BUFFS ARE UNCRITICALLY IN FAVOR
OF ANYTHING THAT SEEMS "HIGH TECH"?
I  WOULD  HOPE THAT BY NOW, AFTER THE ABYSMAL SAFETY  RECORD  OF
NUCLEAR POWER PLANTS,  AND THE FACT THAT IT HAS BECOME CLEAR  THAT
THEY ARE NEITHER SAFE NOR ECONOMICAL NOR RELIABLE,  THAT IT SHOULD
BE  CLEAR  TO  EVERYONE BUT  THE  MOST  DIEHARD  ELECTRICAL-UTILITY
OPERATORS THAT IT WOULD BE SHEER INSANITY TO BUILD ANY MORE PLANTS,
AND  THAT  THE  TOP  PRIORITY  SHOULD BE  FIGURING  OUT  THE  MOST
EXPEDITIOUS  WAY OF DISMANTLING THE ONES CURRENTLY  IN  OPERATION,
WITH  THE  MINIMUM  DISRUPTION  OF  THE  ECONOMY  AND  NEEDED POWER
CAPACITY.  EVEN IF THEY ARE ALL SHUT DOWN NOW,  IT WILL BE DECADES
BEFORE  WE  SOLVE THE PROBLEMS OF DISPOSING OF  THE  NUCLEAR  WASTE
THAT ALREADY EXISTS!
       +++ SUBMESSAGES +++
   SCARY-ROADS             10-MAY-83
   PROS-AND-CONS           11-MAY-83
   B-SMART                 12-MAY-83
   NUKES:SOME-FACTS        14-MAY-83
```

LISTING 10-2 (continued)

```
COMMAND? read b-smart

*** B-SMART              12-MAY-83
   PARENT=NUKES             USAGE=  6
I wish all of you brains would realize that there are two types of
NUCLEAR ENERGY.
There is both FUSION AND FISSION!!!!
One  use  radioactive materials to generate power,  the other  use
Hydrogen Isotopes.
The second type is NON-RADIOACTIVE and the waste produce is  steam
(WATER).
Additionally,  I know that our Government is suppressing alternate
energy  supplies from the public.  We have the technology and the
resources  to  start building a cleaner  tommorow, with  all  the
energy we could ask for or need. DO YOUR HOMEWORK
SIGNED ==========>     JOHN B.
       +++ SUBMESSAGES +++
   HEY-JOHN!             12-MAY-83

COMMAND? read hey-john
HEY-JOHN ? NOT FOUND
COMMAND? read hey-john!

*** HEY-JOHN!            12-MAY-83
   PARENT=B-SMART           USAGE=  5
HEY JOHN B.!
   YOU ADDED TO THIS CONVERSATION BUT DIDN'T READ ALL THE ENTRIES.
IF  YOU READ 'PROS-AND-CONS' YOU'LL SEE IT DOES INCLUDE A PART  ON
FUSSION!!!
      DO !YOUR! HOMEWORK!!!!!!!!

       +++ NO SUBMESSAGES +++
```

OTHER TIMESHARING SERVICES

In the United States, more than 4000 organizations called *service bureaus* provide a combination of computing services—both programs and raw computing power—and consultation. You may use these organizations in different ways. At one level, you work with a consultant to solve a particular computing problem, such as automating your company payroll. The consultant recommends and perhaps modifies software, establishes procedures for preparing data for input, develops tailored report formats, and in general performs all the hand-holding functions necessary to implement a system. At the other end of the spectrum, you may simply set up an account, purchase manuals, and use the system yourself by either programming or using available software such as a file management package or a large statistics package. These large programs have their own documentation.

More and more service bureaus are adding communications capabilities, and you can access many of the large ones through the communications networks. For example, Tymeshare, the parent company of TYMNET, runs a large service bureau as one of its services. Some specialize in subject areas such as energy, engineering, and health or in program areas such as accounting or graphics. Major capabilities of large service bureaus are general data processing, modeling, payroll, taxes, inventory, graphics, leasing of intelligent terminals, online access, and database management. See Appendix I for the addresses of the six largest: ADP, Boeing, GEISCO, MCAUTO, Tymshare, and Xerox. These are general bureaus in that they offer a wide variety of services mentioned. See the *Datapro Directory of On-line Services* in the DIRECTO-

RIES section of the bibliography for an extensive descriptive listing of service bureaus. Some special-purpose organizations of interest are listed below.

GMS

GMS Systems, Inc.
12 West 37th Street
New York, NY 10018
(212) 947-3590

Originally called Graphic Management Systems, GMS specialized at first in computer-produced graphics. While it has since branched out, its major products remain graphics plotting and graphics analyses (called from client databases) that are used in producing reports for management.

Edunet

Edunet
P.O. Box 364
Princeton, NJ 08540
(609) 734-1878

Edunet is an international service providing computer programs and communications services to members—more than 160 colleges, universities, and related non-profit educational and research organizations. Sixteen member organizations are online vendors of programs that are mainly oriented toward research and instruction, giving users access to a vast array of software produced at major U.S. universities such as Stanford and the Massachusetts Institute of Technology.

Edunet provides electronic mail and EIES teleconferencing services. An extensive Member's Guide gives details of suppliers' services, including directories of software. Edunet also has a hotline that handles general inquiries and consulting. The annual institutional fee varies from $450 for small colleges (less than 1,000 full-time students) and non-profit organizations (less than 100 staff) to $1,800 for large universities and organizations. Online communications are through TYMNET and TELENET, and charges depend on the particular service used.

TeleLearning Network

TeleLearning Systems, Inc.
505 Beach Street
San Francisco, CA 94133
(800) 22L-EARN (Outside California)
(800) 44L-EARN (California)

TeleLearning Systems announced the "world's first electronic university" in September 1983. The basic idea is to unite the concept of traditional correspondence courses with micro and online computer technology. While currently offerings include about 170 courses, mostly in computer literacy, plans are to cover the gamut of subjects for adults, children, and people in business. Courses are developed by college faculty and other experts. Fifteen universities were involved in the pilot programs.

Students are required to purchase the TeleLearning Knowledge Module, a package that contains a 300-baud modem, all connections, and communications software that dials, logs on, and tells you what is going on. Modules are ready for the IBM PC and for the Apple II at $229.95 and for the Commodore 64 for $129.95; versions for Atari, Radio Shack TRS-80 Model III, and possibly the Coleco Adam will follow. You will need one disk drive.

Courses are sent to students either on floppies or through online, lesson-by-lesson communications. Computer literacy instructors staff the hotlines (numbers above) each day. Students and course instructors may communicate online in a "chat" mode or through electronic mail with instructors committed to answering student questions and returning completed assignments within 24 hours. Courses cost between $35 and $200.

Chapter 11
The Future

The overriding trend in online access is easily summed up in one word: more. We can expect to see: more organizations entering the field as vendors; many more databases; much more use; more searchers, as individual users take up online in ever increasing numbers; and finally, more diversity of every kind. Just keeping up with developments is becoming a full-time activity in itself.

There is so much momentum right now that it would take a serious catastrophe outside the industry itself to slow things down. The major fuel, of course, is the microcomputer boom. Online capability is available for less than $100 over the cost of a micro, thus placing it within reach of millions of people. The potential for this technology to touch and change lives is so great, the degree to which it could pervade society so large, that the long-term future can only be considered within the context of many societal forces. This means a very cloudy long-term crystal ball.

Proper analysis of any technology within the societal context, especially a technology as important as online, could fill a dozen books. Since this work is meant to be a practical guide, not a scholarly treatise, we cannot cover these issues in any depth. It is useful and interesting, though, for those of us who are online pioneers, to consider the larger picture from time to time. For this reason, the final section of this last chapter will look at some of the political, social, and economic factors that influence online technology—*and* may be influenced by it.

VENDORS

In addition to more vendors entering the market, there is a trend toward diversification of services among existing vendor organizations. Many would like to provide "one-stop" communications and information services for their customers. Thus, Dialcom, which pioneered electronic mail, has augmented their product line with word and text processing, executive calendar scheduling, database information services, electronic publishing, and other related products. BRS, which began as a vendor of scholarly databases, has developed offline software and plans to include electronic mail, software delivery, and at-home shopping in its After Dark service. Dow Jones now offers electronic mail and is gradually adding databases unrelated to the stock market. And the new AMA/GTE service has begun providing both information and electronic mail to health professionals.

Another indication of this one-stop trend is the "pass-through" or "gateway" phenomenon. Vendors are offering their users access to the services of other vendors through their own computers and accounting systems. Mead, Delphi, and Dialcom all have pass-through service to Dialog, for example.

As a kind of tug in the opposite direction, there is more *vertical integration*—database producers are vending their own databases. Chemical Abstracts Service and the Institute for Scientific Information, both producers of large scientific databases, have become online vendors within the past two years, and INSPEC, the Institution of Electrical Engineers, recently started an online data and retrieval service.

DATABASES

As more databases come online, the most important trend is toward source databases, the kind that have all the required information rather than only references to other documents. Most legal and business databases have always been of this type—stock quotes, news articles, full case reports, and economic data are some examples—and source databases are now found frequently in other areas.

Directories, dictionaries, numeric databases, and full text of both monographs and journals are the most common types. Obviously it is more convenient to find all the information you want online, in one place. But another important advantage of these databases is that, in theory, they can always be up-to-date. Several years elapse between editions of major medical textbooks, for example, during which time the state of medical knowledge expands at an ever-increasing pace. A major advantage to a physician would be a textbook that always reflects the very latest medical thought and that is based on the latest research. Online systems can fill this need.

SIMPLIFIED SEARCH PROTOCOLS

The search process can be simplified either through easier, more "user-friendly" languages supplied by vendors or through transparent search aids such as some of the equipment and software described in Chapter 9. To date, in commercial systems, simplification has tended to mean menu-driven protocols, while command-driven systems are at the other end of the spectrum—not "user-hostile" but definitely requiring more training and practice before use. There are also combination protocols, which are partly menu-driven and partly command-driven, and many variations. Whether a radically different approach will be found as a result of all the research in this area remains to be seen.

What is clear is that, though easier for inexperienced persons, menu-driven languages are slow and more costly when used by experienced searchers because they require more online time. Probably, more services will develop several levels of protocols to accommodate this range of users; The Source and CompuServe, for example, are searchable in either menu-driven or command-driven modes.

Also contributing to command-language simplification are the language translators that allow you to search several vendors with one language, e.g., the Common Command Language on several of the European hosts and Sci-Mate, which can be used in menu-driven mode to search several major vendors.

Research continues as well on techniques for helping with search-strategy problems, particularly with the selection of search terms. Developments in this area include the automatic matching of keywords to lists of synonyms by CSIN and the preformulated strategies planned for the Orbit SearchMaster.

EXTENDED USE

Extended use refers to further utilization of downloaded information for creation of a private database or for performing analyses. Until microcomputers and word processors with offline storage devices became common, downloading was not possible for most searchers. Now we see the development of software, such as Sci-Mate and the Dow Jones Market Analyzer, to be used with the downloaded data. Many more packages of this type are certain to appear. Users and information providers will need to work out copyright questions in a manner that will be fair and convenient for all.

INTEGRATION OF TECHNOLOGIES

The future of online services is inevitably linked with that of related technologies.

Electronic Mail

Electronic mail competes in many situations with TWX, TELEX, facsimile, and courier delivery as well as the U.S. mail. Some electronic mail providers are actually taking advantage of these other services by tying into them directly. For example, you can utilize the TELEX system through Dialcom.

Videotex

In the consumer information area, *teletext* and *videotex* offer information products strikingly similar to those of the information utilities. In fact, the utilities are themselves sometimes called videotex services. In the most general sense, *videotex* refers to frame-by-frame, or page-by-page, delivery of information. In a stricter sense, *videotex* is terminology approved by the International Telephone and Telegraph Consultative Committee for the process of receiving information that is either sent over the airways or transmitted through a communications link (e.g., telephone or cable) to a television set modified to receive it. Sometimes videotex is used interchangeably with *viewdata*, which is interactive, two-way videotex stored in a computer system. *Teletext* is the simpler, broadcast version of videotex. It takes advantage of a limited portion of a television channel for one-way transmission of information. Basic videotex services are news, weather, banking, shopping, finance, and entertainment such as movie reviews, but subscribers to the British Prestel service may now access over 200,000 pages of information from 130 different database providers.

Videotex has several thousand subscribers in Europe, but it is not yet a commercial success. The cost of equipment is high, although according to projections it could drop to about $100 with mass production. While it is not generally available in the United States, there are indications that this technology is about to explode. AT&T and Knight-Ridder are developing advanced systems, and a Knight-Ridder subsidiary, Viewdata Corporation of America, Inc., is beginning full-fledged commercial service in the Miami area. Charges in Miami are about $15 per month after an initial outlay of approximately $600 for a terminal.

At the same time, both NBC and CBS are planning to broadcast teletext free of charge, and Time, Inc. is about to deliver teletext through cable at a cost of about $10 to $15 per month. The nationwide CBS system, Extravision, will require decoders at a cost of about $125 each. Extravision will start with about 100 pages covering weather, the stock market, airline schedules, and movie and theater listings. CBS is also considering videotex.

Microcomputer equipment and software to tie into videotex are now expensive, but equipment currently in the prototype stage will likely bring down the costs of combined television/computer terminals. How consumers ultimately use videotex and online information services together, and in relation to other information and entertainment media such as television, cable, radio, and magazines, is an open question.

Videodisk

In scholarly and business database publishing, some analysts are already predicting that online is a transitional technology! This is due to the tremendous storage capacity of low-cost *videodisks*. *Videodisks* are a durable storage medium that can be searched. The Pergamon Video Patsearch described in Chapter 9 is an example of a combined microcomputer-online-videodisk system. LaserData, Inc. of Woburn, Massachusetts recently announced a microcomputer-based disk system that stores *and searches one million pages* of text on one $79.95 disk. Very large local retrieval systems are thus a real possibility. Whether publishers or users will prefer this to online is debatable; much depends on the economic arrangements.

FEE STRUCTURES

Unlike many other computer technologies, online has not seen a trend toward lower costs; nor are costs likely to be lowered in the near future. One reason is that the volume of online use has not yet been great enough to make vending of online services a very profitable business. A more important reason is that the creation of most online databases is still a labor-intensive activity for which costs will continue to increase. As users switch from purchase of printed products derived from databases to online use, it is necessary for producers to recover a greater share of their database creation costs from royalties for online use, thus keeping charges up.

What is changing in the cost picture is the nature of charges. There is a trend toward charging for actual received information in addition to connect time. Thus, many online producers and vendors now have fees for online "hits," and electronic mail services are charging for characters transmitted in and out in addition to connect time.

SOCIETAL FACTORS

Technological pessimists usually describe one of three scenarios. Most common is the picture of the individual *isolated* in his or her home with only a computer for company. Then, there is the specter of Big Brother, whose databank knows everything about everyone and who can use this information to control us; at the very least, these pessimists say, Big Brother's databank is a violation of our right to privacy. Finally, concern revolves around the relationship between information and power: because online access is expensive, they say, the rich will become richer (more powerful), and the poor, even less powerful.

You can probably empathize with all these arguments while recognizing other sides. Many people view the possibility of working at home—*telecommuting* or *teleworking*—as highly desirable. People unable to enter the work force (e.g., mothers of young children and people with certain handicaps) would be able to find meaningful work. Bedridden children could "attend" classes. Others would simply prefer the freedom and flexibility of staying at home, conserving energy, avoiding rush-hour traffic, saving travel time, and not having to wear a business suit. Some feel that productivity would increase.

In defense of Big Brother, collecting information in large databanks permits quick credit checks, enables the police to locate criminals, and makes available a great deal of demographic data. As for the question of power and information—through online services, more people have access to more information than ever before in history. That has value.

Online services can save time by making certain professional and personal tasks more efficient. Even more, they allow us to seek information that we would not have considered trying to find previously.

Certain people—librarians, postal workers, newspaper employees, and authors, for example—may see their jobs change radically. These are some obvious changes, but there will be other impacts that we cannot foresee and that will be influenced by factors outside the online technology. These include changes in copyright and communications legislation, tax regulations regarding deductions for using home space for business, public attitudes, competing technologies, pollution, demographics, energy availability, and so forth. The list is limitless—as is the potential for online communications to transform our lives.

Glossary

ABBS   *See* Computer Bulletin Board System.
ACCESS POINT   *See* FIELD.
ADJACENCY SEARCHING   Searching for terms that are next to each other in a field.
ACOUSTIC COUPLER   A type of modem containing two rubber cups into which the telephone handset is placed to make the connection between the computer or terminal and the telephone lines.
ANALOG SIGNAL   A continuous signal that varies in proportion to the strength of the signal input; used by the telephone system.
ANSWER MODE   State in which a device is ready to receive transmission from a computer in ORIGINATE MODE.
ANSWER-PROVIDING DATABASES   *See* SOURCE DATABASES.
ASCII   A popular code used for computer transmission; stands for American Standard Code for Information Interchange.
ASYNCHRONOUS TRANSMISSION   Data transmission in which time intervals between the data sent are not equal, the usual situation in interactive online communications; compare to SYNCHRONOUS TRANSMISSION.
AUTO-DIALING   *See* DIRECT DIALING.
BASIC INDEX   The subject index on Dialog that can be searched without qualifiers; usually the basic index consists of title words, abstract words, descriptors, and identifiers.
BAUD   Number of bits of data transmitted per second; approximately 10 times the number of characters transmitted per second.
BIBLIOGRAPHIC DATABASES   Databases containing references to publications.
BIT   The smallest unit of information in the binary system of notation used by computers; bits have values of either 1 or 0.
BOOLEAN OPERATORS   Logical operators used to combine sets; in online searching, the most frequent operators are AND, OR, and NOT.
BUFFER   A computer storage area, typically between input and output devices, where data is stored temporarily to make up for differences in flow speed.
CATHODE RAY TUBE   An electronic display device.
CBBS   *See* Computer Bulletin Board System.
CHEMICAL STRUCTURE SEARCH   Search for information about a chemical substance on the basis of its structure.
CHEMICAL SUBSTRUCTURE SEARCH   A search for information on chemical compounds that satisfy certain structural criteria.

CITATION SEARCH   A search for documents citing a specific document or author.
CITED AUTHOR SEARCH   A search for documents citing a particular author.
COMMAND-DRIVEN SYSTEM   A type of system, operation of which is initiated by a user giving commands; contrast to MENU-DRIVEN SYSTEM.
COMMANDS   Instructions given by users to computer networks and services.
COMMON COMMAND LANGUAGE   A standardized command language that can be used for searching many of the European vendors.
COMMUNICATING WORD PROCESSORS   Word processors that can be used to interact with computers.
COMMUNICATIONS INTERFACE   In microcomputer communications, the hardware link between the computer and modem; more generally, all the software and hardware linking computers.
COMMUNICATIONS SOFTWARE   Programs that allow a computer to communicate with other computers.
COMPUTER-ASSISTED INSTRUCTION   A tutorial in which the student responds to questions from the online program. The program "branches" according to student responses.
COMPUTER BULLETIN BOARD SYSTEM   Small online system usually run by an individual or local group to provide a means for exchanging information and public-domain software; called CBBS, RBBS, (Remote Bulletin Board System), RCPM (Remote CP/M), ABBS (Apple Bulletin Board System), and other names.
COMPUTER CONFERENCING   Ongoing online discussion that permits participants to exchange information and ideas; conferences have been compared to panels, forums, debates, and round tables.
COMPUTER MESSAGING   Any type of message transfer by computer; includes electronic mail, online discussions, computer conferencing, and electronic bulletin boards.
CONCEPTS (SEARCH)   Separate ideas implied by a search topic.
CONNECT TIME   Length of time a user is in communication with an online system.
CONTROLLED VOCABULARY   Online indexing terms that are selected from an authorized list, such as a thesaurus; contrast to FREE TEXT.
COVERAGE (database)   The extent or scope of a database according to characteristics of included items, such as date and type.
CRASH   System failure that interrupts or prevents service.
CRT   See CATHODE RAY TUBE.
CUSTOMER SERVICE NUMBERS   See HOTLINES.
DATABASE   A collection of records in computer-readable form.
DATABASE MANAGEMENT SYSTEM   A computer-based system for formatting, inputting, storing, retrieving, modifying, and outputting information.
DATABASE PRODUCERS   Publishers of computer-readable databases.
DEFAULT   The value at which a variable is set unless specifically instructed otherwise.
DESCRIPTORS   Index terms; usually descriptors are selected from a controlled vocabulary.
DICTIONARY DATABASES   Databases containing synonyms, most commonly for chemical substances.
DIGITAL SIGNAL   A series of electrical impulses that transmit information in computer circuits.

DIRECT-CONNECT MODEM   Modem which is connected directly to the telephone outlet, bypassing the telephone.

DIRECT DIALING   Dialing from a computer keyboard instead of from a telephone.

DIRECTORY DATABASE   Databases containing the type of information found in printed directories.

DISK   *See* MAGNETIC DISK.

DOWNLOADING   Capturing data transmitted from a remote computer on the storage medium of a terminal; contrast to UPLOADING.

DUMB TERMINAL   A terminal the only function of which is to communicate with a computer; a dumb terminal is not capable of processing information.

ELECTRONIC BULLETIN BOARDS   Online services for posting messages to be read by anyone with access to the system.

ELECTRONIC MAIL   Sending of message(s) through a computer communications network to specified recipient(s).

ELECTRONIC MESSAGING   *See* COMPUTER MESSAGING.

ELECTRONIC NOTEBOOKS   Personal online files for gathering thoughts and organizing materials.

END USERS   People wanting information for their own use.

EXTENDED USE   Utilization of downloaded information, usually to create a private database, to do further searching, or to perform analyses.

FIELD   Searchable element in a record; examples are author field or subject-term field.

FILE   *See* DATABASE.

FREE TEXT   Words in title or abstract that may be searched using online systems; contrast to CONTROLLED VOCABULARY terms, which are selected from an authorized word list such as a thesaurus.

FULL DUPLEX   A transmission mode in which data can be sent and received simultaneously; contrast to HALF DUPLEX.

FULL TEXT   The complete document, as opposed to a representation, such as a reference to the document.

FUNCTION KEYS   Keys on a keyboard that, when struck, instruct the computer to perform a task, such as printing a reference.

GATEWAY SERVICE   Service by which a user gains access to one online vendor through the computer of another vendor.

HALF DUPLEX   Transmission in only one direction at a time; contrast to FULL DUPLEX.

HITS   *See* POSTINGS.

HOSTS   Term most commonly used in Europe for VENDORS.

HOTLINES   Telephone services staffed by consultants who answer users' questions.

IDENTIFIERS   Index terms, assigned to documents, that are not selected from the database vocabulary, e. g., from a thesaurus.

INFORMATION RETRIEVAL   In computer technology, searching computer databases for information.

INFORMATION UTILITY   A vendor that provides a wide range of business and home-use information services, electronic mail, and other online computing capabilities.

IMPACT PRINTER   A type of printer in which printing consists of hammering paper through a ribbon.

INTELLIGENT TERMINAL A terminal that performs local data processing functions such as word processing.

INTERMEDIARIES Librarians and other information professionals who search for information on behalf of others.

LANGUAGE TRANSLATOR Program for converting one or more command languages to a different language.

LINE NOISE Extraneous interference with data transmission; usually, line noise consists of strings of characters not typed by the user or transmitted by the computer system.

LOGGING OFF The process of disconnecting from a remote computer.

LOGGING ON The process of connecting to a remote computer.

LOGICAL OPERATORS See BOOLEAN OPERATORS.

MAGNETIC DISK A random-access storage medium for computer-readable data.

MAGNETIC TAPE A serial storage medium for computer-readable data.

MENU-DRIVEN SYSTEM Online system that asks the user questions, provides a "menu" of allowable responses, and explains how to select one; contrast to COMMAND-DRIVEN SYSTEM.

MESSAGING See COMPUTER MESSAGING.

MODEM An abbreviation for MOdulation-DEModulation; modems are devices for connecting computers or terminals to the telephone network. They translate digital signals from the computer to sound for transmission over telephone lines (modulation) and convert incoming sound to digital signals (demodulation).

NESTING A logical search technique in which one logical combination is contained within another; for example, "*insecticide* AND (*apples* OR *oranges*)" is a nested statement.

NETWORK NODE An access point to a telecommunications network.

NODE See NETWORK NODE.

NUMERIC DATABASES Databases containing numeric data.

OFFLINE Refers to computer processing performed without direct interaction between user and computer.

OFFLOADING See DOWNLOADING.

ONLINE Refers to computer access in which user interacts directly with computer.

ONLINE DISCUSSIONS Direct, interactive conversations between online users, either one-to-one or in a group.

ORIGINATE MODE Status of a microcomputer or other communications device when initiating transmission; mode used to communicate with most remote computers; alternately, the state for receiving data from a computer in ANSWER MODE.

PARALLEL DATA Data transmitted more than one bit at a time; contrast to SERIAL DATA.

PARITY BIT In ASCII code, the eighth bit, sometimes used to check for transmission errors. This bit is set to 0 or 1 and is added to the others so that the sum is either always even (even parity) or always odd (odd parity).

PASS-THROUGH SERVICE See GATEWAY SERVICE.

PASSWORD A unique identification code assigned by online systems to each user; billing is done on the basis of passwords.

PHOTOCOMPOSITION Creation of type images on a photographic medium for printing.

PORT   A channel for entrance to or exit from a timesharing computer.
POSTINGS   The number of items retrieved in a search.
PRESTEL   The British interactive videotex service.
PRIVATE FILE   A database searched by a restricted group of users.
PROTOCOLS   Conventions determining the format for exchange of messages in communications. *See also* COMMANDS.
PROXIMITY SEARCHING   A search for terms that are a specified distance from each other, usually in a title or abstract.
PUBLICLY-ACCESSIBLE SYSTEMS   Systems that can be accessed by people not associated with the proprietary organization.
RANDOM-ACCESS STORAGE DEVICE   Computer storage device that allows data to be read directly, no matter where it is located physically on the storage medium; random access usually implies that the time to access any location is the same. Compare to SERIAL ACCESS.
RBBS   *See* Computer Bulletin Board System.
RCPM   *See* Computer Bulletin Board System.
RECORD   A unit of related information; for example, in a bibliographic database, all information about one document (author, title, date, et cetera) is one record.
REFERENCE DATABASES   Databases that serve primarily as pointers to original sources of information; BIBLIOGRAPHIC DATABASES are one type.
REFERENCE VENDORS   Vendors primarily in the business of providing information to the academic and business communities.
REFERRAL DATABASES   Databases that contain descriptions of an information source other than a document; common types contain directory information or description of research projects.
REGISTRY NUMBER   A unique identification number assigned by Chemical Abstracts Service to chemical substances discussed in its publications.
REMOTE COMPUTER   Computer at a physical location different from that of the person using it.
RESEARCH FRONT SPECIALTY   An area of intense research identified through analysis of citation patterns; used primarily as a search concept for the ISI search system.
RESPONSE TIME   Time between the submission of a piece of information to a remote computer and the return of results.
SDI   *See* SELECTIVE DISSEMINATION OF INFORMATION.
SEARCH AIDS   *See* USER AIDS.
SEARCH STRATEGY   Plan for grouping and combining terms in a computer search.
SEGMENTED DATABASES   Databases divided into parts (usually by date) that must be searched separately; most often, only very large databases are segmented.
SELECTIVE DISSEMINATION OF INFORMATION (SDI)   A search of updates to databases for the purpose of current awareness.
SERIAL ACCESS   Sequential access to data.
SERIAL DATA   Data transmitted one bit at a time; contrast to PARALLEL DATA.
SERVICE BUREAUS   Organizations providing computing power, programs, and consultation.
SET   Records retrieved in response to a search statement.
SMART TERMINAL   A terminal that can perform some data processing functions locally but fewer than an INTELLIGENT TERMINAL.

SOURCE DATABASES   Databases containing all the information sought; examples are directories or full-text databases. Contrast to BIBLIOGRAPHIC DATABASES, which contain references to publications that contain the information ultimately sought.
STRUCTURE SEARCH   *See* CHEMICAL STRUCTURE SEARCH.
SUBJECT-SPECIFIC VENDORS   Vendors with databases in one subject area such as science or law.
SUBSTRUCTURE SEARCH   *See* CHEMICAL SUBSTRUCTURE SEARCH.
SUPERMARKET VENDORS   Vendors that provide databases in a broad range of subject areas.
SYCHRONOUS TRANSMISSION   Steady-stream data transmission in which time intervals between sent data are equal; compare to ASYNCHRONOUS TRANSMISSION.
SYSOP   SYStem OPerator; person responsible for managing a computer bulletin board system.
TAPE   *See* MAGNETIC TAPE.
TELECOMMUNICATIONS NETWORK   Networks for the transmission of electromagnetic signals; refers here primarily to large international networks for data transmission; examples are TYMNET and TELENET.
TELECOMMUTING   Working at home using online services to communicate with the workplace.
TELETEXT   Simple, broadcast version of videotex that takes advantage of a limited portion of a television channel for one-way transmission of information.
TELEWORKING   *See* TELECOMMUTING.
TERMINAL IDENTIFIER   Code letter, number, or combination used to let online networks know the type of terminal being used.
TERMINAL PROGRAM   *See* COMMUNICATIONS SOFTWARE.
TERMINALS   Devices for communicating with a computer; terminals have keyboards similar to those of typewriters and either printers or video displays or both; *see also* SMART TERMINAL and INTELLIGENT TERMINAL.
THESAURUS   An organized list of approved terms used to index a database; only terms in the thesaurus will appear in certain index fields.
THERMAL PRINTER   A printer that forms characters by imprinting a small matrix of dots on heat-sensitive paper.
TIME SERIES   Data, concerning one measurement, that is presented over a period of time; the cost of living index from 1960 to 1983 is an example of a time series.
TIMESHARING COMPUTERS   Large computers that can be accessed by many people at one time.
TRANSPARENT USER AIDS   Computer hardware and software that assist the search process without the searcher needing to understand how they function.
TRUNCATION   Specification of a word stem in which the characters can vary after a certain point; used in online retrieval to search for terms with variant endings; TEACH$ would locate TEACHING, TEACHER, TEACHES, et cetera.
UNCONTROLLED VOCABULARY   Subject terms, such as title words, that are not selected from a thesaurus or other authorized term list.
UPLOADING   Sending data from a storage device in a local computer to another computer; contrast with DOWNLOADING.

GLOSSARY

USER-FRIENDLY SYSTEMS Systems that are easy to use, particularly for people who are unfamiliar with them.

USER AIDS Computer hardware or software or printed materials (such as manuals) that assist in the search process.

VENDORS Organizations that make remote databases and other computer services available for online access.

VENN DIAGRAMS Drawings of overlapping circles that illustrate the Boolean operations.

VERTICAL INTEGRATION Situation in which database producers act as vendors for their databases.

VIDEODISK A durable, plastic storage device for recorded visual and sound information; a videodisk can store large amounts of digital information in a form suitable for searching.

VIDEOTEX Systems that output information frame-by-frame or page-by-page; or, strictly, terminology approved by the International Telephone and Telegraph Consultative Committee for the process of receiving information that is either sent over the airways or transmitted through a communications link (e.g., telephone or cable) to a television set modified to receive it.

VIEWDATA Interactive, two-way videotex stored in a computer system.

Bibliography

BIBLIOGRAPHIES

Hall, J.L., and Dewe, A. *Online Information Retrieval, 1976–1979: An International Bibliography.* London: Aslib, 1980.

Hawkins, Donald T. *Online Information Retrieval Bibliography 1964–1979.* Medford, NJ: Learned Information, Inc., 1980. (A cumulation of bibliographies appearing in the March issues of *Online Review*, 1977–1979.) Updated in *Online Review* in March 1980 (3d update), April 1981 (4th update), April 1982 (5th update), and April 1983 (6th update).

Pugh, W. Jean, and John, Stephanie C. "A Bibliography of Database and Search System Comparisons." *Online* 6:5 (September 1982) 41–55.

Tenopir, Carol. "DATABASES: Catching Up and Keeping Up." *Library Journal* 108:3 (February 1, 1983) 180–2.

DICTIONARIES

Burton, Philip E. *A Dictionary of Minicomputing and Microcomputing.* New York: Garland Publishing, 1981.

Byerly, Greg. *Online Searching: A Dictionary and Bibliographic Guide.* Littleton Co: Libraries Unlimited, 1983.

Galland, Frank J., ed. *Dictionary of Computing.* Somerset, NJ: John Wiley & Sons, Inc., 1982.

Graham, John. *The Facts On File Dictionary of Telecommunications.* New York: Facts on File, Inc., 1983.

Meadows, A.J., Gordon, M., and Singleton, A. *The Random House Dictionary of New Information Technology.* New York: Vintage Books, 1982.

DIRECTORIES

Services and Databases

Benjamin, William A., ed. *Directory of Industry Data Sources: The United States of America and Canada.* 2d ed., 3 vols. Cambridge, MA: Ballinger Publishing Co., 1982.

Champany, Barry W., and Hotz, Sharon Modrik, eds. *Document Retrieval: Sources and Services*, 2d ed. San Francisco, CA: The Information Store, 1982.

Cuadra, Ruth N, Abels, David M., and Wanger, Judith. *Directory of Online Databases*. Santa Monica, CA: Cuadra Associates, Inc. (Quarterly, or semi-annual, with quarterly updates.)

"Databases Online." *Online Review* 6:4 (August 1982) 353–90.

Data Base User Service. White Plains, NY: Knowledge Industry Publications, Inc. (updated monthly; online version).

Datapro Directory of On-Line Services. Delran, NJ: Datapro Research Corporation. (Updated monthly).

Directory of Computerized Data Files, 1982 Edition. Springfield, VA: National Technical Information Service, 1982.

Directory of Fee-Based Information Services, 1982. Chicago, IL: Information Alternative, 1982.

Directory of Online Information Resources. Kensington, MD: CSG Press, 1982.

Eusidic Database Guide, 1983. Oxford, England: Learned Information, Ltd., 1982.

Hall, James L., and Brown, Marjorie J. *Online Bibliographic Databases*. London: Aslib, 1983. (Distributed in U.S. and Canada by Gale Research Company, Detroit, MI.)

Information Industry Association. *Information Sources 1983–84: The Membership Directory of the Information Industry Association*. Washington, DC: Information Industry Association, 1983.

Information Industry Marketplace 1983, An International Directory of Information Products and Services. New York: R.R. Bowker Co., 1982. (Published outside North and South America as *Information Trade Directory* by Learned Information Ltd., Oxford, England.)

Online Search Services in UK. London: Aslib, 1982.

Schmittroth, John Jr., ed. *Encyclopedia of Information, Systems and Services*. 5th ed. Detroit, MI: Gale Research Co., 1982.

Schmittroth, John Jr., ed. *Telecommunications Systems and Services Directory*. 1st ed. Detroit, MI: Gale Research Co., 1983.

Sessions, Vivian S. *Directory of Databases in the Social and Behavioral Sciences*. New York: Science Associates/International, 1974.

Williams, Martha E., Lannom, Laurence, and Robins, Carolyn G. *Computer Readable Data Bases: a Directory and Data Sourcebook*. White Plains, NY: Knowledge Industry Publications, Inc., 1982.

Warnken, Kelly. *The Information Brokers*. New York: R.R. Bowker Co., 1981.

Equipment

All About Alphanumeric Display Terminals. Delran, NJ: Datapro Research Corporation, 1982.

All About Keyboard/Printer Terminals. Delran, NJ: Datapro Research Corporation, 1982.

All About Modems. Delran, NJ: Datapro Research Corporation, 1982.

Auerbach Computer Technology Reports: Computer Terminals. Philadelphia: Auerbach Publishers. (Monthly reports with quarterly indexes.)

Computer Equipment Review. Westport, CT: Meckler Publishing. (Publishing semi-annually.)

Datapro Directory of Small Computers. Delran, NJ: Datapro Research Corporation. (Update regularly.)

1982-83 Online Terminal/Microcomputer Guide and Directory. 3d ed. Weston, CT: Online, Inc., 1981.

Software

Datapro Directory of Microcomputer Software. Delran, NJ: Datapro Research Corporation. (Updated regularly.)

Online Micro-Software Guide and Directory, 1983-84. Weston, CT: Online, Inc., 1982.

PC Clearinghouse. *Software Directory,* 7th ed. Fairfax, VA: PC Clearinghouse, Inc., 1983.

The Software Catalog, Microcomputers. New York: Elsevier Science Publishing Co., 1983.

MONOGRAPHS

Artwick, Bruce. *Microcomputer Interfacing.* Englewood Cliffs, NJ: Prentice-Hall, Inc., 1980.

Carroll, John M. *Confidential Information Sources: Public and Private.* Woburn, MA: Butterworth Publishers, 1975.

Carroll, John M. *Computer Security.* Woburn, MA: Butterworth Publishers, 1977.

Chen, Ching-Chih, and Schweizer, Susanna. *Online Bibliographic Searching: A Learning Manual.* New York: Neal Schuman Publishers, Inc., 1981.

Computer Technologies and Consumer Information: Interactive Videotex Systems. Lanham, MD: Bernan Associates, 1982

Deasington, R.J. *A Practical Guide to Computer Communications and Networking.* New York: Halsted Press, 1982.

Defler, Frank J. *Microcomputer Data Communications Systems.* Englewood Cliffs, NJ: Prentice-Hall, 1982.

Defler, Frank, Jr. *TRS-80 Data Communications Systems.* Englewood Cliffs, NJ: Prentice-Hall, 1982.

Fenichel, Carol H., and Hogan, Thomas H. *Online Searching: A Primer.* Marlton, NJ: Learned Information, Inc., 1981.

Freeman, Roger. *TeleCommunication Transmission Handbook,* 2d ed. Somerset, NJ: John Wiley & Sons, Inc., 1981.

Glossbrenner, Alfred. *The Complete Handbook of Personal Computer Communications: Everything You Need to Go Online with the World.* New York: St. Martin's Press, 1983.

Harrison, Michael. *Electronic Banking: The Revolution in Financial Services.* White Plains, NY: Knowledge Industry Publications, Inc., 1983.

Hartner, Elizabeth P. *An Introduction to Automated Literature Searching.* New York: Marcel Dekker, 1981.

Henry, W.M., et al. *Online Searching: An Introduction.* London: Butterworth and Co., Ltd., 1980.

Hiltz, Starr Roxanne. *Online Communities.* Norwood, NJ: Ablex Publishing Corp., 1983.

Hoover, Ryan E., ed. *Online Search Strategies*. White Plains, NY: Knowledge Industry Publications, Inc., 1982.

Johnson, Steve. *Information and Communications Technology for the Community*. 2d ed. Portland, OR: Center for Urban Education, 1982.

Katz, Bill, and Fraley, Ruth A., eds. *Video to Online: Reference Services and the New Technology*. New York: The Haworth Press, 1983.

Lancaster, F.W., and Fayen, E.G. *Information Retrieval On-Line*. Los Angeles, CA: Melville Publishing Company, 1973.

Lipnack, Jessica, and Stamps, Jeffery. *Networking: First Report and Directory*. Garden City, NY: Doubleday & Co., Inc., 1982.

Martin, James. *The Wired Society*. Englewood Cliffs, NJ: Prentice-Hall, 1978.

Meadow, Charles, and Cochrane, Pauline. *Basics of Online Searching*. New York: John Wiley & Sons, Inc., 1981.

Nichols, Elizabeth, Nichols, Joseph C., and Musson, Keith B. *Data Communication for Microcomputers*. New York: McGraw-Hill, 1982.

Online Information. Proceedings of the 4th National Online Meeting. (A collection of papers given at the 4th National Online Meeting in New York, April 12–14, 1983). Complied by Martha E. Williams and Thomas Hogan. Medford, NJ: Learned Information, Inc., 1983.

Palmer, Roger C. *Online Reference and Information Retrieval*. Littleton, CO: Libraries Unlimited, Inc., 1983.

Shapiro, Neil L. *The Small Computer Connection*. New York: Micro Text-McGraw-Hill, 1982.

Strauss, Lawrence. *Electronic Marketing: Emerging TV and Computer Channels for Interactive Home Shopping*. White Plains, NY: Knowlege Industry Publications, Inc., 1983.

Vallee, Jacque. *The Network Revolution: Confessions of a Computer Scientist*. Berkeley, CA: AND/OR Press, Inc., 1982

JOURNALS AND NEWSLETTERS

Base & User
Information Marketing Group
Ziff-Davis Database Publishing
One Park Avenue
New York, NY 10016

Byte
McGraw-Hill, Inc.
70 Main Street
Peterborough, NH 03458

Compute
Small Systems Services, Inc.
P.O. Box 5406
Greensboro, NC 27403

Computer Equipment Review
Meckler Publishing
520 Riverside Avenue
Westport, CT 06880

Computers and Electronics
Ziff-Davis Publishing Co.
One Park Avenue
New York, NY 10016

ComputerWorld: The Newsweekly for the Computer Community
376 Cochituate Road
Box 897
Framingham, MA 01701

Creative Computing
Ahl Computing, Inc.
P.O. Box 789-M
Morristown, NJ 07960

Database: The Magazine of Database Reference and Review
Online, Inc.
11 Tannery Lane
Weston, CT 06883

Database Alert
Knowledge Industry Publications, Inc.
701 Westchester Avenue
White Plains, NY 10604

Database Update
Database Update
10076 Boca Entrada Boulevard
Boca Raton, FL 33433

DataCast
Wireless Digital Inc.
345 Swett Road
Woodside, CA 94062

Dial-Out
Dial-Out
175 Fifth Avenue
New York, NY 10010

Electronic Publishing Review
Learned Information Ltd.
Besselsleigh Road
Abingdon, Oxford, OX13 6LG
England

IDP Report (Information and DataBase Publishing Report)
Knowledge Industry Publications, Inc.
701 Westchester Avenue
White Plains, NY 10604

Information Technology: Research and Development
Butterworth Scientific Ltd., Journals Division
Box 63, Westbury House, Bury Street
Guildford, Surrey GU2 5BH
England

Infotecture Europe
Infotecture Europe
11 rue du Marché Saint Honoré
75001 Paris
France

Interface Age
McPheters, Wolfe and Jones
16704 Marquardt Avenue
Cerritos, CA 90701

Link Up: Communications and the Small Computer
On-line Communications, Inc.
6531 Cambridge Street
Minneapolis, MN 55426

Micro Communications
Miller Freeman Publications
500 Howard Street
San Francisco, CA 94105

Modem notes
P.O. Box 408472
Chicago, IL 60640

Monitor
Learned Information Ltd.
Besselsleigh Road
Abingdon, Oxford OX13 6LG
England

Networks: An International Journal
John Wiley & Sons, Inc.
605 Third Avenue
New York, NY 10016

Nibble: the Reference for Apple Computing
Nibble Micro-SPARK
P.O. Box 325
Lincoln, MA 01773

Online: The Magazine of Online Information Systems
Online, Inc.
11 Tannery Lane
Weston, CT 06883

The On-line Computer Telephone Directory
P.O. Box 10005
Kansas City, MO 64111

Online Database Report
Link Resources
215 Park Avenue South
New York, NY 10003

Online Newsletter
Information Intelligence Inc.
P.O. Box 31098
Phoenix, AZ 85046

Online Review: The International Journal of Online Systems
Learned Information, Inc.
143 Old Marlton Pike
Medford, NJ 08055

Other Networks: A Newsletter About Networks of People
P.O. Box 14066
Philadelphia, PA 19123

PC
PC Communications Corporation
One Park Avenue
New York, NY 10016

Personal Computing
Hayden Publishing Co., Inc.
10 Mulholland Drive
Hasbrouck Heights, NJ 07604

Popular Computing
McGraw Hill, Inc.
70 Main Street
Peterborough, NY 03458

Software Review
Meckler Publishing
520 Riverside Avenue
Westport, CT 06880

Today: The Videotex Computer Magazine
P.O. Box 639
Columbus, OH 43216

Videodisc/Videotex
Microform Review, Inc.
520 Riverside Avenue
Westport, CT 06880

VideoPrint: A Twice Monthly Newsletter Covering Technology, User, Product and Legislative Trends in Home Information Systems, Videotex and Teletext Systems and Services
International Resource Development, Inc.
30 High Street
Norwalk, CT 06851

ONLINE NEWSLETTERS

Online Chronicle
Dialog Information Services, Inc.
3460 Hillview Avenue
Palo Alto, CA 94304

Online Hotline
Information Intelligence Inc.
P.O. Box 31098
Phoenix, AZ 85046

FOR FURTHER READING

Chapter 1: Introduction

Ballardo, Trudi. "Scientific Research in Online Retrieval: A Critical Review." *Library Research* 3 (Fall 1981) 187–214.

Blyskal, Jeff. "Technology for Technology's Sake." *Forbes* 131:10 (May 9, 1983) 199–204.

Bourne, Charles P. "Online Systems: History, Technology and Economics." *Journal of the American Society for Information Science* 31:3 (May, 1980) 155–60.

Kiechel, W. "Everything You Always Wanted to Know May Soon Be On-Line." *Fortune* 10:9 (May 1980) 225–40.

McCarn, Davis B. "Online Systems—Techniques and Services." *Annual Review of Information Science and Technology.* Vol. 13. Ed. by Martha E. Williams. White Plains, NY: Knowledge Industry Publications, Inc., 1978, 85–124.

Roberts, S.K. "Online Information Retrieval: Promise and Problems." *Byte* 6:12 (December 1981) 452–61.

Chapter 2: Information Available Online

Bonnelly, Claude, and Drolet, Gaetan. "Searching the Social Sciences Literature Online: SOCIAL SCISEARCH." *Database* 1:4 (December 1978) 10–25.

Luedke, James A., Kovacs, Gabor J., and Fried, John B. "Numeric Data Bases and Systems." *Annual Review of Information Science and Technology.* Ed. by Martha E. Williams. White Plains: Knowledge Industry Publications, Inc., 1977, 119–82.

Plosker, George R., and Summit, Roger K. "Management of Vendor Services: How to Choose an Online Vendor." *Special Libraries* 71:8 (August 1980) 354–7.

Raben, Joseph, and Marks, Gregory, eds. *Databases in the Humanities and Social Sciences: Proceedings of the IFIPS Working Conference on Databases in the Humanities and Social Sciences.* Dartmouth College, August 23–25, 1979. New York: North Holland Publishing Co., 1979.

Williams, Martha E. "Criteria for Evaluation and Selection of Databases and Database Services." *Special Libraries* 66:12 (December 1975) 561–69.

Chapter 3: The Search Process

Bourne, Charles P. *Dialog Lab Workbook: Training Exercises for the Lockheed Dialog Information Retrieval Service.* 3d ed. Palo Alto, CA: Lockheed Corporation, January 1981.

Calkins, Mary. "Free Text or Controlled Vocabulary? A Case History Step-by-Step Analysis . . . Plus Other Aspects of Search Strategy." *Database* 3:2 (June 1980) 53–67.

Conger, Lucinda D. "A Comparison of Basic Index Fields in Multiple System Searching." *Online* 4:3 (July 1980) 25–30.

Conger, Lucinda D. "Multiple System Searching: A Searcher's Guide to Making Use of the Real Differences Between Systems." *Online* 4:2 (April 1980) 10–21.

Fenichel, Carol H. "Process of Searching Online Bibliographic Databases: A Review of Research." *Library Research* 2:2 (Summer 1980) 107–27.

Hawkins, Donald T., and Brown, Carolyn P. "What Is an Online Search?" *Online* 4:1 (January 1980) 12–18.

Knapp, Sara. *ERIC Training Workbook.* Scotia, NY: Bibliographic Retrieval Services Inc., 1981.

Marshall, Doris B. "To Improve Searching, Check Search Results." *Online* 4:3 (July 1980) 32–47.

Print Samples. Weston, CT: Online, Inc. (Six issues in different subject areas.)

Quick*Search Cross-System Database Search Guides. San Jose, CA: California Library Authority for Systems and Services, 1981.

Smith, S.W. "Venn Diagramming for Online Searching." *Special Libraries* 67:11 (November 1976) 510–16.

Chapter 4: Information Utilities

Bellasamo, Gary. "On-line Data Bases for Professional Applications." *Interface Age* 8:3 (March 1983) 137, 139.

Bove, Tony, and Rhodes, Cheryl. "The CompuServe Information Service." *DataCast* No. 004 (March 1982) 9–21.

Cavuoto, Jim. "Previewing the Information Era: a Look at Four Commercial Information Services." *Interface Age* 7:12 (December 1982) 120–2, 182–5.

Ferrarini, Elizabeth M. "A Wise World Awaits Your Computer." *Business Computer Systems* (September 1982) 31–2.

Krajewski, Richard. "On-line Data Bases for Personal Applications." *Interface Age* 8:3 (March 1983) 136, 138, 140, 142.

Levy, Steven. "The Great Electronic Novel." *Popular Computing* 2:8 (June 1983) 84–8.

Magid, Lawrence. "Battle of the Networks: The Source Versus CompuServe." *PC Magazine* 1:9 (January 1983) 180–6, 191–2.

Chapter 5: Reference Vendors with Databases on Many Subjects

Clinton, Marshall, and Grenville, Sally. "Using European Systems from a North American Library." *Online* 4:2 (April 1980) 22–7.

Collier, Harry R. "European Online Users: A Mid-1981 Report." *Online Review.* 6:1 (February 1982) 27–37.

Harper, L.G. "A Comparative Review of BRS, DIALOG, and ORBIT." *Reference Services Review* 9:1 (January–March 1981) 39–50.

Tenopir, Carol. "Dialog's Knowledge Index and BRS/After Dark: Database Searching on Personal Computers." *Library Journal* 108:5 (March 1, 1983) 471–4.

Chapter 6: Scientific, Technical, and Medical Vendors and Databases

Almond, J. Robert, and Welsh, Helen M. "Chemical Substructure Searching—Industrial Applications and Commercial Systems." *Drexel Library Quarterly* 18:2 (Spring 1982) 84–105.

Blair, John C., Jr. "Cross-Database Searching a Chemical Compound: Comparing Lockheed, SDC, BRS, and NLM." *Online* 5:2 (April 1981) 46–61.

Bridges, Kitty. "Environmental Health and Toxicology: An Introduction for the Online Searcher." *Online* 5:1 (January 1981) 27–34.

Doszkocs, Tamas E., Rapp, Barbara A., and Schoolman, Harold M. "Automated Information Retrieval in Science and Technology." *Science* 208:4439 (4 April 1980) 25–30.

Sears, John L. "EMIS: a New Professional Medium for Scientists." *Electronic Publishing Review* 2:1 (1982) 29–34.

Snow, Bonnie. "Online Retrieval of Pharmaceutical Information." *Drexel Library Quarterly* 18:2 (Spring 1982) 64–83.

Tousignaut, Dwight R. "Online Literature-Retrieval Systems: How to Get Started." *American Journal of Hospital Pharmacy.* 40:2 (February 1983) 230–7.

Chapter 7: Business and Economic Vendors and Databases

Chartrand, Robert T., Carr, A. Barry and Miller, Nancy R. "Getting Information to the Farms." *Bulletin of the American Society for Information Science.* 9:3 (February 1983) 10–16.

Gregguras, Fred M., and Carlile, Larry L. "Databases for the Legal Profession." *Database* 3:2 (June 1980) 46–50.

Grosswirth, Marvin. "Getting the Best from Data Banks: Data-Base Retrieval Systems Can Be a Valuable Tool for Any Growing Business." *Personal Computing* 7:5 (May 1983) 111–17, 166.

Hubbard, Abigail. "Online Research for a State Legislature." *Online* 6:4 (July 1982) 27–41.

Mayros, Van, and Werner, D. Michael. *Data Bases for Business.* Radnor, PA: Chilton Book Company, 1982.

McClain, Larry. "Those 'Caviar' Databases." *Popular Computing* 2:4 (February 1983) 56–9.

Provenzano, Dominic. "Nexis." *Database* 4:4 (December 1981) 30–41.

Rothfeder, Jeffrey. "When Congress Asks to See the Bill: The Congressional Budget Office Is Using Personal Computers to Make Sure Its Forecasts Are Right on the Money." *Personal Computing* 7:5 (May 1983) 56–60.

Sze, Melanie. "Business Information Systems Used by Corporate Planning in the Food Industry." *Online Review* 6:4 (August 1982) 329–33.

Wagers, Robert. "ABI/INFORM and MANAGEMENT CONTENTS on Dialog." *Database* 3:1 (March 1980) 12–36.

Chapter 8: Equipment and Communications Software

Benson, Terry, "Data Communications Today." *Interface Age* 8:3 (March 1983) 60–81.

Bove, Tony, and Smith, Kelly. "Free Public Domain CP/M Software! Calling up Remote CP/ M (RCPM) Systems." *DataCast* No. 004 (March 1982) 27–41, 44.

Bruman, Janet L. *Communications Software for Microcomputers.* San Jose, CA: CLASS, 1983.

Miakowski, Stan. "Modems: Hooking Your Computer to the World." *Popular Computing* 2:1 (November 1982) 88–92.

Moskovitz, Robert A. "The Hayes Micromodem II: A Telecommunications System for the Apple II." *Popular Computing* 2:4 (February 1983) 66, 68–72.

Press, Larry. "All About Asynchronous Communications Software." *PC Magazine* 1:9 (January 1983) 88–96.

Radwin, Mark S. "The Intelligent Person's Guide to Choosing a Terminal for Online Interactive Use." *Online* 1:1 (January 1977) 11–19.

Radwin, Mark S. "Choosing a Terminal, Part II." *Online* 1:2 (April 1977) 61–73.

Rhodes, Cheryl, and Bove, Tony. "Modem Software for CP/M Systems: Comparing Reach, Commx, Amcall and Modem7." *DataCast* 004 (March 1982) 51–4.

Shenton, Kathleen E., and Lansberg, Karen M. "Conference Searching at 1200 Baud." *Online* 5:1 (January 1981) 42–3.

Steffenson, Martin B., and King, Kathryn L. "Prerecord Your Online Bibliographic Searches for Time and Money Savings." *Online* 5:1 (January 1981) 47–9.

Thé, Lee. "Data Communications: A Buyer's Guide to Modems and Software." *Personal Computing* 7:3 (March 1983) 99–103, 108–28, 171–75.

Williams, Philip W. "The Use of Microelectronics to Assist Online Information Retrieval." *Online Review* 4:4 (December 1980) 393–9.

Chapter 9: Transferring Files, Search Aids, and Offline Software

Crystal, Maurice I., and Jacobson, Gabriel E. "FRED, A Front End for Databases." *Online* 6:5 (September 1982) 27–30.

Hawkins, Donald T. "Machine Readable Output from Online Searches." *Journal of the American Society for Information Science* 32:4 (July 1981) 253–6.

Horowitz, Gary L., and Bleich, Howard L. "Paperchase: A Computer Program to Search the Medical Literature." *New England Journal of Medicine* 305:16 (15 October 1981) 924–30.

Oberhauser, O.C., and Stebegg, K. "Optimization of Online Searching by Pre-Recording the Search Statements: A Technique for the HP-2645A Terminal." *Online* 6:3 (May 1982) 50–5.

Chapter 10: Computer-Mediated Communication and Other Online Applications

All About Electronic Mail. Delran, NJ: Datapro Research Corporation, 1982.

Bezilla, Robert. "Online Messages, Files, Text and Publishing." *Online* 6:2 (March 1982) 51–5.

Chernicoff, Steve. "Electronic Mail." *Popular Computing* 2:7 (May 1983) 46–53.

Coffey, Michael. "The Better Bulletin Board System." *Creative Computing* 8:12 (December 1982) 20–6.

Connell, Stephen, and Galbraith, Ian A. *Electronic Mail: A Revolution in Business Communications*. White Plains, NY: Knowledge Industry Publications, Inc., 1982.

Derfler, Frank. "Bulletin Boards Continue to Hum: Make Inroads against Big Info Utilities." *Microcomputing* 6:7 (July 1982) 20–8.

Hiltz, Starr Roxanne, and Turoff, Murray. *The Network Nation: Human Communication Through Computer*. Reading, MA: Addison-Wesley, 1978.

International Resource Development, Inc., *Electronic Mail Executives Directory*. White Plains, NY: Knowledge Industry Publications, Inc., 1982.

Kerr, Elaine B., and Hiltz, Starr Roxanne. *Computer-Mediated Communication Systems*. New York: Academic Press, 1982.

Kline David. "Syndicating with Your Osborne: Multiple and Electronic Submission of Freelance Articles." *Portable Companion* (April/May 1983) 34–8.

Lazer, Ellen A., Martin, C.J., and Johnson, James W. *The Teleconferencing Handbook: A Guide to Cost-Effective Communications*. White Plains, NY: Knowledge Industry Publications, Inc., 1983.

Levy, Steve. "Conference Trees." *Popular Computing* 2:7 (May 1983) 70–8.

Online Computer Telephone Directory Poster. Kansas City, MO: Updated Quarterly, ($5.95 from Online Computer Directory Poster, P.O. Box 1005, Kansas City, MO 64111 or call 913-649-1207)

Seger, Katie. "The Electronic Bulletin Board." *PC* 1:9 (January 1983) 214–20.

Vallee, Jacques. "Sitting in on a Computer Conference." *PC* 1:9 (January 1983) 256–68.

Chapter 11: The Future

Butler, Brett. "Beyond the Library—U.S. Online Trends." *3rd International Online Information Meeting.* London, 4–6 December 1979. Oxford and New York: Learned Information, 1979, 385–92.

Broad, William J. "Journals: Fearing the Electronic Future." *Science* 216:4549 (May 28, 1982) 964–8.

Bush, Vannevar. "As We May Think." *Atlantic Monthly.* 176 (January 1945) 101–8.

Cherry, Susan Spaeth. "The New TV Information Systems." *American Libraries* 11:2 (February 1980) 94–110.

Clayton, Audrey. "Factors Affecting Future Online Services." *Online Review* 5:4 (August 1981) 287–300.

Doll, Russell. "Information Technology and Its Socioeconomic and Academic Impact." *Online Review* 5:1 (February 1981) 37–46.

Gregory, Roger. "XANADU: Hypertext from the Future." *Dr. Dobb's Journal* 75 (January 1983) 28–35.

Lancaster, F.W., Smith, Linda C. "On-line Systems in the Communication Process: Projections." *Journal of the American Society for Information Science* 31:3 (May 1980) 193–200.

Schweitzer, James A. *Managing Information Security: A Program for the Electronic Information Age.* Woburn, MA: Butterworth Publishers, 1981.

Sigel, Efrem, ed. *Videotext: The Coming Revolution in Home/Office Information Retrieval.* White Plains, NY: Knowledge Industry Publications, Inc., 1980.

Singh, Indu. *Telecommunications in the Year 2000: National and International Perspectives.* Norwood, NJ: Ablex Publishing Co., 1983.

Slack, Jennifer Daryl. *Communications Technologies and Society: Conceptions of Causality and the Politics of Technical Intervention.* Norwood, NJ: Ablex Publishing Co., 1983.

Tydeman, J., et al. *Teletext and Videotext in the United States.* New York: McGraw-Hill, 1982.

Viewdata and Videotext, 1980–81: A Worldwide Report. White Plains, NY: Knowledge Industry Publications, Inc., 1980.

APPENDIX I

Networks and Major Vendors

ADP (Automatic Data Processing, Inc.)
405 Route 3
Clifton, NJ 07015
(201) 365-7300

Agridata Resources, Inc.
205 West Highland Avenue
Milwaukee, WI 53203
(800) 558-9044
(800) 242-6001 (Wisconsin)

Bibliographic Retrieval Services, Inc.
1200 Route 7
Latham, NY 12110
(800) 833-4707 (Hotline)
(518) 783-1161 (New York state)

Billboard Publications, Inc.
1515 Broadway
New York, NY 10036
(212) 764-7424

BLAISE
The British Library
2 Sheraton Street
London W1V 4BH
England
01-636-1544

Bloodstock Research Information Services, Inc.
801 Corporate Drive
Lexington, KY 40544
(606) 223-4444

Boeing Computer Services Company
177 Madison Avenue
Morristown, NJ 07960
(201) 540-7700

CAN/OLE
Canada Institute for Scientific and Technical Information
National Research Council
Montreal Road
Ottawa Ontario K1A OS2
Canada
(613) 993-1210

Chemical Abstracts Service
2540 Olentangy Road
P.O. Box 3012
Columbus, OH 43210
(800) 848-6533
(614) 421-3698

Chase Econometrics/Interactive Data Corporation
486 Totten Pond Road
Waltham, MA 02154
(617) 890-1234

CITERE-SG2
8, Rue de L'Hotel de Ville
92200 Neuilly-Sur-Seine
France
33 1 747 11 43

CompuServe Information Services, Inc.
5000 Arlington Center Boulevard
Columbus, OH 43220
(800) 848-8990 (Hotline)
(800) 848-8199 (Business)
(614) 457-8600 (Ohio)

Connexions
Professional Data Corporation
55 Wheeler Street
Cambridge, MA 02138
(617) 492-1690

Datacentralen
Retartrej 6-8
DK-2500 Valby
Copenhagen, Denmark
45 (1) 468122

Data Resources, Inc.
24 Hartwell Avenue
Lexington, MA 02173
(617) 863-5100

Data-Star
Willoghby Road, Bracknell
Berkshire RJ6 1HJ
England
44 344 89151

DELPHI
General Videotex Corporation
3 Blackstone Street
Cambridge, MA 02139
(800) 544-4005 (Hotline)
(617) 491-3393 (Massachusetts)

Dialcom International, Inc.
1109 Spring Street
Suite 410
Silver Spring, MD 20910
(301) 588-1572

Dialog Information Services, Inc.
3460 Hillview Avenue
Palo Alto, CA 94304
(800) 227-1927 (Marketing)
(800) 227-8282 (Training)
(800) 982-5838 (California)
(415) 858-3785 (Outside U.S.)

DIMDI
Weisshausstrasse 27
Postfach 42 05 80
D-5000 Cologne 41
Federal Republic of Germany
(49) 221 4724-252

Dow Jones & Company, Inc.
P.O. Box 300
Princeton, NJ 08540
(609) 452-1511 (New Jersey)
(800) 257-5114 (Hotline)
(800) 223-2274 (Marketing)

Dun and Bradstreet, Inc.
99 Church Street
New York, NY 10007
(212) 285-7669

ECHO Service
Commission of the European
 Communities
DG XIII A3
Batiment Jean Monnet
B.P. 1907
Luxembourg
(352) 43011 x2923

Edunet
P.O. Box 364
Princeton, NJ 08540
(609) 734-1878

Electronet/1
Policy Studies Corporation
P.O. Box 2206
Springfield, VA 22152
(703) 455-5103

Electronic Information Exchange
 System (EIES)
Computer Conferencing and
 Communications Center
New Jersey Institute of Technology
323 High Street
Newark, NJ 07102
(201) 645-5211

Electronic Mail & Message System
30 High Street
Norwalk, CT 06851

Electronic Materials Information
 Service (EMIS)
The Institution of Electrical Engineers
Station House
Nightingale Road

APPENDIX I

Hitchin, Hertfordshire SG5 1RJ
England
0462-53331
  or
IEE/INSPEC Service Center
445 Hoes Lane
Piscataway, NJ 08854
(201) 981-0060

ESA-IRS
Esrin
Via Galileo-Galilei
I-00044 Frascati
Italy
06-94011

Euronet Diane (Direct Information
  Access Network Europe)
15, Ave de la Faiencerie
B.P. 777
Luxembourg
(352) 40221
Telex: 3511 Diane LU

FIZ Technik
Ostbahnhofstr. 13
Postfach 60 05 47
6000 Frankfurt/H 60
Federal Republic of Germany
(49) 611 4308-225

GEISCO (General Electric Information
  Services)
401 N. Washington St.
Rockville, MD 20850
(301) 340-4000

GMS Systems, Inc.
12 West 37th Street
New York, NY 10018
(212) 947-3590

GTE Telenet Information Services Inc.
Financial Services Division
100 Wall Street
New York, NY 10005
(212) 425-1470

GTE Telenet Medical Information
  Network
8229 Boone Boulevard
Vienna, VA 22180
(703) 442-2500

Health Education Network (MGH)
MGH Network Coordinator
Massachusetts General Hospital
Laboratory of Computer Science
Boston, MA 02114
(617) 726-3950

Health Education Network (OSU)
OSU Network Coordinator
The Ohio State University
College of Medicine
076 Health Sciences Library
Columbus, OH 43210
(614) 422-6192

Huttonline
E.F. Hutton
One Battery Place Plaza
New York, NY 10004
(212) 745-5000

Inka
c/o Fachinformationszentrum
Mathematic GmbH
D-7514 Eggenstein-Leopoldshafen 2
Federal Republic of Germany
7247 824568

InfoGlobe
The Globe and Mail
444 Front Street West
Toronto, Ontario
Canada M5V 2S9
(416) 598-5250

I.P. Sharp Associates Ltd.
Suite 1900 Exchange Tower
2 First Canadian Place
Toronto, Ontario
Canada M5X 1E3
(416) 364-5361

Institute for Scientific Information
3501 Market Street
Philadelphia, PA 19104
(800) 523-1850
(215) 386-0100

Justice Retrieval and Inquiry System (JURIS)
Information Systems Staff
U.S. Department of Justice
Room 1100, Chester Arthur Building
Washington, DC 20530
(202) 633-5682

Lithium Information Center
Department of Psychiatry
University of Wisconsin-Madison
600 Highland Avenue
Madison, WI 53792
(608) 263-6171

MCAUTO Health Services Division
McDonnell Douglas Automation Company
Health Services Division
5775 Campus Parkway
Hazelwood, MO 63042
(314) 232-7333

Mead Data Central
P.O. Box 933
9333 Springboro Pike
Dayton, OH 45401
(800) 227-4908 (Marketing)
(800) 543-6862 (Hotline)
(800) 762-6626 (Ohio)

Multi-List/McGraw-Hill
1221 Avenue of the Americas
New York, NY 10020
(212) 997-6075

National CSS Inc.
187 Danbury Road
Wilton, CT 06897
(203) 762-2511

National Library of Medicine
8600 Rockville Pike
Bethesda, MD 20209
(301) 496-6193

Newsnet
945 Haverford Rd.
Bryn Mawr, PA 19010
(800) 345-1301
(215) 527-8030

NIH/EPA Chemical Information System
Computer Sciences Corporation
6565 Arlington Boulevard
Falls Church, VA 22046
(800) 368-3432

Occupational Health Services, Inc.
515 Madison Avenue
New York, NY 10002
(800) 223-8978
(212) 752-4530 (New York)

Pergamon Infoline Ltd.
12 Vandy Street
London EC2A 2DE
Tel: 01 377 4650
  or
Pergamon International Information Corporation
1340 Old Chain Bridge Road
McLean, VA 22101
(703 442-0900 (Virginia)
(800) 336-7575

PhotoNet Computer Corporation
500 Park Avenue
New York, NY 10022
(212) 750-1386

Q/L Systems Ltd.
112 Kent Street
Suite 1018, Tower B
Ottawa, Ontario
Canada KIP 5P2
(613) 238-3499

Questel (see Telesystemes Questel)

Sadtler Research Laboratories
3316 Spring Garden Street
Philadelphia, PA 19104
(215) 382-7800

APPENDIX I

SDC Information Services
2500 Colorado Avenue
Santa Monica, CA 90406
(800) 421-7229 (outside California)
(800) 352-6689 (California)
(800) 336-3313 (outside Virginia)
(703) 790-9850 (Virginia)

Source Telecomputing Corporation
1616 Anderson Road
McLean, VA 22102
(800) 336-3330 (Hotline)
(800) 336-3366 (Business)
(703) 734-7500 (Virginia and outside U.S.)

SPI
Department Spidel
98 bd Victor Hugo
92115 Clichy
France
Tel: 01-7311191

Standard & Poor's Compustat Services, Inc.
7400 South Alton Court
Englewood, CO 80112
(303) 771-6510

Telephone Software Connection
P.O. Box 6548
Torrance, CA 90504
(213) 516-9430

Telenet
8229 Boone Boulevard
Vienna, VA 22180
(800) 336-0437
(800) 572-0408 (Virginia)

Telesystemes Questel
40 rue du Cherche-Midi
75006 Paris
France
01-544-3813
   or

Suite 818
1625 I Street, NW
Washington, DC 20006
(800) 424-9600
(202) 296-1604 (Washington, DC)

Tymnet, Inc.
2710 Orchard Parkway
San Jose, CA 95134
(408) 946-4900
(800) 336-0149

Tymeshare, Inc.
20705 Valley Green Drive, VG3
Cupertino, CA 95014
(408) 446-6000
(800) 227-6185

Uninet, Inc.
10951 Lakeview Avenue
Lenexa, KS 66219
(913) 541-4400

VU/TEXT Information Services
P.O. Box 8558
Philadelphia, PA 19101
(215) 854-8297

West Publishing Company
50 West Kellogg Boulevard
P.O. Box 3526
St. Paul, MN 55165
(800) 328-9833

Wharton Econometric Forecasting Associates, Inc.
3624 Science Center
Philadelphia, PA 19104
(215) 386-9000

Project Xanadu
Box 128
Swarthmore, PA 19081

Xerox Computer Services
5310 Beethoven Street
Los Angeles, CA 90066
(213) 306-4000

Appendix II

Selected Databases

ABI/INFORM
    Data Courier, Inc.
    Louisville, KY
    (800) 626-2823

ACADEMIC AMERICAN
  ENCYCLOPEDIA
    Grolier, Inc.
    Danbury, CT

ACCOUNTANTS
    American Institute of Certified
      Public Accountants
    New York, NY

ADTRACK
    Corporate Intelligence, Inc.
    Saint Paul, MN

AGRICOLA
    U.S. Department of Agriculture
    Beltsville, MD

AGRICOMPUTE
AGRIGUIDE
AGRIMART
AGRISCAN
AGRITECH
    Agridata Resources, Inc.
    Milwaukee, WI
    (800) 558-9044

AMERICAN MEN AND WOMEN OF
  SCIENCE
    R.R. Bowker Company
    New York, NY

APILIT
    American Petroleum Institute
    New York, NY

APIPAT
    American Petroleum Institute
    New York, NY

ARTBIBLIOGRAPHIES MODERN
    ABC-Clio, Inc.
    Santa Barbara, CA

AVLINE
    National Library of Medicine
    Bethesda, MD

BI/DATA FORECASTS
BI/DATA TIME SERIES
    Business International Corporation
    New York, NY

BIOSIS PREVIEWS
    BioSciences Information Service
    Philadelphia, PA
    (800) 523-4806

BIOTECHNOLOGY
    Derwent Publications, Ltd.
    London, England

BOOKS IN PRINT
    R.R. Bowker Company
    New York, NY

CA SEARCH
    Chemical Abstracts Service
    Columbus, OH
    (800) 848-6533

APPENDIX II

CANCERLIT
U.S. National Institutes of Health
National Cancer Institute
International Cancer Research Data Bank Program

CAS ONLINE
Chemical Abstracts Service
Columbus, OH
(800) 843-6533

CATLINE
National Library of Medicine
Bethesda, MD

CHEMDEX/CHEMDEX2/CHEMDEX3
Chemical Abstracts Service
Columbus, OH

CHEMICAL INDUSTRY NOTES
Chemical Abstracts Service
Columbus, OH

CHEMLAW
Bureau of National Affairs, Inc.
Fein-Marquart Associates, Inc.

CHEMLINE
Chemical Abstracts Service
Columbus, OH

CHEMNAME
CHEMSEARCH
CHEMSIS
CHEMZERO
Chemical Abstracts Service
Columbus, OH

CIS
Congressional Information Service, Inc.
Washington, DC
(800) 638-8380

CLAIMS/CHEM
CLAIMS/CITATION
CLAIMS/U.S. PATENTS
CLAIMS/UNITERM
IFI/Plenum Data Company
Arlington, VA

COMMERCE BUSINESS DAILY
U.S. Department of Commerce
Chicago, IL

COMPENDEX
Engineering Information, Inc.
New York, NY
(800) 221-1044

COMPREHENSIVE DISSERTATION INDEX
University Microfilms International
Ann Arbor, MI
(800) 521-0600

CROS
Bibliographic Retrieval Services, Inc.
Latham, NY
(800) 833-4707

CTCP (Clinical Toxicology of Commercial Products)
U.S. Environmental Protection Agency
U.S. Food and Drug Administration
U.S. National Institutes of Health
Data from *Clinical Toxicity of Commercial Products* by Gleason, Hodge, Smith, and Gosselin

DBI (DATA BASE INDEX)
SDC Information Services
Santa Monica, CA
(800) 421-7229

DIALINDEX
Dialog Information Services, Inc.
Palo Alto, CA
(800) 227-1927

DISCLOSURE II
Disclosure Inc.
Bethesda, MD
(800) 638-8076

DISEASE INFORMATION
American Medical Association
Chicago, IL

DOW JONES NEWS
DOW JONES QUOTES
DOW JONES SPORTS REPORT
DOW JONES WEATHER REPORT
    Dow Jones & Company, Inc.
    Princeton, NJ
    (800) 257-5114

DRUG INFORMATION
    American Medical Association
    Chicago, IL

ECONOMICS ABSTRACTS INTERNATIONAL
    Learned Information Ltd.
    Oxford, England

EIS INDUSTRIAL PLANTS
    Economic Information Systems, Inc.
    New York, NY

EIS NONMANUFACTURING ESTABLISHMENTS
    Economic Information Systems, Inc.
    New York, NY

ELECTRONIC YELLOW PAGES
    Market Data Retrieval, Inc.
    Westport, CT
    (800) 243-5538

EMBASE
    EXCERPTA MEDICA
    Amsterdam, The Netherlands

ENCYCLOPEDIA BRITANNICA
    Encyclopedia Britannica, Inc.
    Chicago, IL

ENCYCLOPEDIA OF ASSOCIATIONS
    Gale Research Company
    Detroit, MI

ENERGYLINE
    Environment Information Center, Inc.
    New York, NY
    (800) 223-6275

ENVIROLINE
    Environment Information Center, Inc.
    New York, NY
    (800) 223-6275

ENVIRONMENTAL HEALTH NEWS
    Occupational Health Services, Inc.
    New York, NY
    (800) 223-8978

ERIC
    National Institute of Education
    Bethesda, MD
    (800) 336-3728

FEDERAL REGISTER ABSTRACTS
    Capitol Services International
    Washington, DC

FOUNDATION DIRECTORY
    The Foundation Center
    New York, NY

GEOREF
    American Geological Institute
    Falls Church, VA
    (800) 336-4764

GPO MONTHLY CATALOG
    U.S. Government Printing Office
    Washington, DC

HARVARD BUSINESS REVIEW
    John Wiley & Sons, Inc.
    New York, NY

HAZARDLINE
    Occupational Health Services, Inc.
    New York, NY
    (800) 223-8978

HEALTH PLANNING AND ADMINISTRATION
    National Library of Medicine
    Bethesda, MD

HISTORICAL ABSTRACTS
    ABC-Clio, Inc.
    Santa Barbara, CA

APPENDIX II

HORSE
  Bloodstock Research Information Services, Inc.
  Lexington, KY

INFOGLOBE
  The Globe and Mail
  Toronto, Ontario, Canada

THE INFORMATION BANK
  Mead Data Central
  Dayton, OH
  (800) 227-4908

INTERNATIONAL PHARMACEUTICAL ABSTRACTS (IPA)
  American Society of Hospital Pharmacists
  Bethesda, MD

INTERNATIONAL SOFTWARE DIRECTORY
  Imprint Software, Ltd.
  Fort Collins, CO

ISI/BIOMED
ISI/COMPUMATH
ISI/GEOSCITECH
ISI/ISPT+B
  Institute for Scientific Information
  Philadephia, PA
  (800) 523-1850

LABORDOC
  The International Labour Organization
  Geneva, Switzerland

LC/LINE
  Library of Congress
  Washington, DC

LEGAL RESOURCE INDEX
  Information Access Company
  Menlo Park, CA
  (800) 227-8431

LEXIS
  Mead Data Central
  Dayton, OH
  800-227-4908

LITHIUM LIBRARY
  Lithium Information Center
  Department of Psychiatry
  University of Wisconsin
  Madison, WI

MAGAZINE INDEX
  Information Access Company
  Menlo Park, CA
  (800) 227-8431

MANAGEMENT CONTENTS
  Management Contents, Inc.
  Northbrook, IL
  (800) 323-5354

MARKETSCAN
  The Globe and Mail
  Toronto, Ontario, Canada

MATERIALS PROPERTIES FILE
MATERIALS SUPPLY FILE
  Institution of Electrical Engineers
  Herts, England

MATHFILE
  American Mathematical Society
  Providence, RI

MEDIA GENERAL DATA BASE
  Media General Financial Services, Inc.
  Richmond, VA

MEDICAL PROCEDURE CODING & NOMENCLATURE
  American Medical Association
  Chicago, IL

MEDLINE
  National Library of Medicine
  Bethesda, MD
  (301) 496-6193

METADEX
  American Society for Metals
  The Metals Society
  Metals Park, OH

MICROCOMPUTER INDEX
  Microcomputer Information Services
  Santa Clara, CA

MILLION DOLLAR DIRECTORY
    Dun & Bradstreet, Inc.
    Parsippany, NJ

MLA BIBLIOGRAPHY
    Modern Language Association
    New York, NY

NATIONAL NEWSPAPER INDEX
    Information Access Company
    Menlo Park, CA
    (800) 227-8431

NDEX (Newspaper Index)
    Bell & Howell
    Wooster, OH
    (800) 321-9881

NEWSFLASH
    Agridata Resources, Inc.
    Milwaukee, WI
    (800) 558-9044

NEWSEARCH
    Information Access Company
    Menlo Park, CA
    (800) 227-8431

NEXIS
    Mead Data Central
    Dayton, OH
    (800) 227-4908

NTIS
    National Technical Information
        Service
    Springfield, VA

OCEANIC ABSTRACTS
    Cambridge Scientific Abstracts
    Bethesda, MD
    (800) 638-8076

OHM-TADS
    U.S. Environmental Protection
        Agency
    Washington, DC

ONLINE CHRONICLE
    Online, Inc.
    Weston, CT

PAPERCHEM (Paper Chemistry)
    The Institute of Paper Chemistry
    Appleton, WI

PARTICIPATE
    The Source Telecomputing
        Corporation
    McLean, VA
    (800) 336-3366

PASSPORT
    Multinational Computer Models,
        Inc.
    Montclair, NJ

PATDATA
    Bibliographic Retrieval Services,
        Inc.
    Latham, NY

PATLAW
    Bureau of National Affairs, Inc.
    Washington, DC

PATSEARCH
    Pergamon International
        Information Corporation
    McLean, VA
    (800) 336-7575

PESTDOC
    Derwent Publications Ltd.
    London, England

PHARMACEUTICAL NEWS INDEX
    Data Courier, Inc.
    Louisville, KY
    (800) 626-2823

PHILOSOPHERS INDEX
    Bowling Green State University
    Philosophy Documentation Center
    Bowling Green, OH

PIRA
    The Research Association for the
        Paper and Board, Printing and
        Packaging Industries
    Randalls Road, Leatherhead
    Surrey, England

POLLUTION ABSTRACTS
  Cambridge Scientific Abstracts
  Bethesda, MD
  (800) 638-8076

PRE-MED
PRE-PSYC
  Bibliographic Retrieval Services, Inc.
  Latham, New York
  (800) 833-4707

PSYCINFO
  American Psychological Association
  Washington, DC
  (800) 336-4980

PTS INDEXES
PTS PROMT
PTS U.S. FORECASTS and PTS
  INTERNATIONAL FORECASTS
PTS U.S. TIME SERIES and PTS
  INTERNATIONAL TIME SERIES
  Predicasts, Inc.
  Cleveland, OH
  (800) 321-6388

QUICK QUOTE
  CompuServe, Inc.
  Columbus, OH
  (800) 848-8990

RAPRA ABSTRACTS
  Rubber and Plastics Research
    Association of Great Britian
  Salop, England

RINGDOC
  Derwent Publications Ltd.
  London, England

RTECS
  U.S. National Institutes of Health
    National Institute for
    Occupational Safety and Health
  Cincinnati, OH

SCISEARCH
  Institute for Scientific Information
  Philadelphia, PA
  (800) 523-1850

SOCIAL SCISEARCH
  Institute for Scientific Information
  Philadelphia, PA
  (800) 523-1850

SOCIOECONOMIC BIBLIOGRAPHIC
INFORMATION
  American Medical Association
  Chicago, IL

SPIN
  American Institute of Physics
  New York, NY

SUMM
  Agridata Resources, Inc.
  Milwaukee, WI
  (800) 558-9044

SUPERINDEX
  Superindex, Inc.
  Boca Raton, FL

TELEGEN
  Environmental Information Center, Inc.
  New York, NY
  (800) 223-6275

TOXICOLOGY DATA BANK
  National Library of Medicine
  Bethesda, MD

TOXLINE
  National Library of Medicine
  Bethesda, MD

TRIS
  Transportation Research Board
  U.S. Department of Transportation
  Washington, DC

TSCA INITIAL INVENTORY
  U.S. Environmental Protection Agency
  Washington, DC

ULRICH'S INTERNATIONAL
PERIODICAL DIRECTORY
  R.R. Bowker Company
  New York, NY

UNISTOX
The Source Telecomputing
Corporation
McLean, VA

UPI
United Press International
New York, NY

VALUE LINE DATA BASE II
Arnold Bernhard & Co.
New York, NY

VETDOC
Derwent Publications Ltd.
London, England

WALL STREET JOURNAL HIGHLIGHTS
ONLINE
Dow Jones & Company, Inc.
Princeton, NJ
(800) 257-5114

WORLD TEXTILES
Shirley Institute
Didsbury
Manchester, England

WPI/WPIL (The World Patents Index)
Derwent Publications, Ltd.
London, England

ZOOLOGICAL RECORD
BioSciences Information Service
The Zoological Society of London
London, England

Appendix III

Selected Hardware and Software Manufacturers

TERMINAL MANUFACTURERS

ANDERSON JACOBSON, INC.
521 Charcot Avenue
San Jose, CA 95131
(408) 263-8520

BEEHIVE INTERNATIONAL
4910 Amelia Earhart Drive
Box 25668
Salt Lake City, UT 84125

DIGILOG, INC.
1370-T Welsh Road
Montgomeryville, PA 18936
(215) 672-0800

GENERAL ELECTRIC COMPANY
Data Communications Products
    Department
Waynesboro, VA 22980
(703) 949-1188

HAZELTINE CORPORATION
Industrial Products Division
Greenlawn, NY 11740
(516) 261-7000
(800) 645-5300

TEKTRONIX, INC
P.O. Box 1700
Beaverton, OR 97075
(800) 547-1512
(503) 644-0161

TEXAS INSTRUMENTS, INC.
P.O. Box 225474
Dallas, TX 75265
(214) 987-0514

COMMUNICATING WORD PROCESSOR MANUFACTURERS

DIGITAL EQUIPMENT
    CORPORATION
Terminal Products Group
One Iron Way
Marlboro, MA 01752
(617) 467-5111

INTERNATIONAL BUSINESS
    MACHINES
Old Orchard Road
Armonk, NY 10504
(914) 765-1900

LANIER ELECTRONIC
    LABORATORY, INC.
1704 Chantilly Drive, N.E.
Atlanta, GA 30324
(404) 633-9261

WANG LABORATORIES, INC.
1 Industrial Avenue
Lowell, MA 01851
(617) 459-5000

XEROX
High Ridge Park
Stamford, CT 06904
(203) 329-8711

MODEM SUPPLIERS

ANDERSON JACOBSEN INC.
521 Charcot Avenue
San Jose, CA 95131
(468) 263-8520

BELL SYSTEM
(Call your local Bell Business Office)

CHAT COMMUNICATIONS
2462 Wyandotte Street
Mountain View, CA 94043
(415) 962-9670

HAYES MICROCOMPUTER
PRODUCTS, INC.
5923 Peachtree Industrial Boulevard
Norcross, GA 30092
(404) 449-8791

LEADING EDGE PRODUCTS
225 Turnpike Street
Canton, MA 02021

LEXICON CORPORATION
1541 N.W. 65th Avenue
Ft. Lauderdale, FL 33313

MFJ ENTERPRISES, INC.
921 Louisville Road
Starkville, MS 39759

MICROCOM, INC.
1400 A. Providence Highway
Norwood, MA 02062
(617) 762-9319

MICROPERIPHERAL
CORPORATION
2643 151st Place N.E.
Redmond, WA 98052

NOVATION, INC.
20409 Prairie Street
Chatsworth, CA 91311
(800) 423-5419
(213) 996-5060 (California)

PRENTICE CORPORATION
266 Caspian Drive
Sunnyvale, CA 94086

RACAL-VADIC INCORPORATED
222 Caspian Drive
Sunnyvale, CA 94086
(408) 744-0810

TNW CORPORATION
3444 Hancock Street
San Diego, CA 92110

UNIVERSAL DATA SYSTEMS
500 Bradford Drive
Huntsville, AL 35805

U.S. ROBOTICS INC.
1123 West Washington Boulevard
Chicago, IL 60607
(312) 733-0497

ZYCOR LTD.
Gateway House
High Street
Slough, Berks
England

OTHER EQUIPMENT MANUFACTURERS

LASER DATA, INC.
369 Washington Street
Woburn, MA 01801
(617) 938-8844
(Videodisk)

QUADRAM CORPORATION
4357 Park Drive
Norcross, GA 30093
(404) 923-6666
(Interface Board)

APPENDIX III

COMMUNICATIONS SOFTWARE MANUFACTURERS

Basic Packages

Manufacturer	Program	Computer
ATARI 1265 Borregas Avenue Sunnyvale, CA 94086 (408) 745-2000	Telelink	Atari 400/800
COMPUTER STATIONS INC. 11610 Page Service Drive St. Louis, MO 63141 (314) 432-7019	Flexiterm	Apple II
CP/M USERS GROUP 1651 Third Avenue New York, NY 10028	Modem	CP/M Systems
DIGITAL MARKETING CORPORATION 2363 Boulevard Circle Walnut Creek, CA 94596 (800) 826-2222	Micro Link	CP/M Systems Osborne IBM PC Apple II
DOW JONES & CO. P.O. Box 300 Princeton, NJ 08540 (800) 257-5114	Dow Jones packages	Apple IBM PC
HAYES MICROCOMPUTER PRODUCTS INC. 5923 Peachtree Industrial Boulevard Norcross, GA 30092 (404) 449-8791	Hayes Terminal Program or Micromodem Software	Apple
HEADLANDS PRESS P.O. Box 862 Tiburon, CA	PC Talk	IBM PC
LIFEBOAT ASSOCIATES 1651 Third Avenue New York, NY 10028 (212) 860-0300	BSTMS	CP/M Systems Heath TRS-80
LINK SYSTEMS 1640 19th Street Santa Monica, CA 90404 (213) 453-1851	Datalink I Datalink III	Apple II Apple III
LINDBERGH SYSTEMS 41 Fairhill Road Holden, MA 01520 (617) 852-0233	Omniterm	TRS-80 I, II
MICROCOM 1400A Providence Highway Norwood, MA 02062 (617) 762-9310	Micro/Courier Micro/Telegram	Apple

Basic Packages (*continued*)

Manufacturer	Program	Computer
MICROSTUF INC. 1845 The Exchange Suite 140 Atlanta, GA 30339	Crosstalk	CP/M Systems IBM PC
PEACHTREE SOFTWARE 3445 Peachtree Road NE Atlanta, GA 30326 (404) 262-2376	Magic Messenger	CP/M Systems
PHILADELPHIA CONSULTING GROUP, INC. P.O. Box 102 Wynnewood, PA 19096 (215) 649-1598	Pony Express	TRS-80 III
SOLUTION SOFTWARE SYSTEMS 3930 Whispering Trails Hoffman Estates, IL 60195	PC Modem	IBM PC
SSM MICROCOMPUTER PRODUCTS INC. 2190 Paragon Drive San Jose, CA 95131 (408) 946-7400	Transend 1 Transend 2 Transend 3	Apple II Apple II Apple II
SUPERSOFT ASSOCIATES P.O. Box 1628 Suite 401 Champaign, IL 61820	Term II X Term	CP/M
VECTOR GRAPHIC INC. 500 North Ventu Park Road Thousand Oaks, CA 91320 (805) 449-5831	Connect	Vector Graphic Systems
VISICORP 2895 Zanker Road San Jose, CA 95134 (408) 946-9000	Visiterm	Apple
VOLKSMICRO COMPUTER SYSTEMS, INC. 202 Packets Court Suite C Williamsburg, VA 23185 (804) 220-0005	Commwhiz	TRS-80 I, II
WOOLF SOFTWARE SYSTEMS 23842 Archwood Street Canoga Park, CA 91307 (213) 703-8112	Move-it	CP/M Systems

APPENDIX III

Combination Packages

Manufacturer	Program	Computer
HAYES MICROCOMPUTER PRODUCTS 5923 Peachtree Industrial Boulevard Norcross, GA 30092	Micromodem II Micromodem 100	Apple II
MICROPERIPHERAL CORPORATION 2643 151st Place NE Redmond, WA 98052	PC Connection	IBM PC
VEN-TEL, INC. 2342 Walsh Avenue Santa Clara, CA 95051 (408) 727-5721 Includes plug-in model card, cable, and Crosstalk Communications package.	PC Modem	IBM PC

Bulletin Board Packages

Manufacturer	Program	Computer
ADVANCED DATA SYSTEMS 4877 Martin Road Newburgh, IN 47630	Networks	Apple II
B.T. ENTERPRISES 171 Hawkins Road Centereach, NY 11720	Connection-80	TRS-80
CBBS 5219 West Warwick Chicago, IL 60641 (312) 545-8086	CBBS	CP/M
THE COMMUNITREE GROUP 470 Castro Street Suite 207-3002 San Francisco, CA 94114 (415) 861-8733	Communitree	Apple II or II plus
COMPUTER SERVICES OF DANBURY P.O. Box 993 Danbury, CT 06810	Bullet-80	TRS-80
DATEL SYSTEMS, INC. P.O. Box 1318 Lakeside, CA 92040	People's Message System	Apple II
FORUM-80 HEADQUARTERS 7600 East 48th Terrace Kansas City, MO 64129	Forum-80	TRS-80 I, III

INFORMATION ONLINE

Bulletin Board Packages (*continued*)

Manufacturer	Program	Computer
LANCE MICKLUS INC. 217 South Union Street Burlington, VT 05401	ST80-X10 host system ST80-PBB personal bulletin board	TRS-80 I, III TRS-80 I, III
MICROSOFTWARE SYSTEMS Suite 400 7927 Jones Branch Drive McLean, VA 22102	ABBS 4.0	Apple II
MICROSTUF COMPANY P.O. Box 33337 Decatur, GA 30033 (404) 491-3787	Remote North Star Bulletin Board	North Star or CP/M

Software Search Aids

Manufacturer	Program
BIOSCIENCES INFORMATION SERVICE 2100 Arch Street Philadelphia, PA 19103 (215) 587-4800 (Pennsylvania) (800) 523-4806 (Hotline)	B-I-T-S
CAMBRIDGE SCIENTIFIC ABSTRACTS 5161 River Road Bethesda, MD 20816 (301) 951-1400	MicroCAMBRIDGE
COMPUTER CORPORATION OF AMERICA 675 Massachusetts Avenue Cambridge, MA 02139 (617) 492-8860 or CSIN Network Administrator Council on Environmental Quality 722 Jackson Place NW Washington, DC 20036 (202) 395-7285	CSIN
CUADRA ASSOCIATES 2001 Wilshire Boulevard Suite 305 Santa Monica, CA 90403 (213) 829-9972	STAR
DISCLOSURE, INC. 5161 River Road Bethesda, MD 20816 (800) 638-8076 (301) 951-1300 (Maryland)	microDISCLOSURE

APPENDIX III   215

Software Search Aids (*continued*)

Manufacturer	Program	Computer
DOW JONES & COMPANY, INC. P.O. Box 300 Princeton, NJ 08540 (800) 257-5114		Dow Jones Software
ERIC CLEARINGHOUSE ON INFORMATION RESOURCES School of Education Syracuse University Syracuse, NY 13210 (315) 423-3640		MICROsearch (ERIC)
INFORMATION ACCESS COMPANY 404 Sixth Avenue Menlo Park, CA 94025 (800) 227-8431 (415) 367-7171 (California)		Search Helper
INSTITUTE FOR SCIENTIFIC INFORMATION 3501 Market Street Philadelphia, PA 19104 (800) 523-1850		Sci-Mate
PERGAMON INTERNATIONAL INFORMATION CORPORATION 1340 Old Chain Bridge Road McLean, VA 22101 (800) 336-7575		Video Patsearch
SDC Information Services 2500 Colorado Avenue Santa Monica, CA 90406 (800) 421-7229		ORBIT SearchMaster
VISICORP 2895 Zanker Road San Jose, CA 95134 (408) 946-9000		VisiLink
USERLINK SYSTEMS, LTD. 9 Brabyns Brow Marple, Stockport, Cheshire, SK6 7DA England 061-427 5976 *or* C. Olsen and Associates 977 Redmond Avenue San Jose, CA 95120 (408) 268-4586		Userlink

Appendix IV

Selected Bulletin Board Numbers

Berkeley, CA	(415) 538-3580 (FORTH computer language)
Milpitas, CA	(408) 263-2588
Pasadena, CA	(213) 799-1632
Santa Cruz, CA	(408) 475-7101 (Communitree)
Colorado Springs, CO	(303) 634-1158
Atlanta, GA	(404) 892-9627 (Communitree)
Chicago, IL	(312) 545-8086
Logan Square, IL	(312) 252-2136
Greenbelt, MD	(301) 344-9156 (NASA information)
Dearborn, MI	(313) 846-6127
Denville, NJ	(201) 627-5151 (Communitree)
Flanders, NJ	(201) 584-9227
Columbus, OH	(614) 272-2227
Beaverton, OR	(503) 641-7276
Allentown, PA	(215) 398-3937
Cheltenham, PA	(215) 836-5116
Villanova, PA	(215) 337-3414

To obtain a list of over 400 numbers, order:

Online Computer Directory Poster
P.O. Box 10005
Kansas City, MO 64111
(913) 649-1207

$5.95 including shipping and handling
or
Locate numbers in "Public Access Systems," a database in PUBLIC, the user-publication section of The Source, or in the Apple User Group in the user-published Section of CompuServe (GO PCS-50 and Select the Apple User Group).

Index

ABC-Clio database, 14
ABI/INFORM database, 13, 60, 66, 103, 104
Academic American Encyclopedia, 15, 16, 64, 66, 111, 125
Access points. *See* Databases, access points in
Accountants database, 104
Acoustic coupler, 126, 129-131
Adam microcomputer, 171
ADP (Automatic Data Processing) system, 169
ADTRACT database, 104
Advertising & Marketing Intelligence Data Base, 123
AGLINE database, 104
AGRICOLA database, 60, 66, 74
AgriData Resources, Inc., 117
AgriScan database, 118
AgriStar system, 117-118
AMA Drug Evaluations, 77, 96-97
AMA/NET system. *See* GTE TELENET Medical Information Network
American Chemical Society, 14, 64, 74
American Medical Association, 77, 96, 97
American Men and Women of Science, 59, 64, 65, 66
American Petroleum Institute, 70, 75
American Psychological Association, 61, 66
American Society of Hospital Pharmacists, 79
Answer mode, 133, 137, 141
APILIT database, 70
APIPAT database, 75
Apple microcomputer, 138, 139, 141, 142, 150, 151, 153, 154, 155, 171
Aquatic Science and Fisheries Abstracts, 155
Artbibliographies Modern database, 58
ASCII code, 135, 142
Asynchronous operation, 133, 135
AT&T, 174
Atari microcomputer, 132, 150, 171
Auto answer modem, 133
Auto log-on, 136, 143, 144

Auto-Cite database, 123
Autodialing. *See* Direct dialing
AVLINE database, 79

Barrons, 107, 111
Baud rates, 126-127, 131-132, 135
BAZAAR database, 52
Benson, Terry, 138
Bibliographic Retrieval Services (BRS), 7, 9, 10, 11, 18, 56, 62-69, 70, 73, 74, 77, 78, 84, 99-100, 101, 103, 143, 172
history of, 3
see also BRS After Dark, COLLEAGUE system
BIDATA database, 108-109
Billboard database, 125
BIOETHICS database, 80
Biological Abstracts, 14, 73, 74, 75, 76
BIOMED database, 84, 85, 143-150
Biomedical Bibliographic Library, 100
BioSciences Information Service, 66, 79, 153
BIOSIS Previews database, 14, 15, 16, 17, 18, 56, 60, 63, 66, 152
BioSuperfile software package, 153
Biotechnology Index database, 77
BITS service, 153
Black's Law Dictionary, 120
Blaise system, 71
Bloodstock Research Information Services, 125
Boeing Computer Services, 169
Books in Print, 60, 66-68
Boolean operators, 28-29, 146
Bove, Tony, 165
British Library System, 71
BRS After Dark, 56, 64, 65-69, 73, 74, 77, 100, 103, 172. *See also* Bibliographic Retrieval Services
BULLET service, 45, 157
Bulletin boards. *See* Electronic bulletin boards, Computer Bulletin Board Systems
Business information, 14, 37, 45, 103-125. *See also* Financial information

217

Business International Corporation, 107, 109
Business Week, 123
Byte magazine, 123

CA Search database, 14, 15, 16, 18, 74, 92, 93. *See also Chemical Abstracts*
CAI. See Computer-assisted instruction
Cable connections, 128-130
Cambridge Scientific Abstracts, 76, 155
CAN/OLE system, 71
Canadian vendors, 56, 70-71
CANCERLIT database, 16, 80
Career information, 37
CAS ONLINE system, 16, 86, 90-93, 95, 152, 155
CATLINE database, 15, 79
CB SERVICE, 44, 157
CBBS. *See* Computer Bulletin Board Systems
CDI. *See Comprehensive Dissertation Index*
Center for Disease Control, 97
Chat II Message Processor, 139
CHAT service, 37, 157
Chemdex databases, 74-75
Chemical Abstracts, 14, 63, 66, 73, 74, 75, 76, 77. *See also* CA Search database
Chemical Abstracts service, 75, 78, 79, 90, 173
Chemical Biological Activities, 79
Chemical dictionary databases, 74-75
Chemical Industry Notes database, 74, 104
Chemical Modelling Laboratory Database, 86
Chemical Regulations and Guidelines, 107
Chemical Substance Information Network. *See* CSIN system
Chemical substance retrieval, 15, 74-75, 155
  substructure searching in, 8, 16, 85-95
Chemical-Biological Activities, 79
Chemicals in Commerce Information System, 155
Chemlaw database, 74, 107
Chemzero database, 74
Chicago Tribune, 107
Christian Science Monitor, 60, 104, 123
CIS. *See* NIH/EPA Chemical Information System
Cited author search, 145-147
Citere system, 71
CLAIMS database, 15, 77
CLASS report, 138
Clinical Toxicology of Commercial Products, 86, 87-90
COLLEAGUE system, 77, 99-100. *See also* Bibliographic Retrieval Services
Collier, Harry R., 71
Columbia Broadcasting System, 174
Command languages. *See* Search protocols
Command-driven systems, 19, 22-23
Commerce Business Daily, 103, 107

Commodore microcomputer, 128, 132, 150, 154, 171
Common Command Language (Europe), 71, 173
Communications interface, 128
Communications network. *See* Telecommunications networks
Communications services, 36-37, 44-45, 51-52, 156-159. *See also* Electronic mail, Computer conferencing, Electronic bulletin boards
Communications software, 128, 134-139, 140-152, 153-155, 165-166
Communitree system, 166-169
Comp-U-Store, 111
COMPENDEX database, 13, 14. *See also Engineering Index*
Comprehensive Dissertation Index, 14, 15, 17, 58-59, 73
CompuMath database, 84, 85
CompuServe, 7, 9, 11, 17, 19, 34, 42-50, 51, 52, 66, 103, 104-106, 107, 157, 165, 173
  history of, 3, 34
Compustat Services, 125
Computer Bulletin Board Systems, 160-166. *See also* Electronic bulletin boards
Computer conferencing, 37, 51, 157, 158-159, 166-169, 170
Computer Corporation of America, 155
Computer Sciences Corporation, 85
Computer-assisted instruction, 159-160, 170-171
Computer-mediated communications. *See* Communications services
Computing services, 38, 45, 52, 169-170
Concepts (search), 27
Conference Papers Index, 15, 155
Conferencing. *See* Computer conferencing
Congressional Information Service, 15, 103, 107
Connect time, 12, 175
Connexions database, 16, 125
Consumer services. *See* Home services
Control Data Corporation, 34
Controlled vocabulary. *See* Thesauri
Copyright, 142
Corporate information, 104
Council on Environmental Quality, 155
CP/M-based microcomputer, 142, 153
CRC Press, 77
CROS database, 17
Crosstalk software package, 138
CSIN system, 155
Current Medical Information and Terminology database, 97

DARC, 95
Data Base Index, 17, 22, 75-76
Data Courier, Inc., 60, 66

INDEX

Data Resources, Inc. (DRI), 16, 107-108, 115-117, 124, 152
Data series, 108-109, 116, 124, 152
Data-Star system, 71
Database management systems, 143, 146-150, 153
Database producers, 2, 3, 4, 13-18
Databases
   access points in, 8, 18, 25, 73
   bibliographic, 13
   cost of, 2, 12-13, 175
   coverage of, 16-17, 73
   currency of, 18
   databases of, 16-17, 59, 75-76
   definition of, 1
   dictionary, 13, 15, 16, 74, 173
   directory, 13, 15, 16, 173
   evaluation of, 16-18
   full-text, 13, 15-16, 64, 74, 173
   number of, 10
   numeric, 13, 15, 16, 173
   size of, 17
   source, 13, 15-16, 103, 173
   types of, 13-16
Datacentralen system, 71
Datafield database, 77
DataKits databases, 152
Datapro Directory of On-line Services, 169
Deadline Data on World Affairs, 123
DEC VT 100 intelligent terminal, 95
Delaware Corporation Law, 120
Delphi system, 35, 50-55, 173
Derfler, Frank, 165
Derwent Publications, Ltd., 70, 75, 77
Dialcom system, 35, 51, 52, 156, 157, 158, 172, 173, 174
DIALINDEX database, 17, 59
Dialog Information Services, 7, 9, 10, 11, 13, 16, 25-31, 35, 52, 56-62, 64, 70, 71, 73, 74, 77, 78, 84, 93, 101, 103, 104, 107, 139, 143, 154, 155, 173
   history of, 3
   see also Knowledge Index System
DIMDI system, 71
Dining information. *See* Restaurant information
Direct dialing, 133, 137, 144
DISC database, 14
Disclosure database, 11, 18, 103, 104, 111, 123
Dissertation Index, 17, 58-59
Document delivery, 11-12, 17, 56, 59, 61, 64
Dow Jones News/Retrieval Service, 3, 6-7, 9, 11, 19, 43, 104, 107, 109-115, 140, 150-151, 172
Dow Jones Quotes database, 13, 16, 18, 107, 111, 112-114
Dow Jones software, 110, 140-141, 150-151, 174
Dow-A-Lert, 111-112

Downloading files, 5, 135, 136, 140, 141-147, 174
DRI. *See* Data Resources, Inc.
Drug Information Base, 96, 97-98
Drugdex, 152
Dun's Market Identifiers, 104
Dunn and Bradstreet, 125
Duplex transmission, 133, 135

EasyLink software, 139
Echo system, 71
Eckstein, Otto, 107
Economic information, 107-109, 111, 124
Economics Abstracts International, 107
Education. *See* Training
Education information, 37
Educational Resources Information Center, 66, 70
Edunet system, 159, 170
EIES system, 157, 158-159, 166, 170
EIS Industrial Plants database, 104
EIS Nonmanufacturing Establishments database, 104
Electronic banking, 45, 52
Electronic Bulletin boards, 37, 39-40, 45, 51, 157. *See also* Computer Bulletin Board Systems
Electronic Information Exchange system. *See* EIES system
Electronic mail, 36, 44, 53-54, 66, 111, 118, 139, 141-142, 156-158, 170, 172, 174
Electronic Materials Information Service (EMIS), 101
Electronic messaging. *See* Communications services
Electronic Yellow Pages database, 13, 16, 59
EMAIL service, 44
EMBASE database. *See Excerpta Medica*
EMIS. *See* Electronic Materials Information Service
Employment services, 37
EMPLOY database, 37
Encyclopedia Brittanica, 123
Encyclopedia of Associations, 59
End users, 3, 4, 7
Energy database, 16, 116
Energy information, 75-76
ENERGYLINE database, 75
Engineering Index, 13, 14, 60, 74, 75, 77. *See also* COMPENDEX database
Entertainment services, 38, 45, 52
ENVIROLINE database, 17, 75
Environmental Health News, 102
Environmental information, 75-77
Environmental Protection Agency, 86, 155
ERIC database, 3, 13, 15, 16, 56, 58, 60, 63, 66, 70-71, 152-153

Errors in searching, 32-33
ESA-IRS system, 71
Euronet Diane network, 10, 71
European hosts, 10, 56, 70-72, 173
Excerpta Medica, 14, 16, 74, 76
Extended use, 174
Extravision, 174-175

Facsimile, 174
Facts and Comparisons, 77
Federal Register database, 86, 107, 123
Federal Tax Library database, 120
FEEDBK service, 45
Fields. *See* Databases, access points in
Financial information, 45, 150-152. *See also* Business information
Fine Chemicals Directory, 101
FIRSTWORLD database, 16
Fiz Technik system, 71
Food and Drug Association, 97
Foundation Directory database, 16, 59
Front ends. *See* Search aids
Future trends, 172-176
FYI Superfile. *See* BioSuperfile software package

Gateway service, 52, 123, 158, 172-173
GEISCO network, 101
GEISCO system, 169
General Videotex Corporation, 35, 50
GeoRef database, 75
GeoSciTech database, 84, 85
Globe and Mail, 125
GMS Systems, Inc., 170
Government information, 37, 107
Government Printing Office database, 60
Government role, 14
GPO Monthly Catalog, 15, 107
Graphics displays, 170
GTE Financial System One, 125
GTE TELENET Medical Information Network, 77, 95-98, 100, 172

H&R Block, 34
Handbook of Chemistry and Physics, 77
Handshaking options, 136
Harvard Business Review, 13, 64, 66, 104
Hayes Micromodem, 132, 138, 139, 151
HAZARDLINE database, 102
Hazard Assessment Chemical System, 155
HEALTH database, 80
Health Education Network, 159-160
Health Effects of Environmental Pollutants, 79
Health Planning and Administration database, 76, 100
HELP lines. *See* Hotlines

Hewlett-Packard graphics terminal, 92
HISTLINE database, 80
Historical Abstracts database, 14, 58
Historical background, 2-3
Home services, 38, 45, 52
Hotlines (vendor and database producer), 11
Humanities information, 14

I.P. Sharp Associates, 108-109, 124
IBM PC microcomputer, 132, 138, 141, 142, 150, 151, 152, 153, 155, 170
IFI/Plenum, 77
Index Medicus, 14
Index terms, 23, 24, 25, 26
Info Globe system, 107, 125
INFOMANIA service, 52
Information Access Corporation, 60, 154
The Information Bank. *See* New York Times Information Bank
Information utilities, 9, 10, 34-55
    definition of, 3
Infrared Information System (IRIS), 102
Inka system, 71
INSPEC database, 60, 77
Institute for Scientific Information, 12, 78, 82-85, 173. *See also* ISI Search Network, Sci-Mate software
Institution of Electrical Engineers, 60, 77, 101, 173
Intermediaries, 3, 7
International Pharmaceutical Abstracts, 16, 61, 77, 79
International Software Database, 61, 139
International Telephone and Telegraph Consultative Committee, 174
Investment information. *See* Financial information, Stock information
IRIS. *See* Infrared Information System
ISI Search Network, 82-85, 143
ISMEC database, 155
ISTP&B database, 84, 85
iXO Telecomputer, 127

Journal of the American Medical Association, 80
Justice Retrieval and Inquiry System (JURIS), 125

Klein, Lawrence, R., 124
Knight-Ridder corporation, 174
Knowledge Index system, 56, 59-62, 64, 73, 74, 103, 104, 139. *See also* Dialog Information Services
Kussmaul Encyclopedia database, 52, 54-55

LABORDOC database, 104
LaserData, Inc., 175
LC/LINE database, 14

Lear Seigler dumb terminal, 95
Legal information, 14, 107, 118-123, 125
Legal Resource Index, 14, 61, 107, 154
Leisure services. *See* Home services
Lexington (KY) Herald-Leader, 125
LEXIS database, 14, 16, 104, 107, 123
Librarians. *See* Intermediaries
Libraries, role of, 4, 7
Library of Congress, 14
Life Sciences Collection databases, 76, 155
Line noise, 132
Lister Hill National Center for Biomedical Communications, 159
Lithium Information Center, 102
Lockheed Information Services. *See* Dialog Information Services
Logging off, 29-31
Logging on, 4, 27
Logical operators. *See* Boolean operators
Los Angeles Times, 107

McCarn, Davis B., 14
McGraw-Hill Encyclopedia of Science and Technology, 77
Magazine Index database, 14, 17, 60, 61-62, 154
MAIL service (on Delphi), 51-52, 53-54
MAIL service (on The Source), 36, 44
Management Contents database, 14, 66, 104
Management information, 104
Marketscan database, 125
Martindales The Extra Pharmacopoeia, 77
Massachusetts General Hospital, 97, 159, 160
Massachusetts Institute of Technology, 170
Materials Properties File, 101
Materials Supply File, 101
Mathematical Modelling System, 86
Mathematical Reviews database, 66, 74, 77
MCAUTO Health Services Division, 169
MCI Communications, 111
Mead Data Central system, 11, 15, 104, 107, 121-123, 173
MED/MAIL service, 96
Media General Financial Services, 104, 111, 112, 114-115
Medical information, 14, 16, 73, 76-77, 78-82, 95-100, 102
MEDLARS system, 73, 78-82
MEDLINE database, 10, 14, 15, 16, 18, 60, 63, 66, 73, 74, 76, 79-81, 100, 104, 143
Menu-driven systems, 19-21, 143-150, 173. *See also* specific systems
Merck Index, 77
Messaging. *See* Communications services
METADEX database, 77
microCambridge software, 155

Microcomputer Index database, 61, 139
MICROcourier software, 139
microDISCLOSURE software, 151
MicroEPS software (on DRI), 117
Microsearch (ERIC), 152-153
Million Dollar Directory, 104
MLA Bibliography database, 14, 58
MODEM software program, 138, 165
Modems, 2, 5, 127, 128-134, 154
  special features of, 133-134
  specifications for, 132-133
  speed of, 131-132
Modern Language Association, 58
Multi-List/McGraw-Hill, 125

National Aeronautics and Space Administration, 3
National Agricultural Library, 60, 66
National Broadcasting Company, 174
National CSS, Inc., 125
National Institute of Education, 60
National Institutes of Health, 86
National Library of Medicine, 2-3, 7, 10, 11, 12, 13, 15, 60, 73, 78, 100, 155
National Newspaper Index, 104, 154
National Science Foundation, 159
National Technical Information Service, 14, 66, 86
NDEX database, 107
Networks. *See* Telecommunications networks
New England Journal of Medicine, 77, 80, 100
New Jersey Institute of Technology, 158
New York Times Information Bank, 15, 17, 104, 123
New York Times, 60, 104, 123
News databases, 14, 38, 103, 104, 107, 111, 124-125
Newsearch database, 14, 104, 154
Newsletters (vendor and database producer), 11
NewsNet system, 16, 107, 124
NEXIS database, 104, 107, 123
NIH/EPA Chemical Information System, 85-90, 92, 155
Novation modems, 151
NTIS Database, 14, 15, 60, 63, 66, 74, 77, 107

Occupational Health Services system, 102
Oceanic Abstracts database, 75, 155
Official Airline Guide, 48-50
Offline searching, 1, 12, 18, 147-150, 152-153
Ohio State University, 159-160
Oil and Hazardous Materials Technical Assistance Data System, 86
The Online Chronicle, 16
Online conversations, 37, 44, 57
The Online Hotline, 16

Online industry, 2-3
Online searching
  advantages of, 8
  definition of, 1
  procedures for, 4-5, 19-33
ONTAP databases, 59
OnTyme system, 51, 157
ORACLE service, 52
ORBIT Search Master software, 70, 154, 173
Originate mode, 133, 141
Osborne Comm-Pac, 138

P/E News database, 104
Paperchem database, 74
Parity, 135
PARTICIPATE service, 37, 157, 166
Pass-through service. *See* Gateway service
Passport database, 125
PATDATA database, 66, 77
Patent information, 8, 77
PATLAW database, 107
PATSEARCH database, 77, 101, 152
PC Modem (Ventel), 138
PConnection modem, 132
Pennsylvania Legislative Database, 125
Pergamon Infoline system, 72, 77, 101, 152
Personal Data manager. *See* Sci-Mate software
PESTDOC database, 70, 75
Pharmaceutical information, 77
Pharmaceutical News Index database, 77, 104
Philadelphia Daily News, 125
Philadelphia Inquirer, 107, 125
Philosopher's Index, 58
PhotoNet system, 125
Physical sciences information, 77
Physicians' Current Procedural Terminology database, 97
Physician's Desk Reference, 77
PIRA database, 101
Poisindex, 152
Political information, 37
Pollution Abstracts database, 75, 155
PORTFOLIO program, 107
POST service, 37, 39-40, 45, 157
Pre-Med database, 3, 64, 100
Pre-Psyc database, 64
Predicasts databases, 16, 103, 107
Prestel videotex system, 137, 174
Printers, 126, 137
Printing search results, 29
Privacy issues, 175-176
Private files, 12
Protocols (communications), 135-136, 137, 138
PSYCINFO database, 14, 15, 16, 58, 60, 63, 66, 76, 104

Psychological Abstracts, 14, 58
Psychology Today database, 16
PTS databases. *See* Predicasts databases
PUNCHLINE service, 52

Q/L Systems, 71
Quadram board, 128
Questel system, 72, 75, 92, 93-95, 152
Quick Quote database, 107

Radio Shack Computer Centers, 43, 117
Radio Shack Direct Connect Modem I, 132
Radio Shack TRS-80 microcomputer, 142, 171
Radio Shack TRS-80 Videotex terminal, 127
Random access storage, 2
RAPRA database, 101
RCA VP-3501 microcomputer, 127
Reader's Digest Association, Inc., 34
Records (database), 25
  definition of, 1
Registry of Toxic Effects of Chemical Substances, 16, 80-82
Remote computers, 1-2, 5-6
Research front specialties, 84
Restaurant information, 40-42
Rhodes, Cheryl, 138
RINGDOC database, 70, 77
RS232C port. *See* Communications interface
Rukeyser, Louis, 111

Sadtler Research Laboratories, 102
SCHEDULER database, 52
Sci-Mate software, 85, 140, 142-150, 173, 174
Science Citation Index, 13, 15, 74, 76, 78. *See also* SCISEARCH database
Scientific and technical information, 14, 38, 73-102
SCISEARCH database, 13, 15, 16, 84, 143. *See also Science Citation Index*
SDC Information Services, 7, 9, 10, 11, 56, 64, 68-71, 73, 74, 75-76, 77, 78, 80, 101, 103, 107, 143, 154, 155
  history of, 3
Search aids, 10-11, 25, 140, 153-155, 173
Search Helper software, 154
Search protocols, 10, 13, 56. *See also* Menu-driven systems, Command-driven systems
Search strategy, 22-27, 31
Searches, types of, 7-8
Searching. *See* Online searching
Selective dissemination of information, 12
Service bureaus, 169-170
Shepard's Citation Index, 107, 120, 123
Shopping services, 37, 52, 66, 111
SIC codes, 11, 18

INDEX

Ski information, 14, 46-48
Smith, Kelly, 165
Social factors in online technology, 175-176
Social sciences information, 14, 58
Social SCISEARCH database, 14, 58, 143
Socioeconomic Research Resources, 97
Sociological Abstracts database, 58
Software, 134-139
  cost of, 138-139
  downloading of, 66, 165
  offline, 140, 147-153
  public domain, 45, 138, 165
The Source, 7, 9, 11, 19, 34-42, 44, 51, 52, 66, 103, 104, 107, 139, 157, 173
  history of, 3, 34
Source*Plus, 37
Spidel system, 72
SPIN database, 74, 77
Sports information, 38, 46-48
Standard and Poor's data, 45, 60, 108, 116, 125
Standard Drug File, 70, 77
Stanford University, 170
Star system, 143
StarGram (on AgriStar), 118
Stock information, 103, 107, 109-115, 140, 150-151
Stop bits, 135
Structure and Nomenclature Search System, 86, 87-89
Substructure searching (chemical). *See* Chemical substance retrieval, substructure searching in
SUNY Biomedical Communications Network, 3
Superindex database, 16, 77
Supermarket vendors. *See* Information utilities
SYSOP, 165, 166
System Development Corporation. *See* SDC Information Services
System protocols. *See* Search protocols

Technical information. *See* Scientific and technical information
Teksim Tektronix Simulator software, 95, 139
Tektronix graphics terminal, 92, 95, 152, 155
Telecommunications networks, 1, 2, 3-5, 10, 22-24, 27. *See also* TELENET, TYMNET, UNINET networks
Telecommuting, 175-176
Teledek TI software, 139
TELEGEN database, 77
TeleLearning Network, 170-171
Telemail, 158
TELENET network, 4, 27, 96, 156, 158
Telephone number directory, 137
Telephone Software Connection, 142
Teletext, 174

Teleworking, 175-176
TELEX network, 139, 174
Telesystemes Questel. *See* Questel system
Terminal programs. *See* Communications software
Terminals, 1-2, 5, 126-128
The', Lee, 138
Thesauri, 10, 18, 24, 25, 26
Time, Inc., 174
Timesharing computers, 1, 2, 5-6
TODAY database, 123
Toxic Substances Control Act database, 74
Toxicology Data Bank, 80
TOXLINE database, 79
Trade and Industry Index, 61
Training, 6-7, 11
Transferring files. *See* Downloading files, Uploading files
TRS-80. *See* Radio Shack TRS-80 microcomputer
TWX network, 134, 174
TYMNET network, 4, 22-24, 156, 169
Tymshare, Inc., 157, 169

U.S. Regional database, 116
UNINET network, 4
UNISTOX service (on The Source), 107
Universal Online Searcher. *See* Sci-Mate software
University of Virginia, 152
University of Wisconsin-Madison, 102
University of Pennsylvania, 124
UPI news, 111
Uploading files, 136
UREST database, 40-42
User aids, 10-11
User support lines. *See* Hotlines (vendor and database producer)
UserLink, 154-155

Value Line database, 45, 103, 104, 105-106, 116
Vax computer, 155
Vector microcomputer, 142
Vendors, 1, 3, 4, 9-13, 56-57, 139, 172-173
  fees charged by, 12, 175
  reference, 9, 10
  selection of, 12-13
  subject specific, 9, 10
  types of, 9-10
Venn diagrams, 28-29
Vertical integration, 173
VETDOC, 70, 76
VicModem, 132
Video Patsearch, 152, 175
Videodisk technology, 152, 175
Videotex, 139, 174-175

Viewdata Corporation of America, 174
VisiCalc, 117, 152
VisiCorp, 117, 151-152
VisiLink software, 117, 151-152
Vocabulary control, 22-25
VU/Text Information Services, 107, 124-125
Wall Street Journal, 60, 104, 107, 111
Wall Street Week transcript, 111, 125
Washington Post, 123
WEATHER database, 46-48
West Publishing Company, 118
Western Union, 139
Westlaw system, 107, 118-121, 123
Wharton Econometric Forecasting Associates, 108, 124

Who's Who database, 59
Wire service news, 104, 111, 123
Word length, 135
Word processors, 126, 137
World database, 125
World Economic Model, 124
World Patents Index, 70, 77
World Textiles database, 77

Xerox Computer Services, 169

Ziff-Davis Publishing Company, 124
Zoological Record database, 77
Zycor, Ltd., 139